Rockites, Magistrates and Parliamentarians

Early nineteenth-century Ireland witnessed widespread and prolonged rural unrest, as groups of labourers and smallholders formed secret societies demanding stabilisation of the occupancy of farms, reduction in rents, protection of wages and lessening or abolition of tithes. One of the most active of these groups – the Rockites – waged a vigorous and sustained campaign of arson, intimidation and houghing (maiming of animals) across the southern half of Ireland in the early 1820s, quickly attracting the attention of the authorities in both Ireland and Britain. Combining analyses of local and economic concerns with wider national political dimensions, this book offers an in-depth and alternative interpretation of the Rockites. Attaching particular importance to the political dimensions of the Rockites, Katsuta demonstrates how their political mindset was created by local circumstances. Styling themselves descendants of the United Irishmen, Rockites drew on the memories of the bitter political struggles in Cork during the 1790s, as well as current political events such as Daniel O'Connell's mass mobilisation to realise Catholic Emancipation. As well as situating the Rockites within the Irish context, the book also offers insights into how British politicians dealt with Ireland in the early years of the Union. The Rockite disturbances became a useful tool for Whigs and radicals in Westminster to blame the Tories for the misgovernment of Ireland. The Tory government was rompted to adopt a new course that proved less a remedy to problems in eland than a response to events within parliament, revealing how the Irish iestion in the early nineteenth-century UK was regarded first and foremost a parliamentary issue.

unsuke Katsuta is Associate Professor in the Graduate School of Humani-es and Sociology at the University of Tokyo.

Rural Worlds: Economic, Social and Cultural Histories of Agricultures and Rural Societies

Series Editor:
Richard W. Hoyle
University of Reading, UK

We like to forget that agriculture is one of the core human activities. In historic societies most people lived in the countryside: a high, if falling proportion of the population were engaged in the production and processing of foodstuffs. The possession of land was a key form of wealth: it brought not only income from tenants but prestige, access to a rural lifestyle and often political power. Nor could government ever be disinterested in the countryside, whether to maintain urban food supply, as a source of taxation, or to maintain social peace. Increasingly it managed every aspect of the countryside. Agriculture itself and the social relations within the countryside were in constant flux as farmers reacted to new or changing opportunities, and landlords sought to maintain or increase their incomes. Moreover, urban attitudes to the landscape and its inhabitants were constantly shifting.

These questions of competition and change, production, power and perception are the primary themes of the series. It looks at change and competition in the countryside: social relations within it and between urban and rural societies. The series offers a forum for the publication of the best work on all of these issues, straddling the economic, social and cultural, concentrating on the rural history of Britain and Ireland, Europe and its colonial empires, and North America over the past millennium.

Series Advisory Board:

www.routledge.com/history/series/RW

Rockites, Magistrates and Parliamentarians

Governance and Disturbances in Pre-Famine Rural Munster

Shunsuke Katsuta

Routledge
Taylor & Francis Group
LONDON AND NEW YORK

First published 2018
by Routledge

2 Park Square, Milton Park, Abingdon, Oxfordshire OX14 4RN
52 Vanderbilt Avenue, New York, NY 10017

Routledge is an imprint of the Taylor & Francis Group, an informa business

First issued in paperback 2020

British Library Cataloguing-in-Publication Data
A catalogue record for this book is available from the British Library

Library of Congress Cataloging-in-Publication Data
Names: Katsuta, Shunsuke, author.
Title: Rockites, magistrates and parliamentarians : governance and disturbances in pre-famine rural Munster / by Shunsuke Katsuta.
Description: New York : Routledge, 2018. | Series: Rural worlds : economic, social and cultural histories of agricultures and rural societies | Includes bibliographical references and index.
Identifiers: LCCN 2017028241 (print) | LCCN 2017030945 (ebook) | ISBN 9781315606774 (ebook) | ISBN 9781472478993 (hardback : alkaline paper)
Subjects: LCSH: Munster (Ireland)—Rural conditions. | Munster (Ireland)—Politics and government—19th century. | Agriculture and state—Ireland—Munster—History—19th century. | Ireland—Relations—Great Britain. | Great Britain—Relations—Ireland. | Land reform—Ireland—Munster—History—19th century. | Farmers—Political activity—Ireland—Munster—History—19th century. | Agricultural laborers—Political activity—Ireland—Munster—History—19th century. | Secret societies—Ireland—Munster—History—19th century. | Social conflict—Ireland—Munster—History—19th century.
Classification: LCC HD1930.3.Z9 (ebook) | LCC HD1930.3.Z9 M864 2018 (print) | DDC 330.9419/081—dc23
LC record available at https://lccn.loc.gov/2017028241

ISBN: 978-1-4724-7899-3 (hbk)
ISBN: 978-0-367-59470-1 (pbk)

Typeset in Sabon
by Apex CoVantage, LLC

To My Parents

Contents

Figures

Maps

Tables

Acknowledgments

I have been blessed with excellent teachers throughout my life. With regard to writing this book, I can name only three of them. To Louis Cullen, I cannot really find appropriate words to express my gratitude and admiration. The combination of great scholarship and high integrity in him has always been a wonder to me. David Dickson's expertise in Irish history, as well as his steady encouragement, has been my inexhaustible source of inspiration and energy. Fascinating works by Kazuhiko Kondo led me to the study of popular movements in the first place, and without his enduring care and support, my life would have been considerably different.

It is a great pleasure to thank my academic friends, junior and senior. First of all, I thank Richard Hoyle and Tony Jenkins for their great kindness in reading an entire draft and for their useful advice on writing. Joanna Innes read Chapter 4 and gave valuable comments. I would also like to express gratitude to people who have been of direct help or encouragement for writing this book, viz. Takeshi Ito, Shusaku Kanazawa, Takashi Koseki, Rohan McWilliam, Tadgh O'Sullivan, Naoki Sakiyama, Shin-ichi Takagami and Akihiro Takei. I have to add that I sincerely thank the unknown referees for their very useful comments on my earlier drafts. I am solely responsible for all the remaining errors.

Many people helped me with studying and living in Dublin, which is now my second home town. I thank, in particular, the excellent staff of the National Library of Ireland, the Coynes of Knocklyon, the Cullens of Blackrock, the Neligans of Glenageary, and last but not least, Mrs Slattery of Kimmage.

Abbreviations

TNA	The National Archives (London)
BL	British Library
BPP	British Parliamentary Papers
CSORP	Chief Secretary's Office Registered Papers
HO	Home Office Papers
NAI	National Archives of Ireland
SOC	State of the Country Papers

Note: Punctuation and the use of capitals have been modernised in all citations from sources.

Introduction

'There will be a general rising'

In the night of 7 March 1823, at around 9 o'clock, a fire was set to Carker Lodge, the residence of Hugh Norcott near Doneraile in County Cork. Because the buildings were thatched, the fire quickly consumed the dwelling house, the barn, haggard (crop store) and the stable. The police arrived, searched around and found a young man in a nearby cabin. His name was John Hickey: he had been employed by Norcott as a gardener and 'experienced many acts of kindness from Mr. Norcott'. Norcott later said to Hickey that 'You are the last man I would have suspected of injuring me'.[1] The police also found in the cabin feathers to ornament a cap, a belt, a whistle and written oaths for initiation into a secret society.[2]

The local authorities were stirred because the feathers had been witnessed several times before in the neighbourhood when houses were 'visited' by a group of men at night, who committed various outrages: seizing arms, beating residents, maiming the cattle or setting fire to houses or haggard.[3] The leader of these nightly disturbers appeared with such feathers on his cap. He was called Captain Rock, his men being called Rockites. They all belonged to a secret society, which made it difficult for the authorities to hunt them down. It seemed, however, that Captain Rock himself was finally caught.[4]

It turned out in the following investigation that Hickey was not the real Captain Rock.[5] However, the investigation revealed that Hickey was a very active Rockite. According to his own statement, he frequently went out of his own locality to commit outrages, making himself known to 300 Rockites.[6] The authorities tried to obtain information from him about his companions in exchange for his turning approver (crown witness) – arson was a capital offence. However, while Hickey gave accurate information about the location of his own arms, he refused to disclose his companions' names.[7] He was sentenced to death on 4 April and hanged on the seventeenth, at the gallows erected on a small hill beside the scene of the arson, surrounded by 150 cavalrymen and 500 infantrymen including yeomen and police, who were mobilised in order to awe the other Rockites.[8]

Not only Hickey but many other Rockites lost their lives. In County Limerick, the birthplace of the Rockite disturbances, thirty Rockites were convicted, mostly sentenced to death, at a special commission court in December 1821.[9] In County Cork, the heartland of the Rockite disturbances, thirty-six men were sentenced to death at the special commission in February 1822, at least fifteen of whom were actually executed.[10] Many others were deported. In the whole of the province of Munster, more than 200 men were sent to Australia between February 1822 and April 1823.[11] In other words, the risk of hanging or deportation did not deter men from becoming Rockites.

From the beginning of the eighteenth century to the end of the nineteenth century rural disturbances haunted Ireland.[12] In particular, in the period from the 1760s to the 1830s large-scale disturbances, by which is meant disturbances covering several counties and lasting for years at a time, occurred in every decade. Contemporaries often called the disturbers 'Whiteboys', a generic term whose origin lies in the fact that on occasion they wore white over-clothes.[13] The Whiteboys were sworn into secret societies and appeared in parties to punish those who disobeyed their 'law' by using violence against person or property. Their 'law', given in the name of mysterious leaders called 'Captain', variously ordered that nobody should take another man's farm, that rents should not be exorbitant, that labourers' employment or wages should be protected and that the payment of tithe should be boycotted. Their 'law' was so effective that disturbers were nicknamed 'midnight legislators'.[14]

Maiming of animals (houghing) and arson were frequently seen in the English countryside as well. However, unlike Irish Whiteboys, English rural disturbers do not seem to have developed underground organisations. Hence, outrages in rural England were more or less sporadic and the actions of individuals who had personal reasons for revenge.[15] More widespread and somehow organised rural disturbances were seen, but, again, they were dimensionally different from Whiteboyism. The Swing Riots, the largest rural disturbances in nineteenth-century England, which mobilised thousands of men in daytime, were a series of localised movements linked together by shared aims. Although the Swing Rioters were more violent than previously thought, violence against the person was exceptional.[16]

Returning to the Rockites, although they were in some ways Whiteboys, they differed in several significant points, which made them unique in the history of Irish rural disturbances. First, the scale of Rockite violence was unprecedented even by the standard of Whiteboyism: they committed more than 300 cases of arson and seized more than 200 firearms between 1821 and 1824 in County Cork alone.[17] Open engagements between the military and thousands of men took place at several locations in the west of Cork in January 1822.

Secondly, Rockite disturbances spread to almost the southern half of Ireland, and they developed a network of underground organisations which covered a wider area than ordinary Whiteboys'. Hickey had an interview with W. H. W. Newenham, a magistrate, the day before his execution:

> Newenham – Are there not committees arranged?
> Hickey – There are: the first in the county is at Mallow, there are others at Buttevant, Doneraile and other places. All catechisms and printed orders come to us as we were informed from Dublin. The head committee is there. Assistance is to be given from France. (this last sentence was not spoken very decidedly) . . .
> Newenham – What is the general plan of arrangement?
> Hickey – Committee men are appointed. A head committee man is ordered to move to the next parish or district and the men composing the committee in said parish are ordered by summons with blank signature to attend on a certain day, hour and place under forfeiture of life and the next head committee man does the same to the next district. One committee man knows the other[;] they also have signs.[18]

Third and last, Rockites entertained more radical ideas than Whiteboys. Hickey told to a parish priest that 'we wished to emancipate the Roman Catholics; we wished to get rid of tithes and taxes.'[19] Hickey's later conversation with Newenham showed how they envisaged their proceedings:

> Hickey – You will be quiet by and [by] in this county, but the business will proceed eastward, it will be slow. When destruction of property and the system is established in each county, then there will be a general rising. – . . .
> Newenham – Do you think the system now pursued will continue?
> Hickey – You may depend upon it. (or words to this effect)
> Newenham – Though many lives would be lost on both sides and much property be destroyed; surely you could not be so mad as to think your party could succeed?
> Hickey – Many lives will be lost. . . .[20]

It was not Hickey alone whose comments implied a rebellion. David Nagle, the real Captain Rock of County Cork, confessed that their scheme was that 'when the people were fully organised, and supplied with pikes, they are [*sic*] bound to turn out, and murder all the Protestants.'[21] Since Protestants virtually monopolised land and the state in early nineteenth-century Ireland, it might be said that Rockites envisaged a kind of social revolution, at least in their minds.

Such words need to be treated with caution, of course. However, Cork Rockites were not the first to refer to widespread violence or social change in the movement. Two police officers, who had considerable experience of dealing with rural disturbances,[22] were dispatched to County Limerick, and they sent a warning to the Irish administration in Dublin that the Limerick Rockites seemed to be aiming at 'overthrowing the Protestant religion and possessing the lands on their own terms' and that their final object was 'the total upset of the established order of things'.[23]

Because Rockites were evidently more dangerous than ordinary White-boys, the authorities took a firmer attitude towards the Rockites. The Home Office of the British government in London, receiving information from the Irish administration, over which it exercised jurisdiction, saw the situation as making 'rapid progress from riot to insurrection, & from insurrection to rebellion', and it promptly sent five regiments of troops to Ireland.[24] Not only strengthening the physical resource of the Irish administration, the British government changed its membership by recalling the top two personnel, the Lord Lieutenant of Ireland and the Irish Chief Secretary, in late 1821, both of whom were judged vacillating and unprepared to deal with the Rockites.[25]

The new Irish administration introduced a new and strong police force and the Insurrection Act, the latter of which, while enforcing curfew and suspending trials by jury, gave magistrates legal power to conduct summary searches of houses for violators of the curfew or for illegal possession of arms. The local authorities used this power extensively. For instance, in one night of early January 1823 they searched 3,000 houses in the north of County Cork.[26] In consequence, nearly 700 men were arrested and tried at the special sessions court under the Insurrection Act between February 1822 and February 1824 in Cork. In the whole of the island, the figure was 2,600.[27] These figures do not include those who were tried at assizes or special commissions.

Thus, the south of Ireland in the early 1820s was in an extraordinary situation, which stirred up the imagination of contemporaries, who took Rockites as the subject of their literary work, for instance, Thomas Moore's *Captain Rock*.[28] While the book depicted the Rockite disturbances as part of a cyclical process of Protestant repression and Catholic rebellion in Irish history, its publication created a sensation and spawned a genre of Rockite books.[29] Furthermore, the Rockite engagements with the troops in Cork in January 1822 became the most significant event in the local history of the area, to the extent that '[e]very event that occurred beforehand or afterwards was dated locally from the year of the battle.'[30] Even as late as the early twentieth century the period of the Rockites was 'constantly spoken of in the South of Ireland as that of "the Rebellion,"' while aged people in numerous instances were 'believed to have confounded its incidents with those of the rebellion of 1798'.[31]

How then, have historians treated the Rockite disturbances, and where does this book lie in the historiography?

Historiography

Because chronic rural disturbances featured prominently in the modern history of Ireland, there have been various previous studies, not only on the Rockites, but also on other groups of disturbers.[32]

Thanks to the works by J. S. Donnelly (the great pioneer in this research field) and others, it is now known that the Irish rural disturbances had several important elements in common with other European rural disturbances. First, mysterious leaders played an important role. In Ireland, not only 'Captain Rock', but also 'Captain Right', 'Captain Thresher' or 'Queen Sive' led the disturbers.[33] In England, 'Captain Swing', as well as 'General Ludd', or 'King John' played a similar role.[34] If such semi-fictional bandit-heroes as Robin Hood, Louis Mandrin, or Stenka Razin are included, the list of these mysterious and mythical leaders can be extended further.[35]

Secondly, the disturbers had a strong sense of the legitimacy of their cause, trying to distinguish themselves from ordinary criminals. The central notion of the rural disturbers in early modern Europe was the idea of 'justice', with which they legitimatised their behaviours.[36] Many of the participants in the Swing Riots behaved, in their thinking, legitimately.[37] The Irish Whiteboys repeatedly stressed the legality of their actions.[38]

Thirdly, the disturbers usually had a conservative or backward-looking mentality. Rural unrest in general needs not be understood as a type of revolution,[39] and the most striking feature of many popular disturbances in modern England was their 'essentially defensive character'.[40] Despite its massive scale of violence, Irish Whiteboyism in the eighteenth and nineteenth centuries can be understood 'as both a means towards the redress of pressing socio-economic grievances and a comment on the failure of the established leadership to come to grips with the implications of change for established pattern of life'.[41]

However, the last point should not be extended too far, because rural disturbers in general could absorb various political ideas including radicalism and millenarianism. Irish Whiteboys, too, particularly those in the nineteenth century, came to have distinct political notions, chiefly because of the revolutionary movements of the radical political organisation of the United Irishmen in the late 1790s, the culmination of which was the uprising of 1798. In this context, it is necessary to investigate the studies of the nineteenth-century Irish rural disturbances more closely.

As to nineteenth-century Irish rural disturbances, the stress was once placed on theoretical analysis rather than an empirical approach, in consequence of which several economic models were produced to explain the agrarian dimensions of the disturbances.[42] However, since 1985, when a summary of these hypotheses was made,[43] attempts at economic modelling for this subject have lain dormant.[44] Since then, detailed and specific studies have been produced, with a focus on their political dimensions.[45]

The question of the political dimensions leads on to the historiographical treatment of the Rockites themselves. Of the studies of that movement,[46] Donnelly's recent book is the most substantial to date. It covers a very wide geographical area (nearly half of Ireland) and describes various aspects of the Rockites themselves, including their typology of outrages, organisation and ideology. While Donnelly admits that economic grievances fuelled the Rockite movement, he stresses that 'millenarian prophecies and sectarian animosities were central to the *mentalité* of the agrarian rebels of 1821–24'.[47] One of Donnelly's major contributions to the historiography of Irish rural disturbances has been finding millenarianism in the Rockite disturbances, but stressing the millenarian aspect can be misleading, because the Rockites' political notions did not necessarily originate in the millenarian prophecy, to which Donnelly attaches great importance.

This book sees the Rockites from different perspectives to Donnelly's. On the one hand, this book tries to offer a more detailed understanding of the Rockites, by focusing on the narrower region of Munster, particularly Counties Limerick and Cork. After investigating the rural society of County Cork and the activities of the Rockites as agrarian disturbers, this book describes and analyses in detail the Rockites' engagements with the troops in Cork, the most violent events in the whole of the Rockite disturbances.[48] In addition, this book identifies several persons who played the role of 'Captain Rock' in Cork and Limerick: one celebrated 'Captain Rock' in Cork turned out to be from an old landowning family connected with Edmund Burke. To attach too great a significance to Captain Rock may be, however, misleading. A 'committee man', imported from a Dublin underground organisation, was as important a figure as a 'Captain'. Thus, this book will also show that the underground network of Cork and Limerick Rockites was a graft of the organisational structure of a Dublin-based political secret society onto local Whiteboy organisations.

On the other hand, this book also tries to offer a more contextualised understanding (the mixture of 'low' and 'high' history) of the Rockites than Donnelly's. First, an attempt will be made to appreciate the impact of the Rockite disturbances more fully. The initial reaction of the authorities to the Rockite disturbances was a strengthening of the machinery of law and order. The next steps led to a more structural change. While a strong and centralised police force was established throughout Ireland for the first time in 1822, the government revised the magistracy in 1822–23, as a result of which about a quarter of the justices of the peace were ejected from the bench, and new courts of law were introduced. It can be seen that the Rockites became an important factor in the process of the transformation of local government in rural Ireland under the Union, which was now moving in the direction of an interventionist state with centralised control over local agencies.

Secondly, the Rockites' mindset was not created by a millenarian prophecy alone, but was developed by both local and national political circumstances. Munster Rockites sometimes styled themselves as descendants of the United Irishmen, and that can be explained only by analysing the evolution of local politics in the early nineteenth century. While thus the interaction between the Rockites' political notions and the dynamism of local politics will be investigated at the level of the parliamentary borough, the influence of Daniel O'Connell's national Catholic politics will be also examined. The mass movement of the Catholic Association in 1824 is generally regarded as a watershed in the history of popular politics in Ireland, but O'Connell's popular mobilisation had already begun in 1821, when the question of the royal veto over Catholic Episcopal appointments was raised in public because of a Catholic relief bill in that year, which contained a veto clause. O'Connell canvassed wide popular support in Munster to oppose the bill, and this book will reveal how his view was reflected in the political thinking of the Rockites when they raised the question of 'the emancipation of the Catholics'.

While the Rockites should thus be analysed in the context of local as well as national politics, this contextualisation can be extended further. This book tries to see the Rockite disturbances in the framework of the United Kingdom as a whole. This attempt may be regarded as unique in the historiography of the nineteenth-century Irish disturbances. Because nineteenth-century Ireland belonged to the United Kingdom, it was the London government based at the Westminster parliament that bore the ultimate liability for coping with Ireland. While what the Irish question was in the early years of the Union has been a rather neglected subject,[49] it cannot be denied that the Rockite disturbances offered the opposition in parliament a good case for criticising the government, at a time when the government saw its position in parliament weakened in the early 1820s.[50] As the government tried to fend off the charges of the misgovernment of Ireland by introducing several measures of reform, the early 1820s became the first 'age of reform' in Ireland under the Union. The case of the Rockite disturbances thus offers a good example for showing how the Irish question played a role in the parliamentary politics of early nineteenth-century Great Britain and Ireland, and, in turn, how the Irish question at that time was regarded first and foremost as a parliamentary issue.

Another thing to add is that Donnelly's coverage of sources is not extensive. To be fair, he never claimed that he had exhausted the available sources, but the study of Rockites is blessed with better and more voluminous sources than the other Irish rural disturbances.

Sources

The main sources for the study of Irish rural disturbances in general are, first, reports sent from magistrates and police or military officers serving in various places in the country to Dublin Castle, the centre of the Irish administration, of outrages committed by Whiteboys, and secondly, newspaper accounts of outrages and the trials of arrested Whiteboys.

Of the reports sent from the country, the most important collection for the study of the rural disturbances in the first three decades of the nineteenth century, including Rockite disturbances, is the State of the Country Papers (SOC), now kept in the National Archives of Ireland (NAI) in Dublin. This collection is divided into two series. The first series covers the period of 1796–1831 and are kept in forty-six boxes, while the second series, covering 1790–1831, are kept in twenty-five boxes. These two series are basically of the same nature.[51] However, while the first series of the State of the Country Papers have been fully calendared, most of the second series remain uncalendared, and hence are relatively little used.[52]

Apart from the State of the Country Papers, the Chief Secretary's Office Registered Papers (CSORP) in the National Archives of Ireland can also be a useful collection, particularly for the study of the Rockites. That collection, letters sent to Dublin Castle from all over the country on various matters, does not as a rule include papers dealing with law-and-order issues. However, for unknown reasons, some of the letters sent to Dublin Castle on the state of the country in the 1820s were not categorised into the State of the Country Papers (either series one or two) as they were for other periods. In consequence, twenty-five boxes of documents dealing with law-and-order issues were classified into a sub-category of Chief Secretary's Office Registered Papers as 'CSORP, State of the Country'. They are essentially of the same nature as the original SOC. Of documents in the twenty-five boxes, those covering 1826–29 have been indexed, but those for 1821 and 1824, exactly the period of the Rockites, have not been indexed or calendared (and are little used).

The study of the Cork Rockites is blessed with another source collection, the Papers of Sir Hugh Gough in the National Army Museum in London. Gough was the commander of the forces in the north of Cork when Rockite activities were at their height. This collection contains not only reports sent to Gough from his subordinate commanders, but also his own memoranda, which were based on his usage of informers and his contact with important Rockites including Hickey and Nagle. Hence, the Gough Papers may be regarded as closer to the activities of the Rockites than papers in Dublin.

As to newspapers, their chief merit is that they are practically the only information source on proceedings of the trials of disturbers because official legal documents which could have been a more detailed and reliable source of proceedings of trials were destroyed during the Irish Civil War. County Cork in the 1820s seems to have been the best covered region in Ireland excepting Dublin, with three Cork newspapers surviving, each of them issued three times a week (*Cork Constitution*, *Cork Mercantile Chronicle* and *Cork Morning Intelligencer*). County Limerick is less well-documented, but *Limerick Chronicle* and *Limerick News* offer detailed information, while Cork papers cover most of the activities of the Limerick Rockites.

In addition to the above sources, four parliamentary committees were set up on the state of Ireland 'with reference to disturbances' in 1824–25, the voluminous minutes of evidence of which offer useful information about the Rockites.[53] In sum, of the county-based studies of rural disturbances in pre-Famine Ireland, the Rockites in Cork and Limerick may have the largest quantity of first-hand information.

Notes

1 *Cork Constitution*, 10 Mar. 1823; *Cork Mercantile Chronicle*, 4 Apr. 1823.
2 Major Carter to W. Gregory, 8 Mar. 1823, National Archives of Ireland (hereafter NAI), State of the Country Papers (hereafter SOC), 2511/43.
3 Major Carter to Gregory, 8 Mar. 1823, SOC, 2511/43.
4 Major General Lambert to Field Marshal Combermere, 1 Apr. 1823, SOC, 2512/5.
5 Lt. Col. Finch to Gregory, 9 Apr. 1823, SOC, 2512/12.
6 Major Carter to Gregory, 21 Mar. 1823, the National Archives, Home Office Papers (hereafter HO), 100/208/91–96; Lord Doneraile to – 2 Apr. 1823, SOC, 2512/3; Col. Arbuthnot to Lt. Col. Finch, 2 Apr. 1823, SOC, 2512/3.
7 Col. Gough to Major General Lambert, 21 Mar. 1823, SOC, 2511/56; Major Carter to Gregory, 21 Mar. 1823, HO 100/208/91–96; Lord Doneraile to – 2 Apr. 1823, SOC, 2512/3; Col. Arbuthnot to Lt. Col. Finch, 2 Apr. 1823, SOC, 2512/3.
8 Col. Gough to Lt. Col. Finch, 14 Apr. 1823, National Army Museum, Gough Papers, 8303/105/111.
9 British Parliamentary Papers (hereafter BPP), Return of number of persons indicted and tried: at assizes, and special commissions in Ireland, 1816–23, 1823 (305) (306) XVI. 625, 639.
10 W. C. Plunket to Lord Wellesley, 26 Feb. 1822, HO 100/203/320–327; *Cork Morning Intelligencer*, 26, 28 Feb., 5, 7, 9 Mar. 1822; *Saunders's Newsletters*, 8 Mar. 1822. Cf. Jeremiah O'Mahony, *West Cork and its story* (Tralee: Kerryman Ltd, 1961), pp. 264–265.
11 BPP, Return of persons tried in counties in Ireland under Insurrection Act, 1823, 1823 (311) XVI. 687.
12 Samuel Clark and James S. Donnelly Jr. eds., *Irish peasants: violence and political unrest 1780–1914* (Dublin: Gill & Macmillan, 1983); C. H. E. Philpin ed., *Nationalism and popular protest in Ireland* (Cambridge: Cambridge University Press, 1987).
13 George Cornwall Lewis, *Local disturbances in Ireland* (Cork: Tower Books, 1977, reprint, first published in 1836), p. 2.
14 Galen Broeker, *Rural disorder and police reform in Ireland, 1812–36* (London: Routledge & Kegan Paul; Toronto: University of Toronto Press, 1970), p. 8.
15 John E. Archer, *'By a flash and a scare': incendiarism, animal maiming, and porching in East Anglia 1815–1870* (Oxford: Clarendon Press, 1990), pp. 2, 220.
16 John E. Archer, *Social unrest and popular protest in England 1780–1840* (Cambridge: Cambridge University Press, 2000), p. 19; Carl J. Griffin, 'Swing, Swing Redivivus, or something after Swing? On the death throes of a protest movement, December 1830-December 1833', *International Review of Social History*, vol. 54, no. 3, Dec. 2009, p. 465.
17 Compiled from *Cork Constitution*, *Cork Morning Intelligencer*, *Limerick Chronicle*, State of the Country Papers and Chief Secretary's Office Registered Papers.
18 Newenham to –, 13 Apr. 1823, SOC, 2512/16.
19 Evidence of Rev. O'Brien, 10 May 1825, BPP, Select committee to inquire into state of Ireland with reference to disturbances, minutes of evidence, 1825 (129) VIII. 1, pp. 584–586; Major Carter to Gregory, 21 Mar. 1823, HO 100/208/91.
20 Newenham to –, 13 Apr. 1823, SOC, 2512/16.

21 'Extract from the confession of David Nagle taken before Lt. Col. Hill', Jan. 1823[1824], Gough Papers, 8303/105/335.
22 Stanley H. Palmer, *Police and protest in England and Ireland 1780–1850* (Cambridge: Cambridge University Press, 1988), pp. 204–205, 212.
23 Majors Willcocks and Warburton to C. Grant, 23 Oct. 1821, HO 100/202/25.
24 Lord Sidmouth to Lord Talbot, 23 Oct. 1821, HO 100/201/154; same to same, 8 Nov. 1821, HO 100/202/55–56.
25 Lord Sidmouth to Lord Liverpool, 21 Nov. 1821, Devon Record Office, Sidmouth Papers, 152M/1821/OI/56; same to same, 22 Nov. 1821, *ibid.*, 152M/1821/OI/57.
26 Col. Gough to Lt. Col. Finch, 11 Jan. 1823, SOC, 2511/6.
27 BPP, Return of persons tried in counties in Ireland under Insurrection Act, 1823, 1823 (311) XVI. 687; BPP, Return of persons committed under Insurrection Act in Ireland, 1823–24, 1824(174) XXII. 189.
28 Thomas Moore, *Memoirs of captain Rock, the celebrated Irish chieftain: with some account of his ancestors* (London: Longman, Hurst, Rees, Orme, Brown, and Green, 1824); Mortimer O'Sullivan, *Captain Rock detected: or, the origin and character of the recent disturbances and the causes, both moral and political of the present alarming condition of the south and west of Ireland, fully and fairly considered and exposed by a Munster farmer* (London: T. Cadell, 1824); Anon., *Captain Rock in London: or, the chieftain's gazette* (London: James Robins and Co., Joseph Robins, Junr. and Co., [1825–26]); Mrs. S. C. Hall, *The Whiteboy: a story of Ireland in 1822* (London: Chapman and Hall, 1845); Charlotte Elizabeth, *The Rockite: an Irish story* (fourth and enlarged edition, London: James Nisbet & Co., 1846, originally published in 1829).
29 Patrick O'Sullivan, 'A literary difficulty in explaining Ireland: Tom Moore and Captain Rock, 1824', in Roger Swift and Sheridan Gilley eds., *The Irish in Britain 1815–1939* (Savage: Barnes & Noble Books, 1989), pp. 243–252; Luke Gibbons, 'Between Captain Rock and a hard place: art and agrarian insurgency', in Tadhg Foley and Seán Ryder eds., *Ideology and Ireland in the nineteenth century* (Dublin: Four Courts Press, 1998), p. 29. Interesting accounts of some of the Rockite activities and even of the person of Captain Rock can be seen in R. Shelton Mackenzie, *Bits of Blarney* (New York: Redfield, 1854). However, I cannot find a corroboration of Mackenzie's accounts in other sources. His accounts seem to have been a mixture of oral local tradition and fiction, as Mackenzie was born in Mallow only in 1809 according to Friel. Mary Friel, *Dancing as a social pastime in the south-east of Ireland, 1800–1897* (Dublin: Four Courts Press, 2004), p. 11. See also note 49 of Chapter 2 of this book.
30 Brian Brennan, *Máire Bhuí Ní Laoire: a poet of her people* (Cork: The Collins Press, 2000), p. 44.
31 Henry F. Berry, 'Story of the attack on Lavally Cottage, Ballymagooly, near Mallow, in 1823', *Journal of the Cork Historical and Archaeological Society*, vol. xv, no. 81, 1909, p. 1.
32 Thanks to the empirical studies of Donnelly and others, considerable light has been shed on eighteenth-century rural disturbances. See Maureen Wall, 'The Whiteboys', in T. Desmond Williams ed., *Secret societies in Ireland* (Dublin: Gill & Macmillan; New York: Barnes & Noble Books, 1973); M. R. Beames, 'Peasant movements: Ireland, 1785–1795', *Journal of Peasant Studies*, vol. ii, no. 4, 1975; James S. Donnelly Jr, 'The Rightboy movement 1785–8', *Studia Hibernica*, nos. 17/18, 1977–78; *idem*, 'The Whiteboy movement, 1761–5', *Irish Historical Studies*, vol. xxi, no. 81, 1978; W. A. Maguire, 'Lord Donegall and the Hearts of Steel', *Irish Historical Studies*, vol. xxi, no. 84, 1979; J. S. Donnelly Jr, 'Hearts of Oak, Hearts of Steel', *Studia Hibernica*, no. 21, 1981;

idem, 'Irish agrarian rebellion: the Whiteboys of 1769–76', *Proceedings of the Royal Irish Academy*, section C, vol. lxxxiii, no. 12, 1983; David W. Miller, 'The Armagh troubles, 1784–95', in Clark and Donnelly eds., *Irish peasants*; Thomas Bartlett, 'Select documents XXXVIII: Defenders and Defenderism in 1795', *Irish Historical Studies*, vol. xxiv, no. 95, 1984–85; Maurice J. Bric, 'Popular protest movements in Kerry, 1770–1800', *Journal of the Kerry Archaeological and Historical Society*, no. 18, 1985; *idem*, 'The Whiteboy movement in Tipperary, 1760–80', in William Nolan in association with Thomas G. McGrath eds., *Tipperary: history and society: interdisciplinary essays on the history of an Irish county* (Dublin: Geography Publications, 1985); S. J. Connolly, 'Law, order and popular protest in early eighteenth-century Ireland: the case of the Houghers', in Patrick J. Corish ed., *Radicals, rebels and establishments: Historical Studies XV: papers read before the Irish Conference of Historians, Maynooth, 16–19 June 1983* (Belfast: Appletree Books, 1985); Maurice J. Bric, 'Priests, parsons and politics: the Rightboy protest in County Cork, 1785–1788', in Philpin ed., *Nationalism and popular protest in Ireland*; Thomas Bartlett, 'An end to moral economy: the Irish militia disturbances of 1793', in Philpin ed., *Nationalism and popular protest in Ireland*; S. J. Connolly, 'The Houghers: agrarian protest in early eighteenth-century Connacht', in Philpin ed., *Nationalism and popular protest in Ireland*; S. J. Connolly, 'Violence and order in the eighteenth century', in Patrick O'Flanagan, Paul Ferguson and Kevin Whelan eds., *Rural Ireland 1600–1900: modernisation and change* (Cork: Cork University Press, 1987); L. M. Cullen, 'The political structures of the Defenders', in Hugh Gough and David Dickson eds., *Ireland and the French revolution* (Dublin: Irish Academic Press, 1990); David W. Miller ed., *Peep O'Day Boys and Defenders: selected documents on the disturbances in County Armagh, 1784–1796* (Belfast: Public Record Office of Northern Ireland, 1990); Jim Smyth, 'Popular politicisation, Defenderism and the Catholic question', in Gough and Dickson eds., *Ireland and the French revolution*; *idem*, *The men of no property: Irish radicals and popular politics in the late eighteenth century* (reprint, London: Macmillan; New York: St. Martin's Press, 1998, first published in 1992); David W. Miller, 'Politicisation in revolutionary Ireland: the case of the Armagh troubles', *Irish Economic and Social History*, vol. xxiii, 1996; Eoin F. Magennis, 'A "Presbyterian insurrection"? Reconsidering the Hearts of Oak disturbances of July 1763', *Irish Historical Studies*, vol. xxxi, no. 122, 1998; Ivan F. Nelson, '"The first chapter of 1798"?: restoring a military perspective to the Irish militia riots of 1793', *Irish Historical Studies*, vol. xxxiii, no. 132, 2003; James G. Patterson, '"Educated Whiteboyism": the Cork tithe war, 1798–9', *History Ireland*, vol. xii, no. 4, 2004; Martyn J. Powell, 'Popular disturbances in late eighteenth-century Ireland: the origins of the Peep of Day Boys', *Irish Historical Studies*, vol. xxxiv, no. 135, 2005; James G. Patterson, 'Republicanism, agrarianism and banditry in the west of Ireland, 1798–1803', *Irish Historical Studies*, vol. xxxv, no. 137, 2006; *idem*, *In the wake of the great rebellion: republicanism, agrarianism and banditry in Ireland after 1798* (Manchester and New York: Manchester University Press, 2008). For the studies on the nineteenth-century disturbances, see below. Cronin offers a summary of a longer-term than this chapter covers. See Maura Cronin, *Agrarian protest in Ireland 1750–1960* (Dundalk: Dundalgan Press for the Economic and Social History Society of Ireland, 2012).

33 E.g. Donnelly, 'The Rightboy movement 1785–8', p. 133; *idem*, 'The Whiteboy movement, 1761–5', pp. 26–29; Bric, 'Priests, parsons and politics', p. 183; S. J. Connolly, 'Jacobites, Whiteboys and republicans: varieties of disaffection in eighteenth-century Ireland', *Eighteenth-Century Ireland*, vol. xviii, 2003, p. 73.

34 *Standard*, 6 Sept. 1830; E. J. Hobsbawm and George Rudé, *Captain Swing* (London: Pimlico, 1993, first published in 1969); E. P. Thompson, *Customs in common: studies in traditional popular culture* (New York: The New Press, 1991), chaps. 5 and 8, *passim*.
35 Eric Hobsbawm, *Bandits* (London: Abacus, 2001, first published in 1969), chap. 10.
36 Hugues Neveux, préface de Jean-Claude Perrot, *Les révoltes paysannes en Europe (XIVe-XVIIe siècle)* (Paris: Albin Michel, 1997), chap. 3.
37 Archer, *Social unrest and popular protest in England 1780–1840*, p. 19; Adrian Randall, '"Captain Swing": a retrospect', *International Review of Social History*, vol. 54, no. 3, Dec. 2009, p. 423.
38 Michael Beames, *Peasants and power: the Whiteboy movements and their control in pre-Famine Ireland* (Sussex: The Harvester Press; New York: St Martin's Press, 1983), p. 89.
39 Victor V. Magagna, *Communities of grain: rural rebellion in comparative perspective* (Ithaca: Cornell University Press, 1991), pp. 22–23.
40 John Stevenson, *Popular disturbances in England, 1700–1832* (second edition, Harlow and New York: Longman, 1992, first published in 1979), p. 316.
41 Bric, 'The Whiteboy movement in Tipperary, 1760–80', p. 168. See also Connolly, 'Jacobites, Whiteboys and republicans', p. 73.
42 Gale. E. Christianson, 'Secret societies and agrarian violence in Ireland, 1780–1840', *Agricultural History*, vol. xlvi, no. 3, 1972; Joseph Lee, 'The Ribbonmen', in Williams ed., *Secret societies in Ireland*; Samuel Clark, 'The importance of agrarian classes: agrarian class structure and collective action in nineteenth-century Ireland', *British Journal of Sociology*, vol. xxix, no. 1, 1978; Joseph J. Lee, 'Patterns of rural unrest in nineteenth-century Ireland: a preliminary survey', in L. M. Cullen and F. Furet eds., *Ireland and France 17th–20th centuries: towards a comparative study of rural history: proceedings of the first Franco-Irish symposium on social and economic history* ([n.p.]: Éditions de l'Ecole des Hautes Études en Sciences Sociales, 1980); David Fitzpatrick, 'Class, family and rural unrest in nineteenth-century Ireland', in P. J. Drudy ed., *Ireland: land, politics and people: Irish studies II* (Cambridge: Cambridge University Press, 1982); James W. O'Neill, 'A look at Captain Rock: agrarian rebellion in Ireland, 1815–1845', *Éire-Ireland*, vol. xvii, no. 3, 1982; Beames, *Peasants and power*; J. S. Donnelly Jr, 'The social composition of agrarian rebellions in early nineteenth-century Ireland: the case of the Carders and Caravats, 1813–16', in Corish ed., *Radicals, rebels and establishments*; M. R. Beames, 'Rural conflict in pre-Famine Ireland: peasant assassinations in Tipperary, 1837–1847', in Philpin ed., *Nationalism and popular protest in Ireland*; Alfred Zeller, *Irische Agrarbewegungen 1760–1880* (Frankfurt am Main: Peter Lang, 1989). Cf. J. W. Knott, 'Land, kinship and identity: the cultural roots of agrarian agitation in eighteenth- and nineteenth-century Ireland', *Journal of Peasant Studies*, vol. xii, no. 1, 1984.
43 David Fitzpatrick, 'Unrest in rural Ireland', *Irish Economic and Social History*, vol. xii, 1985, pp. 100–101.
44 An important exception is the study of Huggins who attempts to use the model of 'moral economy' to interpret disturbances in nineteenth-century Roscommon. While Huggins analyses these disturbances in the context of social relations in pre-Famine Irish countryside, he does not regard political dimensions as important. Michael Huggins, *Social conflict in pre-Famine Ireland: the case of County Roscommon* (Dublin: Four Courts Press, 2007), pp. 16, 174, 186, 193–194, 200–201.
45 Patrick O'Donoghue, 'Causes of the opposition to tithes, 1830–38', *Studia Hibernica*, no. 5, 1965; *idem*, 'Opposition to tithe payments in 1830–31', *Studia*

Hibernica, no. 6, 1966; *idem*, 'Opposition to tithe payment in 1832–3', *Studia Hibernica*, no. 12, 1972; J. S. Donnelly Jr, 'Pastorini and Captain Rock: millenarianism and sectarianism in the Rockite movement of 1821–24', in Clark and Donnelly eds., *Irish Peasants*; Paul E. W. Roberts, 'Caravats and Shanavests: Whiteboyism and faction fighting in east Munster, 1802–11', in Clark and Donnelly eds., *Irish Peasants*; Tom Garvin, 'Defenders, Ribbonmen and others: underground political networks in pre-Famine Ireland', in Philpin ed., *Nationalism and popular protest in Ireland*; James S. Donnelly Jr, 'The Terry Alt movement 1829–31', *History Ireland*, vol. ii, no. 4, 1994; Brendan Kiely, *The Connerys: the making of a Waterford legend* (Dublin: Geography Publications, 1994); Shunsuke Katsuta, 'The Rockite movement in county Cork in the early 1820s', *Irish Historical Studies*, vol. xxxiii, no. 131, 2003; Gerald Curtin, 'Opposition to the payment of tithes in West Limerick 1821–1838', *Old Limerick Journal*, no. 26, 2006; Allan Blackstock, 'Tommy Downshire's Boys: popular protest, social change and political manipulation in mid-Ulster, 1829–1847', *Past and Present*, no. 196, 2007; James S. Donnelly Jr, 'Captain Rock: ideology and organization in the Irish agrarian rebellion of 1821–24', *Éire-Ireland*, vol. lxii, nos. 3–4, 2007; *idem*, 'Captain Rock: the origins of the Irish agrarian rebellion of 1821–24', *New Hibernia Review*, vol. xi, no. 4, 2007; Terence Dooley, *The murders at Wildgoose Lodge: agrarian crime and punishment in pre-Famine Ireland* (Dublin: Four Courts Press, 2007); Jennifer Kelly, *'The downfall of Hagan': Sligo Ribbonism in 1842* (Dublin: Four Courts Press, 2008); James S. Donnelly Jr, *Captain Rock: the Irish agrarian rebellion of 1821–24* (Madison: University of Wisconsin Press; Cork: The Collins Press, 2009).

46 Donnelly, 'Pastorini and Captain Rock'; Finbarr Whooley, 'The Rockite movement in north Cork 1820–25', unpublished M. A. thesis, University College, Cork, 1986; Katsuta, 'The Rockite movement in county Cork in the early 1820s'; Stephen Randolph Gibbons, *Captain Rock, Night Errant: the threatening letters of pre-Famine Ireland, 1801–1845* (Dublin: Four Courts Press, 2004); Donnelly, 'Captain Rock: ideology and organization in the Irish agrarian rebellion of 1821–24'; *idem*, 'Captain Rock: the origins of the Irish agrarian rebellion of 1821–24'; *idem*, *Captain Rock: the Irish agrarian rebellion of 1821–24*; Denis A. Cronin, *Who killed the Franks family? agrarian violence in pre- Famine Cork* (Dublin: Four Courts Press, 2009).

47 Donnelly, *Captain Rock: the Irish agrarian rebellion of 1821–24*, chap. 4, p. 342. Italics are original.

48 Donnelly's book only touches on the engagements without any analysis. *Ibid.*, pp. 68–71.

49 By stressing the new development in parliamentary politics concerning Ireland in the early 1820s, this book, in Chapter 4, section 3, tries to revise partly Hoppen's recent works, which see the first thirty years of the nineteenth century indiscriminately. K. Theodore Hoppen, 'An incorporating Union?: British politicians and Ireland 1800–1830', *English Historical Review*, vol. cxxiii, no. 501, 2008, pp. 15–17, 20–21; *idem*, *Governing Hibernia: British politicians and Ireland 1800–1921* (Oxford: Oxford University Press, 2016), chap. 2, esp. pp. 27, 31–34.

50 Boyd Hilton, 'The political arts of Lord Liverpool', *Transactions of the Royal Historical Society*, 5th series, vol. xxxviii, 1988, p. 160.

51 The second series were described as 'an important addition to contemporary papers of this class', meaning the first series of the State of the Country Papers. Public Records in Ireland, *Deputy Keeper's Report*, 49th, 1917, p. 17. For detailed information of the making of the State of the Country Papers, L. M. Cullen, 'The "suppression" of the Volunteers and United Irishmen: sources

and interpretation 1792–4', in Bernard Browne ed., *The Wexford man: essays in honour of Nicky Furlong* (Dublin: Geography Publications, 2007), pp. 67–69.

52 The calendaring of the first series was completed in 1927. *Deputy Keeper's Report*, 56th, 1931, p. 77. Of boxes 154–178 of the second series, only 154–157 (years 1790–1808) have been calendared in an unidentified hand, but no further arrangement has been made to the second series. These uncalendared papers are specified in this book by the date, the sender, the receiver, and the box number. Uncalendared CSORP are specified in the same way.

53 BPP, Select committee to inquire into disturbances in Ireland, minutes of evidence, 1825 (20) VII. 1; *idem*, Select Committee of House of Lords on nature and extent of disturbances in Ireland, minutes of evidence, 1825 (200) VII. 501; *idem*, Select committee . . . minutes of evidence, 1825 (129) VIII. 1; *idem*, Select committee of House of Lords to inquire into state of Ireland with reference to disturbances, minutes of evidence, 1825 (181) IX. 1; *idem*, Select committee of House of Lords to inquire into state of Ireland with reference to disturbances, minutes of evidence, 1825 (521) IX. 249. The last two papers are from the same committee.

1 Rockites as agrarian disturbers

Rural society in County Cork

This chapter deals with the agrarian dimensions of the Rockites, taking an instance of their activities in County Cork. Cork is the biggest of the thirty-two counties in Ireland in terms of geographical size. In terms of population as well, it was the biggest in early nineteenth-century Ireland, having about 10 percent of the total. How have historians looked at its rural society? Although the first half of the nineteenth century can be regarded almost as a 'statistical dark age' for Ireland,[1] censuses offer a good starting point. The first complete census in Ireland was that of 1821. While that census was ideal in date to ascertain the social background of Rockites, it only showed 'the number of persons chiefly employed in agriculture' and did not make any further distinction within that category.[2] The 1831 census is of more use.[3] It divided adult males (above twenty years of age) employed in agriculture into three categories, i.e., farmers (occupiers employing labourers), smallholders (occupiers not employing labourers) and labourers.

According to the 1831 census, there existed in County Cork (excluding the city) 171,873 adult males, of whom 125,726 belonged to the farming community.[4] Of these 125,726, there were 14,862 farmers, 35,613 smallholders and 75,251 agricultural labourers. The census defined farmers as those who constantly hired at least one labourer, which meant they formed the pillar of the middle class in rural Ireland in the early nineteenth century. While smallholders were practically 'family' farmers, they also were basically market producers, forming the lower-middle class in the countryside. At the same time, it was sometimes pointed out that the distinction between them and agricultural labourers was becoming less clear, because of the decline in the living-standard of the smallholders which forced some of them to seek employment by farmers.[5] The agricultural labourers were constantly employed by farmers and formed the bulk of the 'rural poor'. The 1831 census shows that the agricultural labourers formed about 60 percent of the farming community in Cork. This ratio was higher than the national average: in Ireland as a whole, of the total of 1,227,054 men belonging to the farming community 567,441 (46 percent) were the agricultural labourers.

There were several internal differences within Cork. First, in terms of urbanisation and religious composition Cork had a marked gap between north and south. In the early nineteenth century 58 percent of the total Protestant population of the county resided in the south-west of the county, while in 1821 ten of the total fourteen towns of more than 2,000 inhabitants lay in the south.[6] The main theatre of Rockites' activities in Cork was in the rural and Catholic north: four northern baronies of Duhallow, West Muskerry, Orrery and Kilmore, and Fermoy. Secondly, of those four baronies, Fermoy and Orrery and Kilmore can be broadly categorised into a cereal-producing region, while Duhallow (west of) and West Muskerry can be described as a dairy region. The difference between those two regions can be seen in Map 1.1, which shows that the cereal-producing region had a higher land value than the dairy region.

The two regions had a marked difference in another important respect, i.e. social structure. Fermoy barony, to take instance, had a highly stratified society. In 1831 there were 6,385 agricultural labourers employed by 755 farmers, which meant each farmer hired more than eight labourers on average. In contrast, the barony of West Muskerry had 4976 labourers against 1,581 farmers, making the barony less bottom-heavy than Fermoy.[7] Fermoy barony had been an old cereal-producing region since the seventeenth century,[8] and the region was described as 'the garden of Ireland' in the early nineteenth century,[9] with five large flour mills, one of which was allegedly the biggest in Ireland.[10]

The region had a cultural and political centre, Mallow, the second biggest town and the only parliamentary borough in the north of the county.

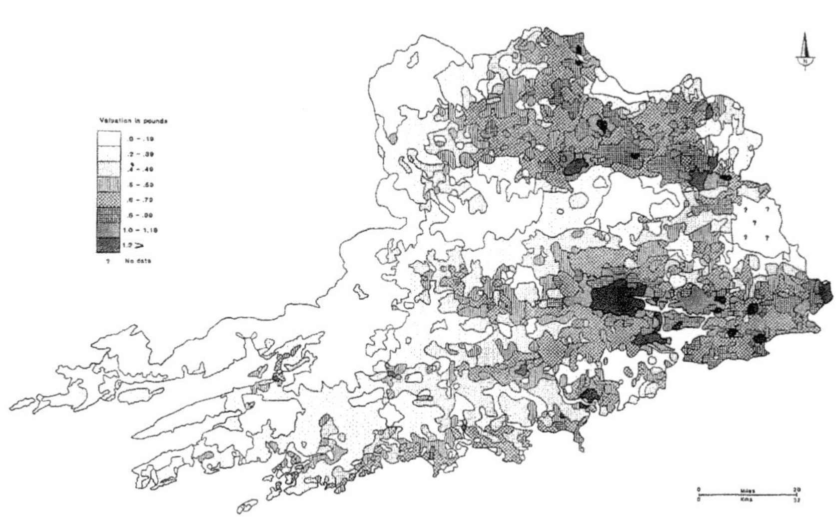

Map 1.1 County Cork's land values, 1851[11]

About fifty gentlemen had their seats around Mallow in the latter half of the eighteenth century, and that made the region Munster's most conspicuously landlord-embellished zone,[12] accompanied with the fastest rate of decline in the use of the Irish language in rural Cork in the early nineteenth century.[13] Although its heyday was gone, early nineteenth-century Mallow was still called the Bath of Ireland, and according to one account, 'Pleasure [was] . . . the object pursued by [its] inhabitants'.[14] The town's keeping its parliamentary seat after the Union played an important role in making it 'a very disaffected place'.[15] It was Mallow which became the most important centre of the Rockites' underground organisations in County Cork.

Some information about agricultural labourers living in the cereal-growing region is provided in a parliamentary committee of 1823. The witness, Sir James Anderson, was a landowner living in the town of Buttevant and running an estate in Fermoy which he inherited from his father. According to him, the agricultural labourer lived and worked in the following way: 'There is a charge made for the potato garden of the labourer, for the grass of his cow, and for his house, and then, on the other side of the account, the number of days he works is put to his credit.'[16] Exchanging labour for land, the agricultural labourer in pre-Famine Ireland was basically a cultivator as well as a labourer, which made contemporaries sometimes call them peasants. The 'charge' he paid and the wage he received were in fact nominal, because of the deficiency in the circulation of cash at that time. While this nominal account system could work to the disadvantage of labourers,[17] the labourer cited above seems to have been in a relatively better position than others of his class. Another witness testified in 1824 that few of the labourers near Mallow could keep a cow.[18]

It should be added that an agricultural labourer had other sources of income, in the form of cash, beyond his own labour, i.e. the potato and the pig. Although an ordinary labourer ate nearly twelve pounds of potato a day,[19] which suggests he ate little else, an Irish acre (i.e. about 1.6 statute acre) of land, the basic unit for renting, would produce more potatoes than any family would consume in one year. Hence in a year blessed with a good harvest he could make some money by selling potatoes to market or using them to fatten his pigs for sale.[20] Though potatoes required much less land than cereals to give the same calorific values, it must be added that the potato was an unreliable crop. There was at least one crop failure somewhere in the island in every two- or three-years in the early nineteenth century.[21] In such bad years the rural poor had to reduce the number of pigs they kept, the food of the man and the pig being the same.[22] The export of pork from Ireland more than trebled over a period of some thirty years in the early nineteenth century. Because the pig existed basically as a poor man's cash-earning beast, the fact not only reflects an increase in the number of the rural poor themselves but suggests a deterioration in the living standard of the Irish farming community as a whole.[23]

The labourer's 'landlord' was not necessarily a landowner but often a farmer who in turn rented a farm from his landowner.[24] Farmers who produced cereals needed to put potato cultivation (by labourers) in the crop rotation for the sake of the rehabilitation of soil. About one-third of the cereal-producing land was constantly devoted to potato cultivation in early nineteenth-century Ireland.[25] In addition, cereal cultivation needed a much greater labour input, estimated at five times bigger than that of dairy farming.[26] These two combined factors in the cereal production, i.e. necessity of potato cultivation and big labour demand, seem to explain the bottom-heavy social structure of the cereal-producing region.

Some information about farmers in the cereal-producing region is obtained from papers of the estates of Viscount Doneraile.[27] On his Buttevant estate there were forty farms and forty-seven 'labourers' cabins' in 1844.[28] Richard Rogers, one of the farmers on the estate, held a farm of forty-three English acres where two labourers' cabins existed. It was generally known then that three families of labourers were needed for the management of a cereal farm of thirty acres, in contrast to which, one family could run a dairy farm of sixty acres.[29] Rogers kept in fact fourteen acres of his farm for wheat cultivation, eleven acres for oats, some of which must have been under potato cultivation. Rogers also had nine cows, eight sheep, two horses and seventeen pigs,[30] which shows that he ran a mixed farming holding.

The dairy region of the west of Duhallow or West Muskerry presented a striking difference from the cereal-producing Fermoy or Orrery and Kilmore. As is shown in Map 1.2, the region was hilly and mostly under pasture.

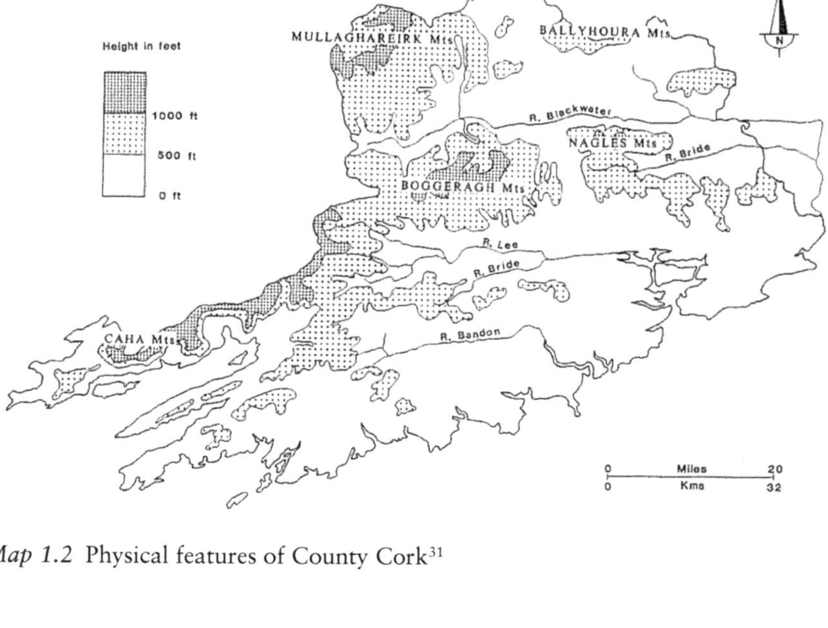

Map 1.2 Physical features of County Cork[31]

The development of this region was relatively recent. In the west of Duhallow transhumance continued well into the eighteenth century, and it was only after the 1740s that pockets of permanent settlement began to be established there.[32] Even in the early nineteenth century most of the land was unreclaimed,[33] and the road structure was in a primitive state.[34] The value of land was estimated by the number of cows which it could support.[35] These facts suggest that the traditional 'Irish' way of life survived here to some extent. A witness testified in a parliamentary committee in 1825 that he conceived the west of Duhallow 'of all parts of Ireland, to have been the one most imperfectly subjected to the English conquest, or to the English laws.'[36] While there were only two towns in Duhallow, Kanturk and Newmarket,[37] neither of them had a resident magistrate before the outbreak of the Rockite disturbances.[38]

West Muskerry was more or less at a similar stage of development. The barony had no more than three towns which deserved the name, i.e. Macroom, Millstreet and Blarney.[39] Macroom together with Millstreet played their role as frontier towns.[40] A landlord who came to live in Macroom in the early eighteenth century deplored the virtual absence of Protestants in the surrounding region.[41] Even in the early nineteenth century Millstreet was described as deriving its chief support from a small military barrack and inns.[42] The proportion of the number of Protestant inhabitants in this region was not more than 2 percent in the first half of the nineteenth century, in contrast to the county average of about 9 percent.[43]

The butter production of this region was controlled by butter buyers based in Cork City. A butter buyer gave producers (dairy farmers and smallholders) an advance at the commencement of the season (April) for paying rent or preparing for butter production. Between July and October producers made returns to the butter buyer from the money made by the sale of butter at Cork City. Butter of the best quality was exported to London and Lisbon. While one butter buyer might make advances amounting to £15,000 in a season to producers of various sizes, what a 'poor farmer' could borrow reached only £5 a year for his butter production with three or five cows.[44] These poor farmers, probably smallholders in the 1831 census, appeared as 'little farmers' in the following account by a London surgeon who visited Millstreet in 1822:

> Stopped a few minutes in Millstreet, where the beggars were as numerous as at Macroom . . . The country still badly cultivated, and wearing a desolate appearance; the cabins excessively wretched. Met a great many little farmers driving their stunted horses with back-loads of butter, three casks each, to the Cork market.[45]

It was in this dairy region that thousands of people had gathered and fought with the troops in January 1822 in daytime. In comparison, Rockites in the cereal-producing region were clandestine and small-scale in their activities. Before looking at their activities in each region, however, it is necessary to investigate the question of poverty in rural Ireland before the Famine.

Poverty

Poverty was a common-place topic of the day. Some of the contemporary literature seems to have been politically motivated in arguing that misgovernment was the cause of misery. Here reports of the Board of Health, a government institution, may be a good starting point. The Board commissioned informed men in the country in 1820 to report on the condition of their localities. A clergyman of the Church of Ireland in the parish of Clondrohid near Macroom returned the following report:

> The cabins are mostly constructed of stones with clay mortar . . . windows very few, what there are do not open, but the glass in them is generally broken, and of course there is an admission of air. . . . The interior of their houses is generally dirty . . . they have not cattle, except pigs, which in some cases are kept in the house at night. . . . Many of the inhabitants have feather beds, such as have not, sleep on straw, almost all have bedsteads and blankets. . . . Their food consists almost exclusively of potatoes, generally in sufficiency . . .[46]

Another but more graphic description is given in the picture in Figure 1.1, which was of a poor man's cabin in County Clare in the 1830s.

Figure 1.1 A poor man's cabin (Connery, 1837, p. 44)

Nobody would deny that people living in such conditions were poor. However, poverty, like famine as is mentioned below, itself rarely causes people to rise. What matters here is the relative poverty. The Irish administration commissioned another investigation of the condition of the poor in the country in 1813. A clergyman of the Church of Ireland in the parish of Macroom answered that 'The general food of the people in the country is potatoes and milk; few of them have meat . . . except on a Sunday. . . . Go into the poorest cabin in the country, and they will cheerfully offer you share of their potatoes and milk, butter and eggs, and be affronted if you refuse them.'[47]

These two accounts, put together, suggest that there was certain deterioration in the condition of the poor in this region between 1813 and 1820, which may be confirmed by the account by the surgeon mentioned above. A deterioration in conditions can be inferred from other accounts. The Rev. H. Townsend, who left a detailed account of County Cork at the beginning of the nineteenth century, wrote that the agricultural labourers in the barony of Duhallow in 1810 enjoyed 'very sufficient means of comfortable subsistence'.[48] In early 1822, however, it was regarded as 'luxurious' for the poor in that region to drink milk.[49] In the cereal-producing region as well, Anderson, the above-mentioned landowner, testified in 1823 that 'The distress is very great, and has been since 1817, but has considerably increased for the last two years.'[50]

What may have been the reason for the deterioration? Anderson pointed out as the primary cause the general shortage of employment, which was reflected in a fall in wages. According to him, the general rate of wages in his region was six pence per day, but he was perfectly confident that he 'could get five hundred individuals to work at four pence per day'. He added that 'I have known many instances in which the anxiety of people for employment was evinced so far as to lead them to exertions beyond their strength. They would work ten hours a day for 4d.'[51] A fall in wages was reported from other districts as well. The average wage for one day's labour in the diocese of Cloyne in the north of County Cork was about eight pence, having fallen from about eleven pence around 1809.[52] In Duhallow in the early 1810s a casual labourer could earn a shilling a day including meals (eighteen pence without food), while in Fermoy in the same period the average wage was estimated to be five shillings a week.[53] Thus, it is fairly safe to conclude that there was a steep fall in employment in the early 1820s. That phenomenon was not confined to Cork. A witness from Kerry testified in a parliamentary committee in 1823 that there existed 'the greatest possible anxiety on the part of the people to procure employment'.[54]

As a cause of this want of employment, a rapid increase in population, particularly among the rural poor, was often mentioned.[55] The Rev. Townsend gave the following account to Dublin Castle in an investigation of the condition of the country in 1819:

> . . . agricultural wages are rather fallen. Indeed they cannot rise in a country where population encreases faster than the demand for labour and in some places than the means of subsistence. This is principally ascribable to that total unconcern for future welfare which belongs to every ignorant and half-civilised population. . . . A young pauper of 21 marries a girl of 18 equally poor tho' with a certainty of soon having half a dozen children which they must be unable to maintain. When severely pinched the husband takes a spade on his shoulder and sets off looking for work in England or other parts of Ireland. The wife travels up & down the country with her little flock begging & sometimes stealing. . . . This pilgrimage generally takes place in the spring when the little stock of potatoes is out & continues till the new ones come in, about August. I am sure not less than 10 or 15 flocks come daily to my house during that interval, few women having less than six children & several having more.[56]

It is true that population was growing quite fast at that time. County Cork saw its population more than doubled between 1766 and 1821.[57] Taking Ireland as a whole, the population in the century before the Famine grew by 300 percent, the highest rate (possibly excepting Finland) in Europe of the day,[58] which caused the country to have the highest rate of farming population/arable land in Europe in 1845.[59]

However, this population increase was a long-term trend which cannot fully explain why there was a particular fall in employment in the early 1820s. The want of employment in the early 1820s was, in fact, not created by the employee (the rural poor) but by the employer, i.e. the farmer. The Buttevant estate owned by Lord Doneraile in the north of County Cork offers a striking example. Most of the farms on the estate were leased at about 1810. The sum total of rent arrears on the estate was £615 in May 1820, but it jumped to £4,839 in November 1823. The sum total of the estate rent was only about £2,424 per year,[60] which suggests that the tenant farmers were under severe hardship. This estate was no exception. From near Macroom it was reported in 1821 that on an estate with a rental of £5,000, arrears of £11,000 had accumulated over about the preceding five years.[61]

One factor behind the economic hardship of the early 1820s was the widespread bank failure which hit Munster in June 1820. A magistrate of County Kerry reported that 'the state of the country is truly pitiable, what constituted the circulating medium of the south & south west of this kingdom is now little better than waste papers'.[62] The impact of the bank failure caused butter buyers in Munster to stop using their own notes which they had issued to butter farmers in advance,[63] though the crisis itself was over in several weeks.[64]

Another and more important cause of the hardship was the drastic fall in agricultural prices, shown in Table 1.1. Already in 1814, a warning was sent from County Cork to Dublin Castle that 'Farmers who took grounds

Table 1.1 Agricultural prices in the south of Ireland, 1812–1824 (Shillings/cwt.)

	Wheat	*Barley*	*Oats*	*Butter*
1812	22.71	14.06	11.29	116.70
1813	18.53	11.65	11.05	112.50
1814	12.64	8.88	7.50	118.00
1815	12.16	5.43	5.77	116.75
1816	17.10	7.19	7.14	93.00
1817	19.67	11.22	9.93	99.13
1818	17.05	12.75	10.73	123.63
1819	13.82	10.06	8.04	98.25
1820	11.64	6.19	5.77	85.88
1821	9.74	5.23	4.84	85.75
1822	7.46	5.36	4.95	72.88
1823	9.83	6.92	5.46	82.38
1824	12.64	9.25	7.16	91.88

(Kennedy and Solar (2007), appendix tables)

within these last ten or dozen years will be ruined should the present prices of grain continue'.[65] Nevertheless, prices declined further, to create severe agricultural depression in the early 1820s. All market producers, from rich farmers to poor smallholders, found it difficult to pay rent to their landlords, while the rural poor were also indirectly affected. As potato cultivators, they were not greatly affected by price falls, but as labourers did suffer adversely. As Anderson testified, the gentry and farmers were 'in a state of distress to diminish or rather almost wholly extinguish their means of giving employment to the poor.'[66]

One thing remains to be considered. In addition to the price falls, rural society in the south of Ireland at the time of the Rockite disturbances experienced another hardship, i.e. the famine of 1822. The direct cause of the famine was the bad harvest of the preceding year and the subsequent heavy rain which severely damaged the potato crop stored underground.[67] In November 1821, a magistrate in County Clare foresaw 'as bad a spring & summer as the south of Ireland ever saw'.[68] In January 1822 'Captn. John Rock' at 'Millst. head quarters' prohibited forestalling or sending corn out of the country, as he had 'received several petitions from the lower classes of the inhabitants of . . . [the] county of Kerry complaining of the heavy pressure of the times and the great scarcity apprehended'.[69] In County Cork the same year 'John Rock Commander in Chief of the United Irishmen' ordered against bringing potatoes into the market in March.[70] However, it is difficult to argue that the famine of 1822 played any significant role, psychological shock apart, in Rockite disturbances. Popular disturbances in general were not motivated by famine in itself.[71] In the case of the Rockites, notices showing any concern with the anticipated famine, such as the ones cited above, constituted only a very small minority of the total. In addition, the area worst affected by the famine in County Cork was its southern communities,[72] where Rockites were not active. Furthermore, the potato harvest of 1822 was relatively good,[73] but the Rockites remained active after that.

In any event, the most important economic factor in the Rockite disturbances was the fall in agricultural prices in the early 1820s. It is now turn to look at how Cork Rockites tried to cope with the severe agricultural depression.

Rockites as defenders of the status quo

During the night of the first of April 1823, the house of Thomas Regan, a farmer residing in the parish of Caherduggan in Fermoy barony, was 'visited' by seven men. One of them was armed with a gun, another with a bayonet. They forced him to swear to comply with the following notice he had received before:

> Thos Regan
>
> you seems [*sic*] to be ignorant of the new cade of law recently given out by the legislature [*sic*] of Ireland[.] Now I command you on pain of death to give out gardens at 4Gs. [St] plantation acre and houses at one [guinea] each . . . if you presume the liberty of violating those laws in any respect whatsoever you wll [*sic*] not be left. . . [March] 17th 1823 Signed Liut. Deeptought[74]

'The legislature of Ireland' was Captain Rock, under whose authority 'Liut. Deeptought' issued the above notice. Since the charge of four guineas per plantation (i.e. Irish) acre of potato land was entirely normal by contemporary standards,[75] in this case Rockites seem to have been trying to defend the interest of the agricultural labourer.

While the seven men who visited Regan's house cannot be identified, during the next night two other farmers in the same parish were also 'visited' and a notice was served on each of them, which were reportedly similar to that used in the case of Regan.[76] Lest their notices be ignored, Captain Rock's men resorted to violence. On the night of the 22 October 1823, two farmers near Buttevant in the barony of Orrery and Kilmore received Rockite visits. A party of thirty armed men broke into one farmer's house, beat him and broke the windows because he, contrary to Captain Rock's notice posted before, employed strangers, having said that Captain Rock was dead. Labourers from outside were generally hated because they would take local labourers' jobs. Hence, the Rockite party also beat those in-coming labourers employed by him. Then they went to the other farmer's house and beat him as well, as he was too strict on his labourers and occasionally employed outsiders.[77]

Rockites appeared in various other places to defend the interests of the rural poor. Their main issues were access to potato land, its rent, employment and wages. In the four Cork baronies of Duhallow, West Muskerry, Orrery and Kilmore, and Fermoy, eighty-six cases of outrage (using threatening notice, arson, violence against person or cattle) were committed for that purpose between October 1821 and September 1824 (inclusive).[78]

However, Rockite disturbances were not merely a class struggle of the rural poor against the farmers. The agricultural depression in the early 1820s severely affected market producers in general, and Rockites could appear for the purpose of defending their interests, making tenancy of land and rent their chief issues. During the night of 2 March 1823, the house of Patrick Regan was visited by an armed party. The leader served Regan with a notice signed 'General Rock, by the grace of God', threatening to destroy the property and maim his cattle if he persisted in holding a certain piece of land he had lately taken.[79] Of course, non-compliance with Rock's order resulted in punishment. During the night of 3 February 1823, the house of Thomas Quinlan, a 'respectable farmer' near Glanworth in Fermoy barony was 'visited' by an armed party of between twelve and fifteen men. They beat Quinlan's son and burnt his dwelling house as well as his barn and corn. They told him the reason was that Quinlan was a stranger and rented his farm against their 'law'.[80] Here Rockites were practicing a kind of boycott: if there was nobody who dared to take a newly vacant farm, landlords would hesitate to evict the current tenant. That strategy seems to have been fairly common.

In the barony of Orrery and Kilmore, a landlord evicted a tenant, cancelling his arrears of rent and allowing him to remove his crops of the previous season. The tenant left apparently with gratitude, but the farm house was burnt when the new tenant settled in it.[81] In another case, the farm house was burnt down on the very day the former occupier left it.[82] In Duhallow as well, the house from which a farmer was evicted because of non-payment of rent was burnt down the day after he left it.[83] In some cases, arson could be committed even before the scheduled date of the farmer's leaving.[84] In sum, 113 cases of outrage can be identified which aimed at defending the interests of tenants (farmers and smallholders) in the four baronies mentioned before between October 1821 and September 1824 (inclusive).[85]

Thus, Rockites were multi-faceted disturbers. While there is evidence to show that farmers did become Rockites (Chapter 2), Captain Rock even tried to defend both farmers' and labourers' interests at the same time, as is shown in the following notice which was sent to the post office in Kanturk in Duhallow barony to be posted up in February 1822:

> Major Bush . . . experiencing and seeing the yoke and grievances that the lower order of people are labouring under must insist on enforcing and making the following temporary laws perpetual[:] viz landlords

> and landjobbers to give an abatement in their rents adequate to the present times and rates[,] and the under tenents to give a proportional abatement to poor people in their garden or quarter grounds[;] he also expects that . . . gentlemen and rich [?churches] to keep no milkmen dairymen or herdsmen but to let the lands to honest industrious tenants for the value[;] also any person or persons who within those years back canted his on their nabour or fellow creature pot of a farm or tenement is to surrender or give up the same under pain of incuring the displeasure of our hero. . . . By order of the Right Honl. John Rock K.C.B.[86]

Their activities taken together, Rockites as agrarian disturbers seem to have aimed less at promoting than protecting the interests of present occupiers of land, either farmers or labourers, which had been exacerbated by the depression. This defensive attitude makes a contrast to their notions of radical social and political changes mentioned in the Introduction. It is true that John Hickey, the Rockite, referred to 'The getting rid of taxes, tythe and things of that sort' as one of their objectives.[87] David Nagle (Captain Rock in Cork) also mentioned that they intended 'to abolish tithes, to reduce rents, and not to pay any rent which they could possibly avoid'.[88] However, in the real world, Rockites tried to preserve the current state of affairs by setting up their defensive 'law' and punishing one by one those who violated it in each district. In that way, they were similar to traditional Whiteboys, i.e. agrarian nightly marauders with rather limited objectives. The Rockites' vision of a new world where there would be no economic hardships was to be realised in a completely different way, as will be discussed in Chapter 3.

The Rockites' conservatism showed itself in another of the major grievances in the rural society of the day, tithe. Tithe had originally been charged by the Church of Ireland on every product of land, but dairy land became exempt in 1735 and remained so until 1823. Accordingly, Rockite outrages concerning tithe showed a marked regional difference between cereal-growing regions and dairy-farming regions. Seventy-six cases of outrages concerning tithe can be identified in Orrery and Kilmore and Fermoy baronies between October 1821 and September 1824 (inclusive), which should be compared to only ten in Duhallow and West Muskerry in the same period.[89] The parish of Doneraile in Fermoy barony saw particularly violent opposition to tithe.

During the night of 17 January 1822, seven houses in the parish of Doneraile were successively 'visited' by an armed party of Rockites. The leader of the party was described as 'genteely [*sic*] dressed', who said on leaving one of those houses that they had a great deal to do and must be off.[90] The party desired the resident of another house not to pay any tithe and enquired about a tithe haggard in the neighbourhood.[91] Soon afterwards, 'Sir general Rock' sent a threatening notice to Richard Hill, warning that 'no person in the parish of Donerail [*sic*] will not be aloud [to] have the least call to thyths'.[92] This notice was followed by another, which warned the tithe valuator of Doneraile parish not to proceed with his business.[93]

The climax came after the harvest. In September of the same year, another threatening notice was posted, this time warning James Hill, apparently a gentleman farmer,[94] against having anything to do with tithe, which Hill ignored.[95] In consequence, his haggard and cow house were burnt a few days later. The haggard was described as one of the largest and the best preserved in the country.[96] Arson against tithe continued after this incident in Doneraile. In sum, thirty cases of outrage concerning tithe can be identified in that parish alone between October 1821 and September 1824 (inclusive).[97]

However outstanding the case of Doneraile may have looked, what was happening in the parish was in fact no more than a large-scale opposition to a new method of tithe valuation by an enforced boycott. The question of tithe was causing considerable confusion in Doneraile at that time. The tithe farmer of the parish went bankrupt and was committed to gaol for debt by the impropriator of tithe, who had newly employed his proctor. The new proctor began collecting tithe by a new method of valuation. Landlords were so dissatisfied with the new method that they declared they would advise their tenants not to bargain for the tithes. Farmers, encouraged by their landlords' attitude, threatened each other that if anyone should bargain for tithe, his tithe corn would be burnt. It was because James Hill acceded to the payment of tithe by this new method that his haggard was burnt.[98] Thus, Rockites' activities against tithe in that parish were connived at and to some extent encouraged. In fact, Lord Doneraile, the principal landlord, was criticised by Dublin Castle for his conduct on the question of tithe.[99]

In short, prohibition on the payment of tithe did not necessarily mean an attempt at the complete abolition of tithes. It was not in Doneraile alone where Rockites' activities were no more than a localised reaction to a change. In the parish of Kilshannig in Duhallow a proposal for a change in tithe valuation resulted in several notices being posted which showed orders from Captain Rock to parishioners not to pay any tithes.[100] The tithe burden was in fact not so heavy as it may appear. Taking Ireland as a whole, the actual tithe levy was estimated as not a tenth but about 3 percent of the total produce,[101] which made the burden of rent heavier.[102] The real grievance over tithe was its uncertainty both in valuation and payment which 'throws the peasantry completely at the feet of the proctor'.[103] Accordingly, it happened that in other cases of County Cork Rockites either simply fixed a limit to the sum of payment,[104] or aimed at eliminating tithe farmers by ordering tithe payment directly to the vicar.[105]

Rockites, seen as agrarian disturbers facing the agricultural depression of the 1820s, were thus more or less like ordinary Whiteboys. However, it must be shown that in two respects they were unique, i.e. their interest in acquiring arms (to be dealt with in Chapter 2) and their use of arson.

One of the most spectacular cases of Rockite arson was committed against a tithe farmer in the parish of Caherduggan in Fermoy barony in December 1822. Four hundred barrels of corn and several tons of hay were burnt, with the arsonists standing by, firing shots and shouting in exultation as the flames gathered higher.[106] Nagle later confessed he was on the spot as one of the arsonists.[107]

As Captain Rock boasted, his 'fireman' appeared in many places.[108] It was reported that on one night in September 1822 five fires could be observed from Kildorrery, which had command of the surrounding region.[109] Because arson could be used not only for the tithe issue but also for other issues, the number of arson incidents identified in County Cork between October 1821 and March 1825 (inclusive) amounted to no less than 324.[110] It should be noted that not all cases of arson were committed by Rockites. In some cases the proprietor set fire to his own property for the purpose of obtaining compensation from the local grand jury.[111] Nevertheless, when taken as a whole, the Rockite incendiarism may have been an exceptional phenomenon in the history of rural disturbances in the British Isles. While the scale of their activities as arsonists would have seemed staggering to eighteenth-century Whiteboys, the number of arson cases committed in the counties of Norfolk and Suffolk during the Swing Riots in three years of 1830–32 was 175.[112]

One cause of the Rockites' violent incendiarism was the prevalence of thatched houses in rural Ireland. This, however, had been the same in the eighteenth century. Why did Rockites in the nineteenth century resort to arson to such an extent?

Arson can be committed by a small number of men, or even an individual, without much preparation, which means it is an effective weapon of the weak facing the mighty hand and vigilant eye of the authorities. It was, therefore, because the repressive measures of the Irish government were strengthened in the early nineteenth century that Rockites resorted to arson much more frequently than their eighteenth-century predecessors (a point to be made in Chapter 4). It is worthwhile noting that the authorities, including the Irish Chief Secretary, fully admitted the difficulty of containing incendiarists.[113] In September 1822, two large-scale cases of arson occurred near Doneraile, although 'a very great number of houses were searched without finding an individual absent' in the region by the military on that night.[114] In February of the next year the military commander in the north of County Cork confessed that he had begun 'to despair of seeing order and tranquillity established in this part of the country.'[115]

Rockite 'law'

While Rockites committed arson and other outrages as a punishment for those who disobeyed their 'law' and as an indirect warning to others, they seldom used violence without giving a direct warning to the victim in advance. The warning usually took the form of delivering a threatening notice to him or putting it up in a public place. Such notices offer a useful source in describing aspects of the mental world of the Rockites.

In March 1822, the following notice was put up near the town of Doneraile:

> Notice
> To Arthur G. Creagh Esqr
> Sir
> You seem to be ignorant of the 3d article of the statute of the new code of laws as recently given out by the legislator of Ireland, Genl. John Rock. As I am informed you intend to appropriate to your own that part of the lands of [Cloonbane] as lately held by John O'Donoghue by him surrendered last Sep[.] You are not it seems afraid of increasing the General's displeasure nor do you care [for] the industrious poor of your neighbourhood . . . Now Sir I command you in our General's name to set said lands to some industrious man who is not a stranger in your parish[,] at a reasonable rent as likewise to augment the wages of your labourers & all who are employed in your service. Otherwise the consequence of your failure of obeying these command [*sic*] [will] be the destruction of your cattle, consuming your house & effects & [?launching] yourself & family into eternity by the fast sailing [b – y] double [barrels] . . . Aimwell
> Signed by order of General John Rock
> by his Secretary of State
> Major Genl. Deep [T]hought[116]

While this 'proclamation' was probably intended to defend the interests of farmers as well as those of the poor, it is the style rather than the substance which is important here. This '3d article of the statute of the new code of laws' had been already 'proclaimed' in the neighbourhood: 'General John Rock Legislator General of Ireland' gave out 'a new code of laws' decreeing that 'it is unlawful for any gentleman to hold any more lands than that which immediately adjoins his dwelling residence'.[117] Thus, in order to cope with a particular problem in the locality, Rockites issued their order in the style of universal 'law'.

While Rockites borrowed elements of officialdom to put authority to their 'law',[118] the variety of their rhetoric is remarkable (e.g. Figure 1.2). A notice which appeared in Fermoy barony in February 1824 stated 'it is no rhetorical expression or metaphor, but the downright truth, signed at the Secretary Committee Office, by order of Generalissimo of the Royal Irish Radicals at my Hall Dublin the indefatigable'.[119] Sometimes Rock was styled as K. C. B.[120] Another proclamation 'By his excellency John Rock Captain General, and Supreme Director of Irish Liberators' appeared in the parish of Kinneigh in East Carbery barony in January 1822, which made Baron Carbery suspect that 'there are some persons concerned in this wicked business above the common order.'[121] In a 'proclamation' in the parish of Caherduggan in March 1823 'the [Deboneir] Captain Rock' warned that 'Your infidelity and your transgressions against the [new] established laws of this

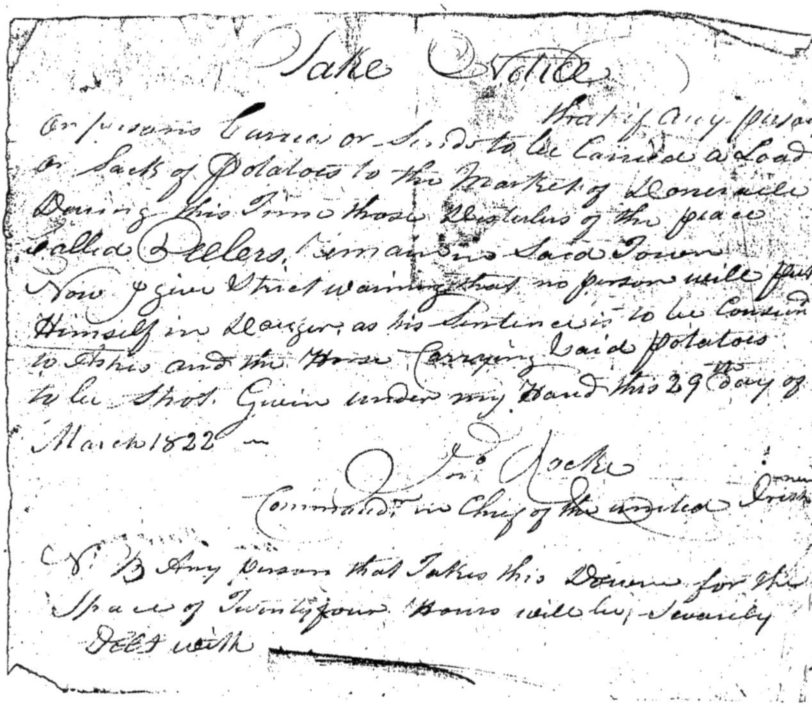
Take Notice
That if any person or persons carries or sends to be carried a load or sack of potatoes to the market of Doneraile during this time those [illegible] of the place called Dealers remaining said town
Now I give strict warning that no person will put himself in danger as his sentence is to be [illegible] to ashes and the horse carrying said potatoes to be shot. Given under my hand this 29th day of March 1822 —
Jno. Rocke
Commandr. in Chief of the United Irish
N. B. Any person that takes this down for the space of twentyfour hours will be severely delt with

Figure 1.2 A Rockite notice, signed 'John Rock, Commander in Chief of the United Irishmen'[122]

land which were founded on the laws of God, must be represented before the Senaters [*sic*] at the illustrious Senate House'.[123]

Among the various rhetorical styles used by Rockites, what looked most authoritative to the contemporaries may have been that of official proclamation. The following notice which appeared in Duhallow barony in March 1823 offers an example:

> A Proclamation.
> To All Whom It May Concern.
> It is hoped that no person will display the rudeness of taking down this paper until satisfactory [*sic*] read, the motive of it being, to preserve from ruin property life and family, by acquainting the publick of a few capital errors which ought to be particularly avoided as the ignorance of them might lead people blindfold to be hurled down the steep and rugged precipice of destruction – Behold my sword is unsheathed to mow down offenders my fire is kindled every night to consume their propertys my resolution is fixed, therefore I hope, that no person will be so infatuated as [thro'] a violation of my laws to lay his head on the block or thrust himself and all his possessions into the flame that opens widely. . . . 'Tis true we have been deprived of some of our associates by hanging and transportation, but this has only

encreased our strength, as weeding a garden encourages the growth of the genuine plant[,] consequently I expect that due adherence will be paid to the following articles as the violation of any of them deserves shooting and burning besides several other excruciating tortures —

Article 1st – That no person or persons shall propose for or take into possession directly or indirectly any house, farm, or lot of lands, wrested form a tenant by his landlords, until the expiration of 7 years after the ejection.

2nd – That no person shall pay tithe money to the minister or any person acting under him.

3rd – That no wolfish proctor shall sue for tithe money.

4th – That no person shall serve a process or processes for tithe money. Any person or persons transgressing any of these will suffer shooting burning &c. &c. &c.

N. B. – A voracious minister screams aloud in dreary Tartarus for a merciless proctor and for sworn process servers[;] let Charles M'Carthy, Barrett and Darird prepare as they are considered very fit persons to fill a situation in hell.

Captain Rock

By the Grace of God.

This 'proclamation', copies of which were seen in various places in Duhallow barony, was reportedly written in a beautiful handwriting.[124]

While Rockite notices included primitive ones as well as stylish ones cited above, the question as to who wrote these notices is elusive. In March 1823 Cornelius Morrissy was arrested by a military patrol near the river Blackwater, when a Rockite notice was found on him.[125] The notice, signed by 'G. J. Rock, Commander-in-Chief of the Irish forces', advised 'the bloody tyrants to drop their designs . . . or to expect the fulfillment of the writer's denunciation in having plenty of Irish beef, and plenty of fire to boil it'. A magistrate identified the handwriting as being the same as that of the notices addressed to his tenants.[126] Nevertheless, it would be overhasty to conclude that this Morrissy was the author of the notice. Rockites could use an amanuensis, in order to avoid being traced by means of the handwriting. In that context Daniel Connor and one Sullivan were brought to trial in County Cork in April 1822. Connor was charged with delivering a threatening notice to Francis Burton, and Sullivan, a writing master, was charged with penning that notice. Sullivan admitted his handwriting, but maintained that he was forced to write it by a party of Rockites who came to his house. While Connor was convicted, Sullivan was discharged.[127]

In addition, Captain Rock could also use messengers. In March 1822, John Connors, who was considered to be weak in his intellectual powers, visited Edward Leahy, apparently a gentleman living about 2.5 miles away from Connors. Connors, afraid and crying, handed a letter to Leahy which he said he was forced to deliver by some men who had called on him and beat him the night before. The substance of the letter was that Captain Rock regarded Leahy's steward as a man of bad character and that he should dismiss him. Leahy then received to the same effect a second letter, which further stated he could do whatever he liked to Connors.[128]

About 200 Rockite notices and 'proclamations' can be identified in County Cork between 1821 and 1824.[129] Because Rockites were dealing with individual problems in each district, it is natural that Captain Rock's 'law' specified in these notices differed from district to district even when 'the law' was applied to the same kind of issue. Not only the case of tithes as mentioned above, but that of land tenancy shows this differentiation. In one case it was decreed that three years should elapse before a new proposition for a lease could be made for the farm from which the former occupier had been evicted.[130] In another, the gap period was defined as seven years.[131] In some cases, what became the object of sanction was not the length of time but the number of farms which could be held by a single individual.[132] Even the above-mentioned '3d article of the statute of the new code of laws' of March 1822 changed its content with the passing of time. In September of the same year, that 'article' decreed 'not to buy tithes or bargain for them from any tythe farmer, tythe minister, or impropritor [*sic*] of it'.[133]

Then, who was Captain Rock, who appeared, armed with 'official' authority, in various places for the purpose of coping with the specific agrarian issues of each locality? Was there a real person nicknamed Captain Rock who led all other Rockites and issued his 'laws', perhaps written by someone, to cope with various specific issues? That was practically impossible. Then were there numerous small Captains Rock, who used the same name but acted more or less independently in each district? This explanation is more plausible but not sufficient, since a doubt remains as to why disturbers in various places in the south of Ireland could act under the same leader's name.

The tradition of captain

It was already a well-established custom for rural disturbers in early nineteenth-century Ireland to follow and accept the authority of a mythical 'Captain': e.g. Captain Sive, Captain Cropper and Captain Thumper had appeared in County Tipperary in the 1760s and 1770s;[134] Rightboys followed their leader, Captain Right, in the south in the 1780s.[135] Of course, the title 'Captain' was not a specifically Irish phenomenon. In Tudor England 'Captain Poverty' had appeared who acted as a popular hero[136] and 'Captain Swing' led the Swing rioters in England in the 1830s.[137]

Not only as a disturber but as a literary figure, the term captain had a wide appeal. Here again the Irish case was not unique. In the Picaresque literature in eighteenth-century France, such leaders appeared as Mandrin the '"Généralissime" commandant un "Capitane", des "Lieutenants" et une troupe disciplinée de "Soldats"'.[138] It is argued that the motif of outlaw captain in the eighteenth-century English popular books was appropriated to Ireland in the form of *A genuine history of the lives and actions of the most notorious Irish highwaymen, Tories and rapparees*, which contained several accounts of outlaw captains. The book was probably published first in the 1740s, and went through at least ten editions in the course of the eighteenth century.[139] Thomas Crofton Croker, a folklorist, who travelled in the south of Ireland in 1821–22, wrote about that book as 'one of the most popular books amongst the peasantry . . . circulated to an extent that almost seems incredible'.[140]

It would be unnatural to think that these two types of captain, both somewhat imaginary figures, had no connections. In fact, they could overlap in some cases. In the rural disturbances in County Tyrone in 1790, 'bold Capt. Freney' appeared, who was probably named after the main character of *Life and adventures of James Freney*, a novel which had almost as wide a circulation as that of *Irish highwaymen, Tories and rapparees*.[141] What is more, the image of particular outlaw captains in literature shed some light on the character of mysterious Whiteboy Captain, particularly his authority as well as popularity among the people.

Many of the figures who appeared in *Irish highwaymen, Tories and rapparees* were mere outlaws who often appeared in a society under profound social and political change like post-Cromwellian Ireland. However, some of the characters in the book had a more distinctive quality. The 'captain general of the Irish robbers' was 'a most notorious though a gentleman-like robber' and 'naturally of a generous disposition, frequently giving shares of what he took from the rich to relieve the poor in their necessities.'[142] Another, 'Captain Power', was a Cork man who 'often told the rich, that he took their purses to make a distribution among such as were in want'. In one episode, he saved a farmer by giving money to be used in paying the rent while he punished the landlord who had abused the farmer.[143] The image of these two figures belonged to the tradition of Hobsbawm's 'social bandit'. These were 'peasant outlaws whom the [landlord] and state regard as criminals, but who . . . are considered by their people as heroes, as champions, avengers, fighters for justice, perhaps even leaders of liberation'. Hence, a social bandit, with the support of the people, could act even 'as a parallel government in the peasants' interest'.[144] Of course it would be simplistic to argue that a social-bandit captain in *Irish highwaymen, Tories and rapparees* and a Whiteboy captain were exactly the same.[145] At the same time, it also seems true that rural Ireland had a cultural tradition of social banditry, which opened the way for accepting and following a Whiteboy captain as their champion.[146]

Seeing a Whiteboy Captain as a variation of social bandit makes it easy to explain the care which Captain Rock took about the way he would appear. As people idealised him and turned him into a myth, the captain had to try to live up to his role.[147] The following letter from Captain Rock delivered to an army officer near Newmarket in Duhallow barony in Cork in November 1821 presents an example of this self-recognition:

> Sir
> Being apprized of a demand being made on you and other gentlemen in your neighbourhood in my name for money I beg leave to inform you that such demands are done without my knowledge, and that I hope I shall be able to punish such offender[;] in future therefore I earnestly request

> you will not send a single farthing and that you will acquaint the others concerned, such as you not [to] remit a penny[.] If not too much trouble I would feel exceedingly obliged if you make it publick in Newmarket on Sunday next that I feel much hurt at such libertys being taken in my name and that I will bring the authors of it to justice or loose [*sic*] my life in the attempt[.] Now Sir for your better information that Captain Rock is no doubt the person who sends you this and that at all times he shall bear you and every other person whom I make this request of harmless . . .
> [Gaouse] Lodge John Rock[148]

This letter seems to have been a reaction to a threatening notice demanding money which appeared near Kanturk in October.[149] As will be seen in Chapter 2, Cork Rockites did collect money systematically, but they began to do so only in late 1822 and for the purpose of manufacturing pikes. It was not only the Captain but Rockites in general who seem to be concerned to distinguish themselves from mere criminals. Rockite oaths frequently included an article not to rob or steal.[150] In one case, one Rockite group deprived another of arms as the latter group 'were acting scandelous' and 'not following right rules' in committing robbery.[151]

Captain Rock was, nevertheless, not simply an imaginary leader whose authority had a wide appeal because of his social-bandit character. He was also a real person who led a party of Rockites on the actual occasion of disturbances. A large party (perhaps a hundred) of Rockites attacked the house of Henry Bevan, vicar of Bruree in County Limerick one night in November 1821. The Rockites were led by a leader in a blue coat and pantaloons and dressed with a white sash round his waist, a cocked-hat and white feathers. He was called by his men 'Captain Rock'. As Bevan fired at him, a general confusion was created in the party. One called out, 'murder', another said, 'Captain, supply us with more ammunition, and order up a fresh detachment', while another cried out, 'Lieutenant Sledger advance.'[152]

Though unfortunately nothing is known about this leader, it can be confirmed that a living person played the role of 'Captain Rock'. In some cases, those acting the role of Captain Rock can be identified. The first was Patrick Dillane, a blacksmith near Newcastle in County Limerick. The harsh conduct of a land agent to the Courtenay estates around Newcastle occasioned the assassination of his son in July 1821.[153] The principal of that murder was Dillane, who after that incident was 'baptised' Captain Rock by a school master.[154] Dillane had great popularity around Newcastle because he was a hero who got a blow against the land agent, the common enemy of the locality. When he turned crown witness and appeared in court, people were amazed and declared that 'there was now no trusting any one, as they thought that Paddy Dillane would sooner be hanged than become an informer.'[155] Here a social bandit debased himself by turning informer and became a mere criminal.

It was in fact not Dillane but Walter Fitzmaurice, also a blacksmith near Newcastle, who was the most important Captain Rock in the early phase of the Rockite disturbances.[156] Even Dillane became his 'aid de camp' at one time.[157] When Fitzmaurice appeared in court, his clothes, a large brown loose coat, a grey body coat and a striped waist coat, were described as 'by no means shabby'. He 'stood at the bar with greatest *sang froid*, both his hands in his pockets, and seemed quite indifferent as the respective charges were read by the clerk.' His countenance was 'of a good humoured pleasing cast, what may be termed a jovial looking country fellow.'[158] Unfortunately, there is not much information known about his person.[159]

The most intelligible Captain Rock was a Cork man. A Rockite party 'visited' a glass manufactory and demanded arms near Cork City in May 1823. The leader of the party had a sabre and was dressed in a military uniform, with sash on his blue coat and feathers on his cap.[160] After he obtained some arms, he shook hands with one of the manufacturers. His hand was described as 'soft and unlike that of a person used to manual labour'.[161] Other houses in the neighbourhood were also visited for arms, where a leader appeared with a feather and a belt.[162] In the night of the thirtieth of the same month, the house of a medical doctor was visited near Cork City. His wife gave the following testimony in court:

> . . . some armed men entered the house . . . he [the leader] said, 'now Madam if you please, to show me the arms'— witness then went up stairs, followed by this person and the man whom he called the First Lieutenant . . . the leader turned round and told witness that he was sorry to see her agitated, and asked if she had not a case of pistols in the house, for he was informed there she had – she immediately gave them to him . . . here a man requested leave to speak with the leader – witness heard him say in a low voice that there were many things there which could be useful to them, and asked permission of the leader to take them. The leader stamped on the floor and said in a very angry voice that if the house were filled with gold to the top, they should not lay a finger on one farthing of it. The First Lieutenant begged of witness not to be alarmed, and the Captain said it should be his care to keep her from being injured, and begged of her to compose her mind – at that instance a voice below called out, 'if you don't come down Capt. we will fire up stairs' . . . he looked to the priming and ran to the stairs – he had a view of the hall, and seeing it full of armed men, and four of them standing upon the lower steps of the stairs with their guns pointed up, he presented the piece in his hand at them, and in an angry voice told them to clear out of the hall or that he instantly fire the contents of that amongst them. They retired . . .[163]

This 'Captain' was David Nagle, mentioned in the Introduction, who was the most important Captain Rock in County Cork. Nagle was betrayed by his men after that visit, and was arrested in July 1823. A judge described him as 'a very decent well dressed young man.'[164] He was sentenced to death for that visit, but his sentence was commuted in consideration of his humane conduct on the occasion.[165] He seems eventually to have been sent to Canada as a settler.[166] Before that he had turned informer, and his appearance created a panic in the region of his activity. Nagle's abandonment of the Rockite cause was an important turning point in the Rockite disturbances in Cork.

In any event, Captain Rock was thus a man of double personality. On the one hand, a particular individual (Dillane) first assumed the name of Captain Rock, and the name, rather than the man, became widespread, with authority and popularity being attached to the name, which was predictable from the tradition of Captain. On the other hand, a real person commanding a group of disturbers in each locality modelled himself after that mythical hero, whereby he could have authority over his men, while his men too welcomed being led by the popular hero.

What kind of man then became a Captain Rock? Dillane 'never was better than a poor journeyman blacksmith'.[167] Fitzmaurice was also a blacksmith, but judging from his clothes, he was probably a man of some status. An informer observed that 'Walter seems to exalt in his rank & authority rather than conceal it'.[168] His surname implies that he may have been from a branch of the Fitzmaurices in north Kerry. In the case of Nagle, his family background is more clear and striking. The judge who handed down the death on him 'dwelt upon the appearance of Nagle, and the improbability of supposing a person of his description could be deluded into the commission of an act of this nature.'[169] Lord Doneraile would even call him 'my friend', after the Rockite disturbances were over.[170] The Nagle clan were one of the most extensive Catholic landowning families in Cork, from which Edmund Burke's mother came. The main family of the clan was based in Annakissy in Clenor parish. David Nagle, referring to himself as a 'farmer' who 'was sowing wheat' in December, confessed that he was from Annakissy.[171] While no further information is available on David Nagle, the balance of probability suggests that he belonged to a junior branch of that distinguished clan.

To summarise this chapter, rural Ireland in the early 1820s saw considerable hardship, to cope with which Rockites made their appearance. While they had an aspect of the European 'social bandit', they also inherited several characteristics from Whiteboyism: they were nightly marauders acting in small parties for the sake of defending the status quo in each district. However, Rockites were more than an Irish version of the social bandit or a nineteenth-century version of Whiteboys. They widely appropriated official rhetoric while they committed arson on an unprecedented scale.

Rockites had other distinctive traits: while they showed a strong interest in obtaining arms, they also developed a network of underground organisations in which not only a captain but a committee man played an important role. That network was brought in from Dublin City by a political secret society functioning there, as will be seen in the next chapter.

Acknowledgments

Parts of this chapter were originally published in "The Rockite movement in County Cork in the early 1820s," *Irish Historical Studies*, vol. xxxiii, no. 131, May 2003, pp. 278–296.

Notes

1 Cormac Ó Gráda, *Ireland before and after the Famine: explorations in economic history, 1800–1925* (second edition, Manchester and New York: Manchester University Press, 1993), p. 57.
2 BPP, Abstract of answers and returns pursuant to act for taking account of population of Ireland; enumeration abstract, appendix, 1824 (577, 1823) XXII. 411, pp. 378–379.
3 BPP, Abstract of answers and returns under the population acts, 55 Geo. III, chap. 120, 3 Geo. IV, chap. 5, 2 Geo. IV, chap. 30, 1 Will. IV, chap 19, enumeration, 1831 (1833).
4 See also David Dickson, *Old world colony: Cork and south Munster 1630–1830* (Cork: Cork University Press, 2005), p. 315.
5 Margaret MacCurtain, 'Pre-Famine peasantry in Ireland: definition and theme', *Irish University Review*, vol. 4, no. 2, 1974, p. 193; Michael Beames, *Peasants and power: the Whiteboy movements and their control in pre-Famine Ireland* (Sussex: The Harvester Press; New York: St Martin's Press, 1983), pp. 16, 54.
6 Abstract of answers and returns pursuant to act for taking account of population of Ireland . . . 1824 (577, 1823) XXII. 411, pp. 148–167; Ian d'Alton, *Protestant society and politics in Cork 1812–1844* (Cork: Cork University Press, 1980), pp. 8–9, 13.
7 Abstract of answers and returns under the population acts . . . 1831 (1833), pp. 158–159. The figure for the labourers of West Muskerry is 5076 in another table of the same census. See *ibid.*, p. 157.
8 Dickson, *Old world colony*, pp. 219–220.
9 T. Crofton Croker, *Researches in the south of Ireland, illustrative of the scenery, architectural remains, and the manners and superstitions of the peasantry: with an appendix, containing a private narrative of the rebellion of 1798* (London: John Murray, 1824), p. 130.
10 The Rev. Horatio Townsend, *A general and statistical survey of the county of Cork*, 2 vols (second edition, Cork: Edwards & Savage, 1815), vol. 1, pp. 462–463, 469–470.
11 William J. Smyth, 'Social, economic and landscape transformations in County Cork from the mid-eighteenth to the mid-nineteenth century', in Patrick O'Flanagan and Cornelius G. Buttimer eds., *Cork: history and society: interdisciplinary essays on the history of an Irish county* (Dublin: Geography Publications, 1993), p. 657.
12 Patrick O'Flanagan, 'Three hundred years of urban life: villages and towns in County Cork *c.* 1600 to 1901', in O'Flanagan and Buttimer eds., *Cork: history and society*, p. 441; L. M. Cullen, 'The Blackwater Catholics and county Cork society and politics in the eighteenth century', *ibid.*, p. 535.
13 Garret FitzGerald, 'Irish-speaking in the pre-Famine period: a study based on the 1911 census data for people born before 1851 and still alive in 1911', *Proceedings of the Royal Irish Academy*, Section C, vol. ciii, no. 5, 2003, pp. 202–203.
14 Croker, *Researches in the south of Ireland*, p. 139; O'Flanagan, 'Three hundred years of urban life', p. 421.

15 Brigade Major Croker to R. Peel, 28 Sept. 1813, NAI, SOC, 1544/79.
16 Evidence of Sir James Anderson, 26 June 1823, BPP, Report from the select committee appointed to inquire into the condition of the labouring poor, 1823 (561) VI. 331, p. 118. For Anderson, see Townsend, *A general and statistical survey of the county of Cork*, vol. 1, pp. 466–471.
17 Evidence of P. Mahony, 23 June 1823, Report from the select committee . . . 1823 (561) VI. 331, p. 27; Evidence of Anderson, 26 June 1823, *ibid.*, p. 118.
18 Evidence of W. Wrixon Becher, 2 June 1824, BPP, Select Committee of House of Lords on nature and extent of disturbances in Ireland, minutes of evidence, 1825 (200) VII. 501, p. 146.
19 Cormac Ó Gráda, 'Poverty, population, and agriculture, 1801–45', in W. E. Vaughan ed., *A new history of Ireland V: Ireland under the Union, I 1801–70* (Oxford: Clarendon Press, 1989), p. 112.
20 Evidence of Wrixon Becher, 2 June 1824, Select committee . . . 1825 (200) VII. 501, p. 146.
21 Ó Gráda, *Ireland before and after the Famine*, p. 2.
22 Evidence of Major General Richard Bourke, 16 June 1830, BPP, Select committee on state of poor in Ireland, and means of improving their condition, minutes of evidence (3), 1830 (665) VII. 323, questions 5546–5547.
23 J. S. Donnelly Jr, *The land and the people of nineteenth-century Cork: the rural economy and the land question* (London: Routledge & Kegan Paul, 1975), p. 40; Oliver MacDonagh, 'The economy and society, 1830–45', in Vaughan ed., *A new history of Ireland V*, p. 222.
24 Ó Gráda, 'Poverty, population, and agriculture, 1801–45', p. 114.
25 Cormac Ó Gráda, *The great Irish famine* (Dublin: Gill & Macmillan, 1989), p. 17.
26 David Dickson, *New Foundations: Ireland, 1660–1800* (second revised and enlarged edition, Dublin: Irish Academic Press, 2000), p. 129.
27 The National Library of Ireland, Doneraile Papers.
28 Some of them can be identified in Tithe Applotment Books, parish of Buttevant, film no. 18, NAI.
29 Dickson, *Old world colony*, p. 245.
30 Report of the state and condition of the following farms on the Buttevant estate, April 1844, Doneraile Papers, Mss 34059(3)(1); Report of the nos of labourer's cabins under tenants houses, barns, piggeries, stables and description of walls on the Buttevant estate, April 1844, *ibid.*, Mss 34059(3)(2).
31 O'Flanagan and Buttimer eds., *Cork: history and society*, backcover.
32 Dickson, *Old world colony*, pp. 223–224.
33 Townsend, *A general and statistical survey of the county of Cork*, vol. 1, p. 409.
34 The Rev. F. Hewitt to –, 1 Jan. 1816, SOC, 1769/1; BPP, Report on roads made at public expense in southern district of Ireland, by Richard Griffith, 1831 (119) XII. 61, p. 2.
35 The Rev. James Hall, *Tour through Ireland; particularly the interior & least known parts: containing an accurate view of the parties, politics, and improvements, in the different provinces; with reflections and observations on the union of Britain and Ireland; the practicability and advantages of a telegraphic communication between the two countries, and other matters of importance*, 2 vols (London: R. P. Moore, etc., 1813), vol. 1, p. 211; Evidence of R. Griffith, 19 May 1824, Select committee . . . 1825 (200) VII. 501, p. 37; Evidence of the same, 31 May 1824, Select committee . . . 1825 (20) VII.1, pp. 226–227.
36 Evidence of J. Leslie Foster, 23, 25 Feb. 1825, Select committee of House of Lords to inquire into state of Ireland with reference to disturbances, minutes of evidence, 1825(181) IX. 1, p. 85. A twentieth-century folklorist regarded the region as 'one of the most truly Irish' regions in the country. E. Estyn Evans,

'Peasant beliefs in nineteenth-century Ireland', in Daniel J. Casey and Robert E. Rhodes eds., *Views of the Irish peasantry 1800–1916* (Hamden, Conn.: Aechon Books, 1977), p. 47.
37 Townsend, *A general and statistical survey of the county of Cork*, vol. 1, p. 413.
38 Hewitt to –, 1 Jan. 1816, SOC, 1769/1.
39 Townsend, *A general and statistical survey of the county of Cork*, vol. 2, p. 142.
40 Smyth, 'Social, economic and landscape transformations in county Cork', p. 664.
41 Kevin Whelan, 'An underground gentry? Catholic middlemen in eighteenth-century Ireland', in James S. Donnelly Jr and Kerby A. Miller eds., *Irish popular culture 1650–1850* (Dublin: Irish Academic Press, 1998), p. 122. See also Dickson, *Old world colony*, pp. 229–230.
42 Townsend, *A general and statistical survey of the county of Cork*, vol. 2, p. 143.
43 d'Alton, *Protestant society and politics in Cork*, pp. 8–9.
44 Evidence of W. Fagan, 20 Apr. 1826, BPP, Select committee on the butter trade of Ireland, minutes of evidence, 1826 (406) V. 135, pp. 85–97; Evidence of T. Fitzgibbon, 25 Apr. 1826, *ibid.*, pp. 122–133; Evidence of J. Morgan, 4 May 1826, *ibid.*, pp. 193–203. Cf. Hall, *Tour through Ireland*, vol. 1, p. 211.
45 Thomas Reid, *Travels in Ireland, in the year 1822: exhibiting brief sketches of the moral, physical, and political state of the country; with reflections on the best means of improving its condition* (London: Printed for Longman, Hurst, Rees, Orme, and Brown, 1823), p. 272.
46 *First report of the general board of health in the city of Dublin, most respectfully submitted to the most noble Richard Marquess Wellesley, Lord Lieutenant General and General Governor of Ireland* (Dublin: Graisberry, 1822), appendix, pp. 21–27.
47 William Shaw Mason ed., *A statistical account or parochial survey of Ireland, drawn up from the communications of the clergy*, 3 vols (Dublin: Graisberry and Campbell, for J. Cumming, 1814–19), vol. 1, pp. 567–568.
48 Townsend, *A general and statistical survey of the county of Cork*, vol. 1, p. 411.
49 *Cork Morning Intelligencer*, 4 June 1822.
50 Evidence of Anderson, 26 June 1823, Select committee . . . 1823 (561) VI. 331, p. 117.
51 Evidence of Anderson, 26 June 1823, *ibid.*, pp. 118–119.
52 Cited in Dickson, *Old world colony*, p. 592, note 136.
53 Townsend, *A general and statistical survey of the county of Cork*, vol. 1, pp. 411, 464–465.
54 Evidence of P. Mahony, 23 June 1823, Select committee . . . 1823 (561) VI. 331, pp. 21–22.
55 BPP, Select Committee to inquire into State of Ireland with reference to Disturbances, reports, 1825 (129) VIII. 1, p. 6; R. D. Collison Black, *Economic thought and the Irish question 1817–1870* (Cambridge: Cambridge University Press, 1960), p. 19.
56 The Rev. H. Townsend to –, no date, SOC, 2081/12.
57 Smyth, 'Social, economic and landscape transformations in county Cork', p. 659.
58 Ó Gráda, 'Poverty, population, and agriculture, 1801–45', p. 118.
59 Ó Gráda, *The great Irish famine*, p. 5.
60 Receiver's account of three and an half years from 1 May 1820 to 1 Nov. 1820, Doneraile Papers, Mss 32972(2)(3); Evictions on the Buttevant Estate, *ibid.*, Mss 34022(1)(1).
61 J. [Lesley] to Lord Shannon, 13 July 1821, Public Record Office of Northern Ireland, Shannon Papers, D/2707/A3/1/46.

62 Brigade Major Mahony to W. Gregory, 8 July 1820, SOC, 2184/10. See also Major Warburton to Gregory, 12 June 1820, SOC, 2183/36; Lord Carbery to Gregory, 18 July 1820, SOC, 2182/15.
63 Evidence of Fagan, 20 Apr. 1826, Select committee . . . 1826(406) V. 135, p. 94.
64 Cormac Ó Gráda, *Ireland: a new economic history 1780–1939* (Oxford: Clarendon Press, 1994), pp. 57–60.
65 Brigade Major Croker to Peel, 31 Dec. 1814, SOC, 1560/77; same to same, 30 Jan. 1815, SOC, 1682/8.
66 Evidence of Anderson, 26 June 1823, Select committee . . . 1823 (561) VI. 331, p. 121.
67 Speech of Sir Edward O'Brien, 29 Apr. 1822, *Hansard's parliamentary debates*, first series, vol. 7, c. 146; *Cork Morning Intelligencer*, 4 June 1822.
68 E. O'Brien to C. Grant, 9 Nov. 1821, NAI, CSORP, box 635; same to same, 24 Nov. 1821, CSORP, box 635.
69 A. Morris to H. Goulburn, 5 Feb. 1822, SOC, 2348/37; same to same, 14 Feb. 1822, SOC, 2348/49.
70 Lord Doneraile to Gregory, 2 Apr. 1822, SOC, 2345/52.
71 E. P. Thompson, *Customs in common: studies in traditional popular culture* (New York: The New Press, 1991), pp. 264–266; Ian Gilmour, *Riot, risings and revolution: governance and violence in eighteenth-century England* (London: Hutchionson, 1992), p. 227.
72 E. g., *Cork Morning Intelligencer*, 4 June 1822.
73 Col. Gough to Lt. Col. Finch, 17 Nov. 1823, SOC, 2516/17.
74 A Rockite notice, 17 Mar. 1823, National Army Museum, Gough Papers, 8303/105/643; *Cork Constitution*, 9 Apr. 1823; Col. Gough to Lt. Col. Finch, 12 Apr. 1823, SOC, 2512/18.
75 Evidence of W. H. W. Newenham, 14 June 1824, Select committee . . . 1825 (200) VII. 501, p. 187.
76 *Cork Constitution*, 9 Apr. 1823; Col. Gough to Lt Col. Finch, 12 Apr. 1823, SOC, 2512/18.
77 Major Carter to Goulburn, 23 Oct. 1823, SOC, 2515/58; *Cork Constitution*, 24 Oct. 1823; Col. Gough to Lt Col. Finch, 26 Oct. 1823, SOC, 2515/59.
78 Compiled from *Cork Constitution*, *Cork Morning Intelligencer*, *Limerick Chronicle*, SOC and CSORP.
79 *Cork Constitution*, 5 Mar. 1823; Major Carter to A. Mangin, 8 Mar. 1823, SOC, 2511/45.
80 A. Batwell to Gregory, 4 Feb. 1823, SOC, 2511/18; [G.] Nagle to Goulburn, 6 Feb. 1823, SOC, 2511/21; *Cork Constitution*, 10 Feb. 1823; Major Carter to Mangin, 8 Mar. 1823, SOC, 2511/45.
81 *Cork Constitution*, 30 Apr. 1823; *Limerick Chronicle*, 30 Apr. 1823.
82 Major Carter to Mangin, 8 Mar. 1823, SOC, 2511/45; *Cork Constitution*, 12 Mar. 1823; Major Maxwell to Col. Gough, 17 Mar. 1823, SOC, 2511/55.
83 Col. Gough to Lt. Col. Finch, 1 Apr. 1823, SOC, 2512/5.
84 *Ibid*.
85 Compiled from *Cork Constitution*, *Cork Morning Intelligencer*, *Limerick Chronicle*, SOC and CSORP.
86 S. William to Sir E. Lees, 18 Feb. 1822, SOC, 2344/45.
87 W. H. W. Newenham to –, 13 Apr. 1823, SOC, 2512/16.
88 'Extract from the confession of David Nagle taken before Lt. Col. Hill', Jan. 1823[1824], Gough Papers, 8303/105/335.
89 Compiled from *Cork Constitution*, *Cork Morning Intelligencer*, *Limerick Chronicle*, SOC and CSORP.
90 Information of A. Croker, 18 Jan. 1822, SOC, 2342/55; Major Carter to Gregory, 14 Feb. 1822, SOC, 2344/36.

91 Information of W. Oliver, 19 Jan. 1822, SOC, 2342/55; Information of C. Connors, 19 Jan. 1822, SOC, 2342/55; *Cork Morning Intelligencer*, 22 Jan. 1822. For other visits by this party, see C. Crone to Goulburn, 21 Jan. 1822, SOC, 2342/55; A. Hill to Goulburn, 22 Jan. 1822, SOC, 2355/15; J. Barry to Goulburn, 22 Jan. 1822, SOC, box 170; Major Carter to Gregory, 14 Feb. 1822, SOC, 2344/36.
92 Crone to Goulburn, 21 Jan. 1822, SOC, 2342/55.
93 'John Rock' to W. Fling, [Feb.] 1822, SOC, 2344/01.
94 J. Hill to Goulburn, 19 Sept. 1822, SOC, 2346/50.
95 Major Carter to Goulburn, 14 Sept. 1822, SOC, 2346/60; *Cork Constitution*, 16 Sept. 1822; J. Hill to Goulburn, 19 Sept. 1822, SOC, 2346/50.
96 Information of F. Nash, 14 Sept. 1822, SOC, 2346/51; *Cork Constitution*, 16 Sept. 1822.
97 Compiled from *Cork Constitution*, *Cork Morning Intelligencer*, *Limerick Chronicle*, SOC and CSORP.
98 Col. Gough to Lt. Col. Finch, 10 Nov. 1823, SOC, 2516/8; Evidence of the Rev. O'Brien, 10 May 1825, BPP, Select committee to inquire into state of Ireland with reference to disturbances, minutes of evidence, 1825 (129) VIII. 1, pp. 586–587.
99 Goulburn to Peel, 18 Oct. 1822, TNA, HO 100/206/238–239.
100 *Cork Constitution*, 2 Aug. 1822; J. Lloyd to – 30 July 1822, SOC, 2346/21.
101 Brian Jenkins, *Era of emancipation: British government of Ireland, 1812–1830* (Kingston and Montreal: McGill-Queen's University Press, 1988), p. 30.
102 Gregory to Goulburn, 12 Apr. 1822, Emory University, Gregory Papers, 624/13.
103 Speech of Sir Henry Parnell, 23 June 1812, *Hansard's*, first series, vol. 22, c. 724; Speech of Grant, 22 Apr. 1822, *Hansard's*, second series, vol. 6, c. 1513–1514; Speech of Parnell, 13 June 1822, *ibid.*, vol. 7, c. 1037–1039.
104 E. Hutchinson to Grant, 15 Nov. 1821, CSORP, box 633.
105 Major Carter to Goulburn, 9 Nov. 1823, SOC, 2516/6; 'Proclamations of Rock', 11 Dec. 1821, SOC, 2299/12.
106 Major Carter to Goulburn, 12 Dec. 1822, SOC, 2347/50; A. Hill to Col. Gough, 12 Dec. 1822, SOC, 2347/53; *Cork Constitution*, 16 Dec. 1822.
107 Major Carter to Gregory, 8 Aug. 1823, SOC, 2514/36; Statement and further statement of P. Daly, [12 Feb. 1824], Gough Papers, 8303/105/334.
108 *Cork Constitution*, 21, 24, 31 Mar. 1823.
109 The Rev. R. Woodward to –, 27 Sept. 1822, SOC, 2346/68.
110 Compiled from *Cork Constitution*, *Cork Morning Intelligencer*, *Limerick Chronicle*, SOC and CSORP.
111 *Cork Constitution*, 21 Oct. 1822; A. Crossby to Major Carter, 22 Oct. 1822, SOC, 2347/19; Col. Gough to Lt. Col. Sorell, 31 Oct. 1822, CSORP, 1822/2654.
112 John E. Archer, *'By a flash and a scare': incendiarism, animal maiming, and porching in East Anglia 1815–1870* (Oxford: Clarendon Press, 1990), pp. 70–71. A recent analysis has shown that there were 1,292 incidents of arson during the whole Swing Riots. Cited in Adrian Randall, '"Captain Swing": A retrospect', *International Review of Social History*, vol. 54, no. 3, 2009, pp. 425–426.
113 Major Carter to Goulburn, 22 Sept. 1822, SOC, 2346/54; Goulburn to Peel, 12 Oct. 1822, HO 100/206/228–229.
114 Col. Gough to Lt. Col. Sorell, 4 Oct. 1822, SOC, 2347/3.
115 Col. Arbuthnot to Lt. Col. Finch, 28 Feb. 1823, SOC, 2511/39.
116 Lord Doneraile to Gregory, 17 Mar. 1822, SOC, 2345/28.
117 *Ibid.*
118 Captain Rock's 'laws' imitating official law in their styles may have appeared comical to the authorities. Citations of Captain Rock's law at court could cause

burst of laughter. *Limerick Chronicle*, 9 Mar. 1822; *Cork Constitution*, 11 Nov. 1822.

119 Col. Arbuthnot to Lt. Col. Finch, 2 Feb. 1824, SOC, 2614/30.
120 S. William to Sir E. Lees, 18 Feb. 1822, SOC, 2344/45.
121 Lord Carbery to –, 15 Jan. 1822, SOC, 2342/33.
122 Lord Doneraile to Gregory, 2 Apr. 1822, SOC, 2345/52. See also *Cork Constitution*, 24 Mar. 1823, 23 Sept. 1824.
123 Captain Craster to Col. Gough, 1 Apr. 1823, SOC, 2512/5.
124 *Cork Constitution*, 24 Mar. 1823.
125 *Cork Constitution*, 4 Apr. 1823; Col. Arbuthnot to Lt. Col. Finch, 15 Apr. 1823, SOC, 2512/17.
126 *Cork Constitution*, 2 May 1823.
127 *Cork Morning Intelligencer*, 23, 27 Apr. 1822; Information of D. Connors [Connor], 23 Sept. 1823, SOC, 2515/31.
128 *Cork Morning Intelligencer*, 30 Apr. 1822.
129 Compiled from *Cork Constitution*, *Cork Morning Intelligencer*, *Limerick Chronicle*, SOC and CSORP.
130 Lord Carbery to –, 15 Jan. 1822, SOC, 2342/33.
131 *Cork Morning Intelligencer*, 26 Feb. 1822; *Cork Constitution*, 24 Mar. 1823.
132 *Limerick Chronicle*, 16 Apr. 1823.
133 Major Carter to the Chief Secretary, 29 Sept. 1823, SOC, 2515/39.
134 Maurice J. Bric, 'The Whiteboy movement in Tipperary, 1760–80', in William Nolan in association with Thomas G. McGrath eds., *Tipperary: history and society: interdisciplinary essays on the history of an Irish county* (Dublin: Geography Publications, 1985), pp. 153, 162.
135 James S. Donnelly Jr, 'The Rightboy movement 1785–8', *Studia Hibernica*, nos. 17/18, 1977–78, p. 133; Maurice J. Bric, 'Priests, parsons, and politics: the Rightboy protest in county Cork, 1785–8', in C. H. E. Philpin ed., *Nationalism and popular protest in Ireland* (Cambridge: Cambridge University Press, 1987), p. 183.
136 M. L. Bush, 'Captain Poverty and the pilgrimage of grace', *Historical Research*, vol. lxv, no. 156, 1992, p. 17.
137 E. J. Hobsbawm and George Rudé, *Captain Swing* (London: Pimlico, 1993).
138 *Histoires curieuses et véritables de Cartouche et de Mandrin*, textes présentés par Hans-Jürgen Lüsebrink ([n. p.]: Montalba, 1984), p. 40.
139 Niall Ó Ciosáin, 'The Irish rogues', in Donnelly and Miller eds., *Irish popular Culture*, pp. 78–79.
140 Croker, *Researches in the south of Ireland*, p. 55.
141 J. R. R. Adams, 'Swine-tax and eat-him-all-magee: the hedge schools and popular education in Ireland', in Donnelly and Miller eds., *Irish popular culture*, pp. 107–108.
142 J. Cosgrove, *A genuine history of the lives and actions of the most notorious Irish highwaymen, Tories and rapparees, from Redmond O'Brien, the famous gentleman-robber, to Cahier na Gappul, the great horse-catcher, who was executed at Maryborough in August, 1735* (Belfast: N. I., 1776), pp. 6–7.
143 *Ibid.*, pp. 34–36.
144 E. J. Hobsbawm, *Primitive rebels: studies in archaic forms of social movement in the 19th and 20th centuries* (third edition, Manchester: Manchester University Press, 1971), pp. 20–21. Mandrin was described as '"prétendu Prince" revendiquant tous les droits d'un véritable monarque'. Lüsebrink, *Histoires curieuses et véritables de Cartouche et de Mandrin*, p. 40.
145 One major difference between them is that Captain Rock or Captain Right does not seem to have the function of re-distributor of wealth.

146 This implies that the authority of captain in Irish rural disturbances was not derived from such elements of distinctively Irish popular culture as magic or fairy. Cf. James Warner O'Neill, *Popular culture and peasant rebellion in pre-famine Ireland*, Ph. D. thesis, University of Minnesota, 1984.
147 Hobsbawm, *Primitive rebels*, p. 13.
148 Ensign Lindsay to –, 12 Nov. 1821, SOC, 2296/38; Major General Aylmer to Col. Broke, 4 Dec. 1821, SOC, 2293/36.
149 A notice from Captain Rock, 29 Oct. 1821, SOC, 2347/23.
150 Major Maxwell to Gregory, 28 Feb. 1823, SOC, 2511/37; Col. Gough to Lt. Col. Finch, 5 Mar. 1823, SOC, 2511/41; *Cork Constitution*, 24 Mar., 11 Apr. 1823; Information of J. Hurien, 22 July 1823, SOC, 2513/74; Confession of Nagle, [23] Aug. 1823, SOC, 2514/55.
151 Confession of Nagle, [23] Aug. 1823, SOC, 2514/55; Confession of Nagle, 25 Aug. 1823, Gough Papers, 8303/105/387.
152 *Limerick Chronicle*, 17 Nov. 1821; Captain Gunn to Lt. Col. Gordon, 14 Nov. 1821, SOC, 2296/40; A. Preston to –, 15 Nov. 1821, CSORP, box 636; Information of W. McDonnell, 15 Dec. 1821, SOC, box 169.
153 *Limerick Chronicle*, 28 July, 1 Aug. 1821.
154 *Cork Constitution*, 5 Aug. 1822; *Limerick Chronicle*, 16, 23 Oct. 1822.
155 M. Barrington to Gregory, 1 Aug. 1822, SOC, 2354/11; Major Willcocks to Gregory, 2 Aug. 1822, SOC, 2354/14.
156 *Cork Morning Intelligencer*, 16 Apr. 1822; Major Carter to Gregory, 3 Aug. 1822, SOC, 2346/22.
157 Col. Thornton to Lt. Col. Sorell, 1 Apr. 1822, NAI, Chief Secretary's Office Official Papers, 1002.
158 *Limerick Chronicle*, 27 July 1822; *Cork Morning Intelligencer*, 30 July 1822.
159 It was not a case of Whiteboyism, but that of abduction which was chosen for obtaining his conviction, in which he was involved as an accomplice while he was evading law in mountains in the north of Duhallow barony. Major Carter to Gregory, 3 Aug. 1822, SOC, 2346/22; *Cork Constitution*, 5, 26 Aug. 1822; Information of H. Goold, 10 July 1823, SOC, 2517/47.
160 J. Browne to Gregory, 5 June 1823, SOC, 2513/55.
161 *Cork Constitution*, 5 May 1823.
162 *Cork Morning Intelligencer*, 3 May 1823; *Cork Constitution*, 5 May 1823. This year's *Cork Morning Intelligencer* does not exist in the National Library of Ireland, but this day's issue is enveloped in SOC, 2513/2.
163 *Cork Constitution*, 15 Aug. 1823.
164 Barrington to Gregory, 13 Aug. 1823, SOC, 2514/43.
165 J. McCarthy to Gregory, 3 July 1823, SOC, 2514/4; *Cork Constitution*, 4 July 1823; Barrington to Gregory, 13 Aug. 1823, SOC, 2514/43; M. Blacker to Goulburn, 17 Oct. 1823, SOC, 2515/53; Evidence of J. McCarthy, 16 June 1824, Select committee . . . (200) VII. 501, pp. 206–207.
166 Endorsements to CSORP, 1824/10851 and CSORP, 1825/11210; Goulburn to Gregory, 11 Oct. 1824, Gough Papers, 8303/105/378.
167 Major Vokes to Goulburn, 9 Nov. 1823, CSORP, 1823/7142.
168 – to Col. Gough, no date [1822], Gough Papers, 8303/105/259.
169 *Cork Constitution*, 15 Aug. 1823; *Cork Mercantile Chronicle*, 15 Aug. 1823.
170 Lord Doneraile to Blacker, 22 Apr. 1825, CSORP, 1825/11210.
171 'Extract from the confession of David Nagle taken before Lt. Col. Hill', Jan. 1823 [1824], Gough Papers, 8303/105/335; Confession of Nagle, [23] Aug. 1823, SOC, 2514/55.

2 Rockite organisation and activities

Dublin and Limerick

The first Rockites were Limerick men. Donnelly traces the origins of Rockite disturbances in the region around Newcastle in County Limerick, where exacting management by the land agent of the Courtenay estates prompted the emergence of the first Rockites in 1821.[1] This chapter, by interconnecting Newcastle, Rathkeale (also in County Limerick), and Dublin City, argues that the first Rockites in County Limerick were part of a wider underground network of organisations.

In December, 1820 the following catechism was found in Rathkeale, which was allegedly circulated among tradesmen:

> . . . What is that in your hand[?] / A laurel branch.
>
> Where did it grow[?] / In America, blossomed in France and took root in Ireland.
>
> When will [we] have new moon? / When heresy is banished out of Irish nation and the Tree of Liberty circulated throughout the Irish. . . .
>
> I, A. B. swear that I . . . support freedom and liberty or else the republican uniform green.[2]

This is not the sole example of republican rhetoric of the late eighteenth century. In September the same year, another catechism was found in Newcastle which ran as follows: '. . . What is that in your hand? A bush. Where did it grow? In France. Where is the fruit? In Ireland.'[3] Catechisms containing such phrases were found in other places as well. A County Leitrim version was, '. . . Where did it grow[?] It grew in America[.] Where did it spread[?] In all Ireland[.] Where blossom[?] In France. . .',[4] while in County Roscommon a similar catechism went: '. . . Where did it grow – In America, was blossomed in France, it came . . . to shew religion rights in Ireland . . .'[5]

Not only catechisms but also other documents suggest that there existed an underground network connecting various places in early nineteenth-century Ireland. Dublin Castle succeeded in penetrating an underground society in Dublin City and established a flow of information from its spies in the 1820s.[6] In the information they gathered, it can be shown that the society there required the following 'obligations' and 'regulations' in late 1821:

> OBLIGATIONS FOR THE FRATERNAL SOCIETY
> I B. A. (with the sign of the cross) do declare and promise, in the name, and through the assistance of the blessed trinity, that I will endeavour to keep inviolate all the secrets of this BOARD, or FRATERNAL SOCIETY, from all, but those whom I believe to be regular members, and bound in the same fraternal ties.
>
> 1st. I declare and promise, without any dread or compulsion, allegiance to his present Majesty. [N.B. This phrase was a precaution in case of detection of this document.][7]
>
> 2nd. That I will be true and steadfast to my brethern [*sic*] of this society, dedicated to St Patrick, the holy patron of Ireland, in all things lawful, and not otherwise; and that I will duly and regularly attend where any lawful superior shall think proper, and conform myself to the regulations made by them so long as those who are, or may be in trust, think proper. . . .
>
> 4th. I also declare and promise . . . that I shall endeavour to propagate brotherly love and friendship, among such of my acquaintance as may be thought worthy. . . .
>
> 6th. That in towns and countries, I will give the preference in dealing to those attached to our national interest, according as circumstances may answer me. . . .

> GENERAL REGULATIONS FOR THE PATRIOTIC ASSOCIATION, OR SONS OF SHAMROCK
> [1.] Resolved that as far as our system has [extended] throughout each parish in the kingdom they shall be divided into bodies of 36 each, who are to elect 3 committee men[,] a [treasurer], and a master, and to represent them at the parish[,] and [that] a book is to be kept by the master, & one of the committee, & by that means no defraud can be committed. . . .
>
> 3 That the different bodies before each parish meeting, do hold a meeting in order to represent the state of their bodies to parish master's[,] in like manner, before the county, or district meeting; where they are to divide each county into two, or more districts; who are to send delegates to the provincial meeting, in order to make or repeal laws for the benefit of the institution: and those delegates shall in 4 days after their return, hand down the returns for the ensuing quarter.[8]

When the organisation was raided by the authorities in June 1822, one of its members possessed those 'obligations'.[9] Copies of the 'obligations' and 'regulations' were found also in County Kildare,[10] Killaloe in County Clare,[11] County Down,[12] and Newport in County Tipperary.[13] The Down copy was a printed one.[14] These documents were probably used also in Limerick City, and in Rathkeale and Newcastle, which were the early centres of the Rockite disturbances. Although no copies were discovered in those three places, the police officer referred to the contents of the 'regulations' accurately, and he testified they were in use there.[15]

Those obligations and regulations were still being used in the 1830s in Sligo City, County Meath, and in the County or City of Armagh,[16] while copies of a document whose contents were very similar to the 'regulations', and which seem to have preceded them, were found in County Monaghan,[17] County Leitrim,[18] and Drogheda in County Louth.[19]

It often happens that such underground organisations existed only on paper. However, in this case the real existence of the organisations can be shown by human connections between localities. In October 1821, Major Going, the police officer whose headquarters were at Rathkeale, was assassinated.[20] The immediate cause was his treatment of the corpses of the two men shot at an engagement between the police and a party of local Whiteboys in August of the same year.[21] When Going ordered their burial, one of the corpses was still warm and looked as if the man was alive. A rumour spread that he had not been yet dead.[22] As a result, Going became an enemy of the people and was murdered.

The trials for Going's murder were held in March 1823 and March 1824. Altogether three men were convicted and executed. According to a principal in this case who turned informer, two other men, Madigan and O'Brien, were also involved and that Madigan was a brother-in-law to 'Callaghan', who had been one of the two men shot dead and buried by the police.[23] When the trial was finally held in March 1823, both Madigan and O'Brien were still on the run. However, they had been known to an underground organisation in Dublin City immediately after the murder of Going. According to spies in Dublin, a man by the name of Henry O'Brien was introduced in less than a week after the murder of Going to a 'committee' in Dublin, and that this man explained that he, together with his two brothers-in-law, had fled from Limerick.[24] In the next month, the murder was further mentioned in a committee meeting when it was stated that a man of the name of 'Thomas Maddigan, brother-in-law to John Callaghan who was killed by the police', was also suspected.[25] That details in the information from Dublin respecting events Limerick broadly tallied,[26] suggests that some commutation had been established between Dublin City and County Limerick by the time of the outbreak of the Rockite disturbances.

The members of the organisations were called Ribbonmen. The obligations and regulations show that at least on paper Ribbonmen had a national network. According to preceding studies, Ribbonmen had branches not only in Ireland but in the Irish communities in Liverpool, Manchester and Glasgow.[27] Ribbonmen were not primarily agrarian disturbers: many were artisans.[28] Here it might be recalled that Patrick Dillane and Walter Fitzmaurice, the first Captains Rock at Newcastle, were blacksmiths,[29] while several important Rockite leaders in Cork were also artisans, as will be shown later. In short, the true origin of the Rockite organisation lay in that of the Ribbonmen.

Ribbonmen themselves were descendants of Defenders, a Catholic revolutionary organisation who played a key rôle in the politicisation of the rural population in the 1790s by bridging the urban-based, elitist United Irishmen and the rural Catholic communities.[30] The Defenders envisaged a French-assisted Catholic rising against the Protestant establishment,[31] and a catechism allegedly found in the gaol of County Wexford in 1798, similar in phrases to those of the Ribbonmen, ran as follows: 'What have you in your hand? A green bough. Where did it first grow? In America. Where did it bud? In France. Where are you going to plant it? In the crown of Great Britain.'[32]

Ribbonmen in Dublin City and in Limerick City had established communication via the Grand Canal at least by the middle of 1820.[33] However, when disturbances broke out around Newcastle and Ratheale to deal with local issues, the Dublin Ribbonmen lost control of their former comrades who emerged as Rockites. According to intelligence from informers, the Rockites became a subject of discussion in committees in Dublin. While it was said that 'the old members were not concerned in the outrages',[34] Rockites were criticised on the ground that 'nothing of importance will take place until every county and town rises together'.[35] Emissaries were sent from Dublin to Limerick for the purpose of containing premature Rockite movements.[36] However, the attempt was unsuccessful. Although some communication was maintained between Limerick City and Dublin City after that,[37] Rockites in the west of County Limerick began their activities basically as an independent movement. It is now time to look at what was happening in the region around Newcastle, the other centre of the original Rockite disturbances.

The region around Newcastle was owned by Viscount Courtenay. Farms there fell out of lease between 1810 and 1813 and were released at the rents reflecting the high agricultural prices during the Napoleonic War. When the prices began to decline with the ending of the war, farmers found it difficult to pay the rent of their new leases. The land agent made abatement of up to 60 percent of the rent, which won an approval of the local authorities.[38] However, the estates were mortgaged and the trustees in London despatched Alexander Hoskins as their agent for the purpose of reconstructing the financial situation of the estates. On his arrival in September 1818, Hoskins found that arrears of 63,478lb had been accumulated on the rent roll of 14,000lb p.a,[39] and he radically changed the management of the estates. Hoskins suspended the abatement of the rent, and began distraining the cattle of defaulters and evicting them from their farms.[40] He abused his capacity as a magistrate by using the troops for distraining or evicting.[41] Hoskins's conduct was judged to be harsh even by the Dublin Castle authorities,[42] and provoked disturbances around Newcastle, culminating in his son's murder in July 1821 which led to the creation of the first Captain Rock, Patrick Dillane.

Although Dillane, a blacksmith, owed no arrears of rent to Hoskins, he undertook the assassination, as he admitted in court.[43] Hence, there may have been silent backers of his action. There is some evidence to suggest that farmers goaded by the harsh conduct of the land agent were promoting or even joining disturbances.[44] The police officer of Limerick was 'convinced [that] persons of the better class' were involved,[45] which was probably true (as will be shown below).

The primary object of the first Rockites seems to have been to obtain arms (firearms or swords), and they began to collect arms not only in County Limerick but also in the north of County Cork. On 18 August 1821, the town of Newmarket in Duhallow barony was surprised by a party of Rockites. According to a magistrate, their number was about 500 and 'troops of horse paraded the town while the infantry forcibly entered every house breaking the doors with sledges.' They had 'great marks of discipline, being sober, entirely directed by their leaders, acting with firmness & resolution'.[46] The report was possibly exaggerated, but considering the size of the town, which had only about 200 houses in 1831, it cannot be denied that Rockites overwhelmed the town. By the end of October of this year Rockites made two further raids on Newmarket and, moving southward, another on Kanturk (also a town of about 200 houses).[47] Before those raids, the region had shown no symptoms of disturbance.[48]

Arms were also seized in other places in County Cork. In November 1821, a house was raided by an armed party near the town of Buttevant in Orrery and Kilmore barony. It was reported that they were all strangers led by 'a young man of genteel appearance dressed in grey coat.' The 'grey coat' suggests they were from County Limerick, because people of that county were in the habit of wearing grey clothes.[49] The leader desired an inhabitant of the house not to be alarmed as their object was only to take arms. He demanded water, but when pressed to drink spirits or wine, he declined and did not allow his men to drink.[50]

When the magistrates of Duhallow barony held a meeting to discuss the measures to cope with disturbers,[51] they had to admit that they found the Rockites rather mysterious because their sole object appeared to be gathering arms and ammunition, which was different to ordinary Whiteboys.[52] One magistrate warned that 'indeed the mystery & secrecy of their views are among the most alarming symptom'.[53]

Between October 1821 and April 1822, Rockites stole no fewer than 396 firearms in County Limerick.[54] In County Cork in the same period they committed 223 raids in which more than one arm was stolen,[55] some of which must have been committed by Limerick Rockites. One possible reason why the Rockites around Newcastle collected arms was to rescue Michael Shaughnessy, a man who was convicted at the assizes in County Limerick in September 1821, for his visiting with others a man in Hoskins's employment and forcing him to surrender his farm in July.[56] Little more is known about Shaughnessy, but it was the general opinion around Newcastle that Shaughnessy was in fact innocent.[57] Considerable agitation was created in the region,[58] and a plan was allegedly contemplated to rescue him.[59]

Shaughnessy was mentioned in Cork and Kerry as well. When a mounted party of 400 men raided Newmarket in early October 1821, it collected arms from houses allegedly for the purpose of rescuing Shaughnessy.[60] An armed party visited the town of Milltown in Cork, allegedly declaring 'They are determined to put down the government & it will be easy to do it, as they had not force sufficient to hang such a man as Shaughnessy'.[61] From the north of Kerry it was reported that people were 'fully persuaded that [government] are afraid to have Shaughnessy executed,' and that a number of notices were posted stating that all the friends of the 'good fellow' were to meet at Newcastle.[62] Newcastle was where the land agent Hoskins resided and this 'good fellow' seems to have meant Shaughnessy.[63]

Dublin Castle judged, on receiving reports from Limerick, that Hoskins and Shaughnessy were the primary causes of the disturbances, and urged Hoskins to leave the country immediately.[64] They also issued a proclamation to the effect that surrender of arms and suspension of disturbances would bring about an amnesty for Shaughnessy.[65] However, such measures proved ineffective. By the autumn the disturbances were showing signs of becoming more serious than mere local agitation. After Hoskins had left the country and the execution of Shaughnessy had been postponed several times,[66] Dublin Castle sent Majors Warburton and Willcocks, police officers of considerable experiences of dealing with rural disturbances,[67] to the west of County Limerick to investigate the state of the country. After they had looked into matters, they warned in October that 'the views of the leaders are now far extended beyond the object for which they originally associated'.[68] On 8 November Dublin Castle had to warn the London government that 'The audacity of the ruffians is astonishing. The gentry are in a state of inexpressible terror.'[69]

It should be noted that when the Limerick Rockites extended their sphere of activities beyond the west of County Limerick, they were exporting not only disturbances but their organisation. In October 1821, a military patrol found an account book which was 'very carefully concealed' in the house of James Condons near Shanagolden in the west of County Limerick. Condons acknowledged the book to be his property, also all the writing to be his.[70] In the book the following catechism was written:

> . . . What is your art[?] / A deep head and heavy brean quick step and sure ame[*sic*] / What distance is there between the sun and moon[?] / A square foot and Irish heart is its full bloom . . . / How many times did the first cock crow before he flew into [Egypt] [?] / [3] times with devotion / What did he sea [*sic*] / That the Romans would obtain the rights and loyal harts would flow all over Ireland . . .[71]

Within three months the same catechism came to be used in Duhallow. A Rockite who was arrested when he was administering an oath to a man in January 1822 had almost exactly an identical copy:

> What is your art? A deep heart, a clear brain, a quick step, and a sure aim.
> What distance is there between the sun and moon? A square foot, and an Irish heart in its full bloom. . . .
> How many times did the first cock crow? Three times.
> What did he say? That the Romans would obtain their own rights again, and that all loyal hearts should flow over Ireland. . . .[72]

Furthermore, Duhallow men brought that catechism into West Muskerry. On the night of 8 January 1822, the house of Robert Kirchhoffer, a magistrate near Macroom, was attacked by a party of Rockites. Two men seized on the occasion confessed that they were from Duhallow. One of them further stated that he came to this place because people in the region needed a leader.[73] The man had the same catechism.[74] Some of its phrases were found in various other places in Munster,[75] one of which was Doneraile (as is shown by the catechism given by John Hickey[76]). This Rockite catechism was similar in tone with, but somewhat different in wording from the Ribbonmen's catechism mentioned earlier, which again suggests that the first Rockites were Ribbonmen who developed their own organisation.

The end of the Rockite disturbances in Limerick

Dublin Castle tried to contain the Limerick Rockites with 'the most prompt and vigorous measures'.[77] By October 1821, 300 soldiers and 270 policemen were deployed in various locations in the west of County Limerick.[78] Newcastle in particular saw a steep increase in manpower: the numbers of soldiers and policemen stationed there rose from thirty and twenty respectively in August 1821 to one hundred of each in October.[79] In Rathkeale also, the military force was increased from twenty soldiers to fifty,[80] in addition to the fifty policemen already there.[81] The force was used without loss of time. Although the summer assizes were over, a special commission court sat in December. Thirty Rockites were tried, of whom twenty-one were convicted, most of whom were sentenced to death.[82] Major Willcocks, now commanding the police in County Limerick, reported that he had 'never witnessed a more satisfactory proceedings'.[83]

The momentum of the Limerick Rockites was collapsing. By the end of 1821, Fitzmaurice, Dillane and others fled into the Duhallow mountains and remained fugitives there until they surrendered to the authorities in the spring of 1822.[84] By January 1822 Major Willcocks could send reports that the west of County Limerick was quiet.[85] By the late spring of the year Rockite disturbances had evidently run their course in County Limerick. In March 1822 tenants began to pay rents on the Courtenay estates,[86] and the Limerick Rockites began to surrender their arms in hopes that such a move would lead to their comrades who were awaiting trial at the spring assizes being spared.[87] Between 13 and 19 of April, 183 firearms as well as forty-nine swords, sabres and bayonets were surrendered. One hundred and eleven of these 183 firearms were usable,[88] which suggest that the intention behind their surrender was genuine. The result of the assizes betrayed their hopes. Thirty-five men were sentenced to death, most of whom were Rockites. Major Willcocks described the trials as 'one of the most efficient assizes held in the county for many years.'[89] Nevertheless, surrender of arms continued after the assizes.[90] Thus, the Limerick Rockites were abandoning the arms which they had so numerously collected.

However, the authorities did not loosen their grip. With the newly passed Insurrection Act, the authorities conducted extensive house searches. At one time in May 1822 the military commander of the county ordered his men to search sixty-one houses simultaneously, one such search leading to the arrest of forty-eight persons.[91] House searches were a severe measure, which caused one resident landlord to report to Dublin Castle, 'They [local people] are now so frightened and so penitent that I shall think it my duty to urge upon government the expediency of abstaining from very active measures against them during the sowing season provided that they continue perfectly quiet.'[92] Notwithstanding this advice, 445 men were to be tried under the Insurrection Act in County Limerick between March 1822 and April 1823.[93]

Thus, County Limerick was quieted down after the spring of 1822, except for the raid on the village of Glenasheen in April 1823, which was in fact planned and perpetrated by Cork Rockites. It was they who now became the main actors in the disturbances.

The Cork Rockites: victories and defeats

Perhaps because they were preoccupied with the Rockites in Limerick, the authorities were slow to realise the danger in County Cork. It was only in the middle of November 1821 that Dublin Castle fully acknowledged the urgent necessity of making preparations to cope with disturbances in Cork.[94] By this time, however, the region bordering County Limerick was under the authority of Captain Rock. Kanturk and Newmarket were raided more than once between August and October, as is mentioned above. In early November magistrates in the north of the county met at the town of Buttevant, but on that very night Rockites raided the nearby town of Liscarroll and took arms away from certain inhabitants.[95] In the same month, a large party of mounted and armed men entered Kildorrery in the barony of Condons and Clangibbon, with much shouting, who were greeted by several of the inhabitants from their windows, but quickly dispersed on the approach of military.[96] Several men there were robbed of their arms, allegedly for the purpose of attacking the detachment at the town of Mitchelstown in the barony.[97]

By the middle of December, the Rockites had spread their influence further south. A land agent inhabiting in the south of Duhallow was in receipt of a warning from a fellow loyalist that 'there has been a great change in the minds and in the disposition of the people of this neighbourhood who were then quiet but now are . . . almost as bad and as little inclined to pay as in the northern part of this barony.'[98]

The authorities' being slow in County Cork was a double mistake. Rural disturbers in Ireland in general were the most active in winter, because of longer nights and the agricultural off-season. Cork Rockites in the winter of 1821–22 in some ways had the upper hand over the authorities. In late November 1821 the military commander of the north Cork district reported that the Rockites 'overspread a large tract of country in small bodies, lighting signal fires on the hills & firing shots in various directions'.[99] In January 1822 the military officer stationed at Charleville warned Dublin Castle that 'it was the intention of the Whiteboys to draw out the military in small parties by making alarm in different directions'.[100] A magistrate in Mallow uttered a cry for help in the following way:

> I have been sometimes out three entire nights within one week. . . . I seriously apprehend I shall soon be reluctantly compelled to exchange the field for my bed. – There are a few magistrates residing between two & three miles from Mallow some of whom wou'd, I have no doubt, supply my place occasionally, had they timely notice . . . but the orders for patroles are so sudden (sometimes . . . issued half an hour, or less, before they are to take place) as to preclude the possibility of my making any application out of town.[101]

As well as in toying with the troops, Cork Rockites were successful also in obtaining arms. Many of the unprotected towns or seats of gentlemen in the north of the county were disarmed by them one by one,[102] and the military commander of north Cork district observed that the Rockites 'possess the power if they choose to exert it, of inflicting with impunity, far greater evils on the country than they have yet attempted.'[103]

The Cork Rockites could spread their network and disturbances up to a line, roughly speaking, drawn from Cork City to Bantry (Cork and Bantry themselves were to escape troubles). It is noticeable that those southern towns which had experienced sectarian tensions before the coming of the Rockites were not seriously affected. In Bandon, the biggest town in County Cork, Protestants held about 30 percent of the total population of the town, a situation which obtained in few other parts of the south of Ireland.[104] They were described as 'descendants of an English colony totally unconnected with the population of the country'.[105] On the occasion of the Orange procession in the town in July 1821, one Catholic was shot dead and several others were wounded by fire coming from certain Orangemen.[106] It was reported from Dunmanway, another southern town, the next day that the state of the town was 'like that of Bandon'.[107] A few days later, at the fair of Timoleague, a Protestant who was suspected of having taken part in the Bandon incident was murdered.[108] At Innishannon also, a notice was posted ordering Catholics not to have any dealings with Protestants.[109] Why did those southern towns not become sites of Rockite disturbances?

Rockite activities came close to Bandon in late 1821, with several cases of arms raids.[110] While strong animosity was shown in the neighbourhood of Bandon against its Protestant population, the Provost of Bandon sent warnings to Dublin Castle of a suspected attack on the town.[111] The hand of the authorities in the region was soon strengthened. The force of thirty-eight dragoons at Bandon were soon increased to a full company of infantry in January 1822,[112] in addition to which Bandon had two yeomanry corps of about 140 men in total, which meant the town had the largest yeomanry force in the county.[113] In addition, before they could begin any large-scale action against the town the Rockites suffered a defeat in an engagement between a party of their own and the yeomanry near the town on 8 January 1822. Several Rockites were killed and injured.[114] The defeat may have worked as a deterrent to the further Rockite advancement into the south of the county.

Nevertheless, the Rockites in County Cork were not dispirited by that defeat. On the following 11 January, a party of Rockites could repulse Earl of Bantry and five men who followed them from Bantry into the mountains of West Muskerry.[115] What was more, it was in that month that the momentum of the Rockites reached its peak in the mountains of West Muskerry and Duhallow. Thousands of people rose and fought against the troops in the daytime, which was clearly quite different in character from ordinary Whiteboyism or even the usual pattern of Rockite activities. Those engagements have been neglected by historians, but they deserve close attention.[116]

During the night of 20 January people from an area of twelve to fourteen square miles to north-west of Bandon reportedly went into the mountains between Macroom and Bantry to assist the Rockites there.[117] On the following day Lord Bantry with fourteen soldiers as well as thirty-five gentlemen and others made a second expedition from Bantry into the mountains for the purpose of arresting those concerned with the skirmish on the eleventh.[118] After arresting a few men, the party was attacked on their way back to Bantry in the pass of the glen of Keimaneigh. The commanding officer sent a report:

> Their numbers as far as I could judge were above *five hundred*, many well armed with guns and ammunition. They were under some sort of discipline, having a regular bugle which sounded the advance & retreat – they fought in the most resolute & determined manner[.] My party in keeping them in check expended about twenty five rounds a man, and as far as I could ascertain we must have killed about twelve and many wounded.[119]

However, one soldier was 'barbarously murdered' by the furious Rockites.[120]

A local poet who allegedly witnessed the battle later composed the following poem, *Cath Céim an Fhia* (The Battle of Keimaneigh), which remained in the repertoires of many west Cork balladeers even in the twentieth century:

> . . . From the west came the sound of battle of horses' hooves, of armour's rattle
> Which quaked the hills in displeasing fashion, loathsome to report. . . .
> Not a man, woman or child was left in their dwelling or house
> Without grief-cries and thousands of wailings,
> As they watched the guard vigorously surrounding them,
> Shooting and loading and firing in their direction. . . .
> May they come to no better end, those foreign cubs of Calvin's
> Whose God was pomposity and not the Christ, I'm told.
> Many men will fast approach using a ship of vast proportion
> And the French, down south, who are so stoic are ready for the fray. . . .
> Dear beloved sons of Erin, do not stop or retreat,
> For the task undertaken will soon be complete. . . .
> Have your long pikes cleaned and polished,
> Go into battle, don't stay from it. . . .[121]

'The French' will be dealt with in Chapter 3. Their behaviour suggests that the Rockites had some sort of organisation. In addition, it was reported from several quarters that there were outsiders among them,[122] some of whom may have been those who had been seen coming from the north-west of Bandon the preceding night. Scattered traces of encampments were later found in the glen, with beds, provisions, plates, knives, forks and so on.[123]

Immediately after the engagement at Keimaneigh, the commanding officer at Bantry suggested reinforcement of troops in the town of Bantry because Lord Bantry's activities had 'exasperated' the Rockites.[124] The commander of the forces in Munster district responded by removing a portion of the troops stationed at Macroom to Bantry.[125] However, in a few days the Rockites took the offensive not against Bantry but Macroom and other places in West Muskerry and Duhallow. The local authorities concluded that the west of the county was 'in a state of open rebellion'.[126] The Irish Lord Lieutenant, on receiving information from Cork, also judged that the disturbances in Cork assumed 'a still more decided appearance of insurrection'.[127]

In a letter to Dublin Castle dated 23 January, it was reported from Kenmare in Kerry that large parties of men were drilling and exercising in a military manner in the mountains of west Cork.[128] On the morning of the 24th, a commanding officer was alarmed and proceeded from Macroom to Millstreet to find that 'every hill covered with large bodies of . . . at least 8 or 900'.[129] His sergeant later testified in court that 'there was no work going on in any of the fields, and all the houses were deserted.'[130] After they had assembled, they attacked and smashed a mail coach from Cork City.

After that attack, no mail service was possible between Cork and Tralee and Cork and Killarney for two days.[131] The officer ordered his men to pursue the Rockites, and in an engagement at Carriganimmy the military arrested twenty-two men and later collected two dead bodies. The officer reported that the Rockites fought with 'presumption & bo[l]dness altho [they were] so badly armed'.[132] According to newspaper accounts, the Rockites lost twelve men in the engagement.[133] A newspaper correspondent conveyed the tense atmosphere of the surrounded town of Macroom:

> On arriving in Macroom, about a quarter after eleven o'clock, I found the town in a state of alarm, and was informed that an account had arrived about ten o'clock, announcing that the Whiteboys, in large numbers, were collecting about five miles to the west of Macroom . . .
>
> In this state of suspense matters remained until past two o'clock, the town in the [mean] time presenting a very strange appearance; I was assured by a military gentleman, that it literally resembled a place actually besieged, or that dreaded an immediate bombardment, the streets quite thronged with people, business at a stand, and the greatest anxiety to hear any intelligence that may arrive.
>
> . . . At length, a little after three o'clock, an account arrived, announcing for certain, that the Whiteboys were flying in all directions; that several were killed and wounded, and a number taken prisoners. . . . Such are the melancholy details which I have been enabled to collect of this day's proceedings – a day which will be long remembered in the town of Macroom . . .[134]

It was not the end of things, however. On the same day (24 January) the commanding officer at Millstreet reported that 'upwards of 5,000 rebels' were on the hills within two miles of the town. While Macroom had a population of about 2,500, Millstreet had only about 1,500 in 1821.[135] Two encampments were found near the town with beds and every appearance of taking the field in a regular way.[136] The day went off without any event, leaving the town in a tense atmosphere, but the situation had grown worse by the next morning. A detailed account of the day is given in a newspaper:

> Early this morning the inhabitants of the town were alarmed by the sounding of horns in every direction. Captain Wallis and Mr. M'Carthy soon arrived with accounts of the assembling of the Whiteboys in three or four positions of convenience to the town. . . . About two o'clock the out-mounted videttes arrived, with accounts of the insurgents advancing on the town, in three different directions; the first body, about five hundred, appeared on the Small Clara Mountain; the second, greatly exceeding in numbers the first, advanced with white flags between Captain Wallis's deer-park and the castle on the Mallow road; while the third division marched round the Blackwater to Keal-bridge, and formed a

> junction with the Mallow-road party. The entire [body] advanced on the town with horns sounding, and when they reached within a quarter of a mile of it, a small party, under the command of Lieutenant Hart, of the 39th, was sent down to check their advance. They were either suffered, or succeeded, in coming to the Millstreet bridewell, the windows of which they began to destroy, when Lieutenant Hart opened a smart fire on them, which was first received with a terrific yell, but after about ten minutes firing they retreated with all speed up thro' the park and through Tullig; but Captain Wallis, with a small party of the 39th, sallied out from his castle . . . opened a brisk fire on them, which threw them into the greatest confusion. The Clara Mountain party, who attempted to advance through Mount Leader Wood, were fired on briskly by a detachment which had been stationed in Millstreet Chapel by Major D'Arcy, which compelled them also to retreat with great speed . . .[137]

The same 25th saw another engagement on the hill of Deshure between Macroom and Dunmanway. In the early morning of that day, with horns echoing around, a large party of men were witnessed in the north of Palaceanne between Bandon and Dunmanway leaving their houses and moving towards the hill.[138] The commanding officer reported:

> I this morning . . . found the insurgents strongly posted to the am[ount] of at least 2000 people – 1000 of whom upon our approach descended from the heights & came to attack us [from] not less than 100 yards distance[;] they fired three shots at my advanced party & were urged on by a man holding his hat upon a pike, but upon my men advancing in three parties in skirmishing order & commencing firing they immediately retreated. We pursued[,] killed at least 6 of them[,] wounded many & took 30 prisoners.[139]

Also at the east of Rathmore in Kerry, several hundred people assembled and stopped a mail coach. They stole arms from the coach, broke it into pieces and murdered the mail-coach agent.[140] The assemblage of people was reported and gentlemen of the town of Killarney accompanied by soldiers went out and took eight prisoners.[141]

The situation was tense also in Duhallow. From Kanturk a magistrate sent the following warning on 25 January: 'Last night & this morning expresses from the Whiteboys have travelled in every direction about this town calling on the people to assemble at a place near the Blackwater about 3 miles from this place. . . . The fields around are all deserted, not a single man at work notwithstanding the favourable weather.'[142] Eventually Kanturk escaped a Rockite attack, but Newmarket was to witness perhaps the severest engagement of the whole Rockite disturbances. It was reported from Newmarket on the 24th that 'the respectable inhabitants' all residing near the town had been compelled to abandon their houses to seek protection under the military.[143] They were wise to do so. The next day the commanding officer sent the following report, which reads like one from a real battlefield:

> Newmarket four o'clock
> . . . a route having come for the dragoons quartered here, only this morning, immediately after their leaving this the rebel force consisting of some thousands supposing from the small number of the detachments of the 22nd regiment that we could not maintain our post came down immediately over the town, we accordingly expecting an attack stood to our arms, and remained in this state of suspense for some hours – at length when the rebel force did not advance but remained stationary in our view . . . I thought it advisable to advance and meet them[;] I ordered Lieutenant Green in front with 12 men who succeeded in making an impression on the main body and driving them off the road which they occupied, whilst I with the remainder of the party opened a galling fire on their flank, and having completely routed them & having taken three prisoners, we thought it prudent to retire on the town, lest an attack might be made on it from another quarter. . . .[144]

A newspaper account complements the above report: as the military approached, they rose from behind the ditches on both sides of the road; they all shouted, and the advance post fired at the troops without effect; the chief body then took flight, while 'a few boys in white persevered and fired in very quick times'.[145] The commanding officer later testified in court that while the engagement lasted for only about twenty minutes, one soldier was killed.[146] Another military officer wrote to his friend that the loss of lives on the side of the Rockites was twenty,[147] while it was reported later in a newspaper the number reached forty.[148] The latter number seems an exaggeration, but some of those injured at the engagement may have died later.

The engagements of January 1822, which made that month probably one of the most disturbed months in Ireland in the first half of the nineteenth century, stands out in the history of rural disturbances in Ireland. In order to shed light on their nature and causes, it seems convenient to begin with identifying their features.

First, the engagements were more or less organised ones, rather than spontaneous and localised outbursts. While they occurred at several places at almost the same time,[149] at three of the four major engagements, i.e. at Millstreet, Deshure and Newmarket, Rockites entered into engagements in an orderly way, showing some sort of discipline during fighting.

Also, emissaries or 'strangers' appeared to mobilise people. According to a Roman Catholic priest who went to the site of the murder of the mail-coach agent on 25 January, people told him that they had been mobilised by 'Limerick men' but that they received no further directions.[150] In the south of Ireland, it was possible to distinguish people by districts, sometimes even by barony, by physical features and clothes.[151] A witness at the trial of a principal of that murder testified that a mounted party of five to six men came to the principal's house during the preceding night and he told him that they had besieged Millstreet and Macroom and would take Killarney before the next evening.[152] A Roman Catholic priest who attended the execution of those convicted for the engagement at Carriganimmy observed that he had some reason to believe that 'a religious organisation' had been brought in from outside.[153] The fact that there were several traces of an encampment, in addition to those already mentioned, corroborates the case.[154]

Secondly, then, what kind of organisation was there? Although the information is limited, it seems that Duhallow men were the principal leaders. One of them was Timothy Cotter, a blacksmith from Newmarket. Cotter had been identified by the authorities before the January engagements, as a man who was swearing people and organising committees in West Muskerry.[155] Major Carter, the police officer in County Cork who had his own network of spies, judged Cotter to be an important Rockite leader in Duhallow, and one who had not only joined the attack on the mail coach on 24 January,[156] but had played a leading part in the murder of the mail-coach agent the next day.[157] William Barrett, Cotter's comrade, was also a Rockite leader who was living in Millstreet in January 1822 and led the engagement there, but he was later arrested in Duhallow.[158] A newspaper correspondent reported that men from Duhallow bordering on Limerick were mobilising people in West Muskerry for the battle of Deshure.[159] The commander of the forces in the district of Munster was 'quite satisfied that the barony of Duhallow . . . is the seat of every faction, and from whence emanate the principal instigators of all these disturbances.'[160] Here it might be recalled from the account above that it was Duhallow Rockites who brought the catechism, organisation and disturbances into West Muskerry.

What can be said of their Limerick connection? Catechisms used in Duhallow were from the west of Limerick, while the first Captains Rock in Limerick fled into the mountains in Duhallow. Some of those who took part in the battle of Newmarket later made an offer whereby they would help the authorities in achieving the arrest of Walter Fitzmaurice, one of the first Captains Rock in Limerick, in exchange for their own safety.[161] Furthermore, Daniel Ready, a Limerick man fleeing to Duhallow with Fitzmaurice and Patrick Dillane, offered his assistance in the arrest of Cotter mentioned above, on condition of his own pardon.[162] These facts imply that there may have been some relationship between the first Captains Rock and those who led the January engagements. However, the evidence is inconclusive on the Limerick connections.

Thirdly, what was their object? This question is difficult to answer. What is suggestive is the deployment of military forces. It should be recalled that Duhallow and West Muskerry were uplands where the penetration of the authorities was a recent and still incomplete phenomenon. In 1816, neither Newmarket nor Kanturk had any troops.[163] Kanturk at times had a small detachment for a short-term purpose, but it was insufficient in the region where magistrates reported numerous instances 'of an utter contempt for the civil law and of the most gross insult offered to its authorities.'[164] In any event, in early October of 1821 there were soldiers in neither Kanturk nor Newmarket.[165] Millstreet as a barrack town had a detachment, but there was no military at Macroom in 1815.[166] Even in December 1821 the town was described as 'totally without protection' by the commander of the forces in Munster.[167]

Although the authorities were slow to act against Rockites in Cork, they tried to make up for the delay by a massive increase in military force. By the middle of November Kanturk and Newmarket had 108 and 109 soldiers respectively.[168] In Macroom the commanding officer could spare about eighty soldiers from the garrison for the engagement near the town in January 1822.[169]

It is possible that the engagements in January were planned as a counter-offensive against the new and direct threat posed by the garrisons. At the battle of Newmarket, a message was delivered to the proprietor of the town to guarantee that their object was not his person.[170] A yeomanry officer who went near Millstreet and met people gathering there on 25 January sent the following account:

> I met the assistant Roman Catholic clergyman of the parish who told me that he had just returned after expostulating with the people and using all the arguments in his power to dissuade them from their mad projects, to which their reply . . . 'We know from what has already happened in other places that there will be an attempt to hunt us down, we may as well die one way as another, we will not therefore difer [*sic*] our attack upon Millstreet, & if the gentlemen have a disposition to serve us we will listen to them to morrow, after we try what we can do.'[171]

By 'what has already happened' they may have meant the defeat at the engagement in the glen of Keimaneigh.

Fourthly, although there was some sort of organisation and discipline on the side of the assailants, the attitude of the leaders and that of the ordinary 'soldiers' differed. A magistrate observed of the battles of Newmarket and Millstreet, 'The assailants without exaggeration amounted to thousands, but [only] a small proportion of them were at all prepared for battle & by far the greater part were totally unarmed, driven like sheep to a slaughter house.'[172] The commanding officer at Macroom reported, 'they frequently made attempts towards a charge on any small parties they suddenly encountered but a shot or two made them run off instantly'.[173]

While most of those who appeared at the sites of engagements were probably mobilised to be there, 'mobilisation' often simply amounted to an ad-hoc summons. A Catholic clergyman testified:

> . . . a person, since executed for another crime, rode twelve or fourteen miles through the country with a white handkerchief on a pole, calling on a people [*sic*] to attend on the following day, for if they would not they would be annihilated or destroyed in their houses, and this caused

the country to be agitated; some said 'we will go,' others said not, and there was a crowd assembled, and forward they went from this popular impulse.[174]

Fifthly, and finally, this kind of mobilisation was seen outside the immediate regions of engagement. On 26 January, a magistrate wrote from near Doneraile that 'numbers of ill disposed persons have proceeded since last evening to join the insurgents in the neighbourhood of Kanturk and Newmarket and that labourers work is suspended in many parts'.[175] A similar movement was seen around Buttevant.[176] Also, a Rockite who turned informer stated that his party heard about the defeat at the battle of Newmarket when they were on their way there from Charleville.[177] The fact that these movements were noted after the engagements suggests that they were not premeditated ones but rather reactions to the ad-hoc summons. People in Kerry were also mobilised in the same way. On 26 January, the parishioners of Aglish in the west of Killarney deserted the parish to join the Rockites at Inchabeg. They had been mobilised by four 'well dressed strangers', who swore the people to go there on pain of death and destruction. When they reached Killarney, they were remonstrated (possible by a local man of influence) and turned back.[178] During the night of 26 January, some strangers threatened people in the parish of Aghadoe to go off to Millstreet at once or their houses should be burned.[179] Even from Tralee it was reported on the same day that a large party of country people were proceeding towards County Cork.[180] From County Limerick as well, it was reported that a mobilisation was attempted by Cork men.[181]

In short, what was happening on the two days of 24–25 January seems to have been a mixture of planned and perhaps co-ordinated attacks on the newly stationed troops on the one hand and on the other a widespread mobilisation in an ad-hoc and semi-panic manner. What made possible this semi-panic was the psychological state of the people at that time.[182] On 26 January a militia officer wrote to Dublin Castle that 'To those residing in the country, and having intercourse with the lower class of its inhabitants, a very material change is manifest in the manners and disposition of the people[;] petty quarrels, drinking, and rioting at fairs has totally subsided, as previous to the Rebellion of 1798.'[183] In Ireland at that time a notion that something extraordinary was about to happen was prevalent, which was in fact an important factor not only in these engagements but in the whole Rockite disturbances. This question will be dealt with in Chapter 3.

In any event, the Rockites suffered a complete defeat in the uplands in Duhallow and West Muskerry, which pacified the region for the remainder of the period of the Rockite disturbances. Immediately after the engagements, offers were made to the local authorities asking for pardons in exchange for surrendering arms and taking the oath of allegiance.[184] However, Rockites in other regions remained active. In the barony of Orrery and Kilmore in particular, Rockites could again have the upper hand over the authorities.

On the night of 29 January, a magistrate's house near Liscarroll in Orrery and Kilmore was attacked and burnt down together with its barn. The house had been used as military barracks for two months, but the soldiers had been moved a few days before to reinforce the military in the west of the county where thousands of people had risen. Rockites burnt two further houses in Liscarroll on the same day, one of which was under repair for use as a barrack.[185]

The culmination of Rockite enmity came during the night of the 31 January 1822, when the police barracks at Churchtown in Orrery and Kilmore were attacked by a party of several hundred Rockites. During the engagement the Rockites made calls to the eighteen policemen in their barracks to surrender. However, when the exhaustion of their ammunition forced the policemen to surrender, the Rockites assaulted them, killing three men and severely injuring six.[186] A magistrate reported that 'its beyond my capacity to describe the horrid[,] wounded & mangled spectacle they present'.[187]

This victory stirred the Rockites. Two days after at the nearby town of Milford, a party of Rockites proceeded, with the blowing of horns and the firing of shots, to a house which was used as a police barracks. The police, having learned a lesson from the Churchtown attack, had moved to a more secure place. Finding the house vacant, the Rockites burnt it down.[188] According to a newspaper account, the Rockites searched the town for the owner of the house, declaring that they would burn him for his letting the house for barracks.[189]

In February, the same year, an extremely rare instance of Rockite violence against women was committed. Around thirty to forty Rockites attacked wagons carrying the wives and children of the military while the latter were on their way from Kildorrery to Charleville, and raped seven or eight of the women.[190] Several of the harmed women had Protestant-like surnames.[191] However, that does not necessarily mean that the Rockites were targeting Protestants. Officers or non-commissioned officers and their families tended to be Protestants, and a magistrate reported that the Rockites had deliberately targeted the wives of officers or non-commissioned officers.[192] The evidence is too inconclusive to decide whether the Rockites were trying to harm Protestant women or take revenge against the commanders of the military who had killed many Rockites in the January engagements.

The boldness of the Cork Rockites in that winter shocked Dublin Castle, which hurriedly introduced repressive measures. In February a special commission was sent to Cork, where 306 men were awaiting trial, of whom no less than about 200 were considered Rockites.[193] Eventually thirty-six men were sentenced to death,[194] many of them being tried for joining the engagements in January. Some of them seem to have been convicted on the flimsy ground of simply being on the spot,[195] which showed the severe stance of the authorities. The special commission was soon followed by the Insurrection Act, which enforced a curfew and enabled magistrates to conduct summary searches of houses. Furthermore, in the spring assizes of 1822 in Cork (excepting the City) 380 men were tried. While the figure means a substantial increase since 1820 (245 men) and 1821 (225 men),[196] there were many others who were tried at special sessions courts under the Insurrection Act.

Facing such repressive measures, Cork Rockites slowed their activities down in the spring of 1822, but they did so only temporarily. With the beginning of the agricultural off-season and longer nights (and *after* the worst days of the famine were over), Rockites in Orrery and Kilmore, Fermoy, and Condons and Clangibbon baronies resumed their activities. Already in early September of that year Major Carter, the police office of Cork, warned that insubordination was becoming manifest in Fermoy barony.[197] In a little while his warning was confirmed by Colonel Gough, commander of the forces in the north of County Cork, who reported that the 'system of terror' had a dire effect on his neighbourhood.[198] When Major Carter began sending reports of Rockite outrages in succession,[199] the Irish Lord Lieutenant felt at a loss and proposed transferring Major Willcocks and Colonel Thornton from County Limerick to supersede Carter and Gough, respectively.[200]

In the autumn and winter of 1822, Rockites resorted to more traditional tactics of clandestine and nightly activities, avoiding open confrontation with the authorities. It was at that stage that Rockites in the north of Cork committed arson on a massive scale. At the same time, they were not mere Whiteboys. Their activities were based on a network of Ribbonmen-like underground organisations, whose basic unit was a 'committee'.

Rockite organisations: committee and pike

Thanks to Hickey and Nagle, some light can be shed on the Rockite organisations in County Cork, particularly in the second phase of their movement after they resumed their activities in the autumn of 1822.

When he was arrested, Hickey was regarded as Captain (General) Rock. He, however, denied it:

> Newenham —— You are considered the General Rock of your part of the country?
> Hickey —— I was not, they say many things of me that are not true.[201]

In fact, the Captain Rock of Doneraile parish ordered that no persons should attend the execution of Hickey and that no shops should be opened on the day.[202] This show of solidarity was probably intended to undermine the intentions of the authorities to use the occasion to awe other Rockites. In any event, Hickey was, though not a captain, a very active Rockite. Although he joined the organisation only at the end of 1822,[203] by the time of his arrest in March 1823 he could name about seventy-five Rockites as well as the owners of about 150 arms in Doneraile parish alone.[204] In addition, his sphere of activities went well beyond the parish boundary: he was active in Castletownroche, Shanbally, Rockmills, Kildorrery and Marshalstown two weeks before his arrest.[205] Needless to say, he had no material interest in those places. He went there because he was ordered to do so by his organisation.

Hickey gave an account of the Rockite committee organisations in County Cork, as is touched on in the Introduction:

> Newenham —— What is the general plan of arrangement?
> Hickey —— Committee men are appointed. A head committee man is ordered to move to the next parish or district and the men composing the committee in said parish are ordered by summons with blank signature to attend on a certain day, hour and place under forfeiture of life and the next head committee man does the same to the next district. One committee man knows the other[;] they also have signs.[206]

What were the nature and business of a committee? Nagle's information supplies a clue. Nagle wrote confessions (Figure 2.1) in the wake of his death sentence,[207] the accuracy of which was confirmed by Lord Doneraile who wrote that 'the information he had given us was in almost every particular quite correct, with the exception of an occasional flogging administered to a farmer'.[208] Colonel Gough and Major General Lambert joined Lord Doneraile in their judgement on the reliability of Nagle's information.[209]

While Nagle himself attended committees at Mallow, Doneraile and Buttevant, he also provided the names of 'committee men' and captains of the following parishes: Caherduggan, Clenor, Clonmeen, Dunbullogue, Kilbroney, Kilshannig, Rahan, Rathcooney, Monanimy, Mourneabbey, Templesque and Walshtown. These parishes were in baronies of Duhallow, Orrery and Kilmore, Fermoy, Barrymore, Barrets and the liberties of Cork City. Although two other committees can be identified from other sources,[210] it seems certain that Nagle was a key individual in the Rockite organisation and activities of County Cork in the second phase of the disturbances.

According to Nagle, the committee controlled and sanctioned every Rockite activity of the district (parish) under its leadership.[211] Another informant stated that a committee was usually held in a public house where the preparation was made for the next 'visit' including the selection of the leader for the occasion.[212] Among such committees, supposedly the most important was one held in the town of Mallow in November 1822, which Hickey identified as the first committee in the county. At that meeting more than sixty 'committee men' and 'leaders' were present.[213] Nagle gave the following account of the committee:

> Mr. Galvin took the chair[;] the following resolutions were carried on unanimously[.] John Hickey and I sat together[;] John Galvin said he was called upon by Mick Denahy[;] he said he wished to know the strength

> of the country and said it was better [to] have the smiths make pikes in every district all over the country and when they would be prepared to have a general turn out in one night and massacre the Protestants[;] it was seconded by Mr. Denahy and carried on[.] Richard Griffin said that it was not fit to have prisoners going through the country without rescuing them[;] it was supported by Thimothy Keeffe, and Maurice Barret[.] John Hickey moved to say that it was rong [*sic*] to have the police patrolling the country every knight [*sic*] taking every person that came in there [*sic*] way without the least opposition[,] that it was to keep them inside doors, [and that] the only place so as to make an attack was in the wood road leading to Anykisshy[.] [Richard] Griffin seconded the resolution and said he would give him every assistance[.] Jeremiah Leary also said he would have his party goe to attack them[;] it was carried on unanimously —— Mr. Galvin again moved in stating to the house that nothing could be dun [*sic*] until pikes were made[;] it was approved of by the meeting and were accordingly made to my own knowledge[;] the meeting adjourned and was determined to be held in Doneraile the Sunday following at Arthur Coughlan[']s to consider about attacking the police where we met accordingly, accompanied by some of the inhabitants of the town of Doneraile . . .[214]

The Arthur Coughlan mentioned by Nagle appeared in another informant's statement: it was in Coughlan's public house in Doneraile where the attack on the police at Glenasheen was planned,[215] which was carried out in April 1823.[216] To corroborate Nagle and the above informant, a Rockite who was killed in the attack was an associate of John Hickey,[217] while ten men who pleaded guilty at the trial which dealt with this case were mainly from Doneraile.[218]

Richard Griffin, whose name occurred in Nagle's above-cited information as a militant person, appeared in the same character in the information provided by John Dundon, another important Captain Rock in Cork and a wheelwright,[219] who stated that 'He always proposed to fire on the military and police patroles'.[220]

Nagle also provided the occupations of those attending the committee: e.g. Galvin was a blacksmith at Mallow, Denahy a leather cutter, and Griffin a farmer near Mallow. Of the thirty-three men whose occupations were stated by Nagle, one man was a substantial miller, six men were artisans and town labourers, while there were sixteen farmers but only four who were agricultural labourers.[221] Rockites were thus not confined to agricultural labourers, or purely agrarian.

Galvin's words at that committee deserve attention. While as a blacksmith he does not seem to have had any agrarian interest himself, he as chairman attempted to contain the hasty proposals of Griffin and Hickey and tried to turn the direction of the discussion to a more ambitious but less immediate subject, i.e. a general rising to massacre Protestants. Galvin's

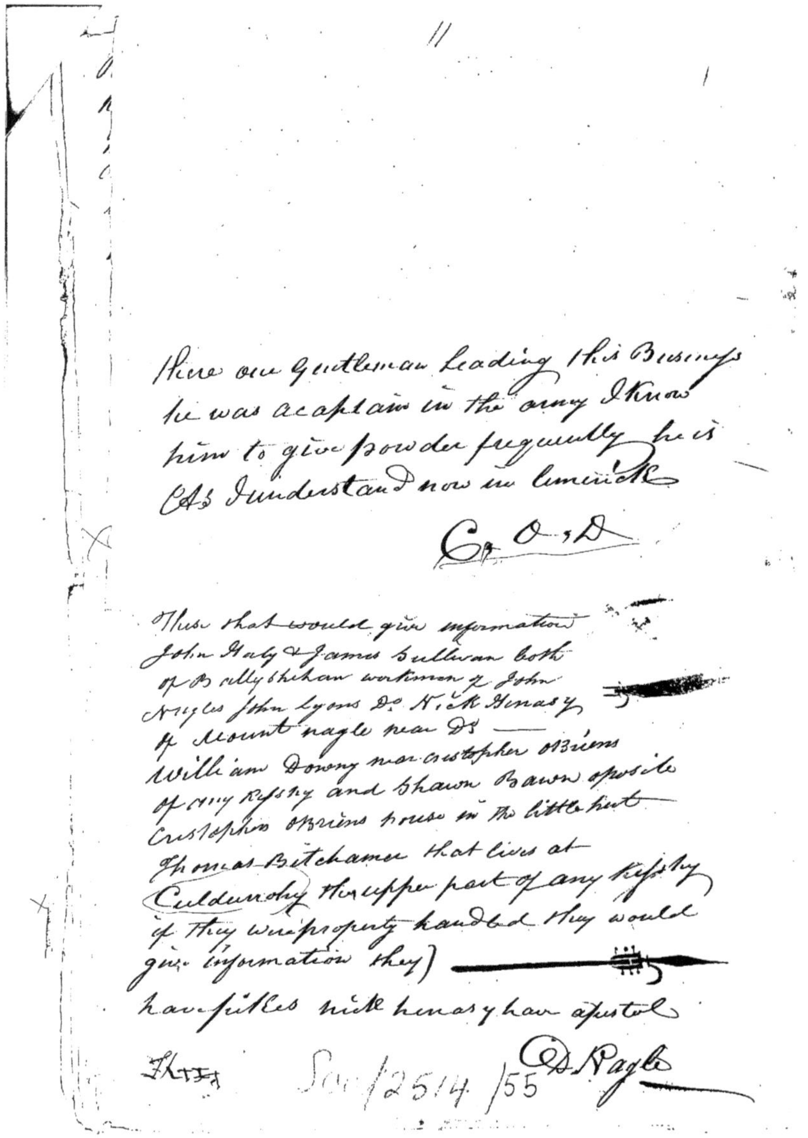

there are Gentleman leading this Business
he was a captain in the army I know
him to give powder frequently he is
as I understand now in Limerick

C. O. D

These that would give information
John Haly & James Sullivan both
of Ballysheehan workmen of John
Nagles John Lyons Do. Nick Henasy
of Mountnagle near Do —
William Downy near Cristopher OBriens
of Arny Kipsky and Shawn Bawn opposite
Cristopher OBriens house in the little hut
Thomas Bitchamer that lives at
Culdunohy the upper part of Any Kipsky
if they were properly handled they would
give information they)
have pistles nick henasy have apistol

C. D. Nagle

Soc/2514/55

Figure 2.1 Nagle's confession, with an illustration of pike near the bottom.[222]

words corroborate Hickey's evidence in that he said that they were contemplating a general rising. Nagle also stated that 'This to be executed by night, the people to massacre the Protestants in their respective parishes.'[223] When Dundon was asked about their object, his answer was 'the overthrow of the government, and the destruction of the Protestants, and that however disparate [*sic*] it may appear, the people were determined and wou'd attempt.'[224] On the side of the authorities, Colonel Gough observed that 'I do not wish it to be understood, I have any idea that any general system of attack or rising is intended this winter, convinced as I am that such is the ulterior object of the insurgent'.[225]

'Massacre of Protestants by Catholics' was in fact a common, and often groundless, phrase appearing at times in seventeenth- and eighteenth-century Ireland. However, such words were uttered in most cases by Protestants who tried to exaggerate or fabricate the danger posed by Catholics.[226] What is unique with Rockites is that Catholics themselves stated it in such an unmistakable way. As is mentioned in the Introduction, annihilation of Protestants would have meant a social revolution. How they could form such a radical idea will be dealt with in Chapter 3. Here other topics of committee discussion should be dealt with.

The resolution for the manufacture of pikes was put into effect, when Nagle and others visited blacksmiths and swore them to perform the work.[227] Nagle stated that pikes were manufactured in four places, one of which was the smithy owned by a certain Jerry Collins in Doneraile.[228] The police found pikes at the workshop of Jeremiah Collins in Doneraile in March 1823.[229] The resolution of the committee to collect money can also be corroborated.[230] Table 2.1 shows an increase in the number of 'visits' for money collecting after the committee had met. Relatively few cases of money collection took place in 1822, which may have reflected Captain Rock's banning of money collection in late 1821, as discussed in Chapter 1. Instances fell in 1824, something which can be accounted for by the decline in Rockite disturbances.

Thus, Cork Rockites were organised to such an extent that they could mobilise members of local districts for the purpose of collecting money and manufacturing pikes.[231] The structure of their organisations can be inferred from the oath of fourteen clauses cited below. A copy of it was found with Hickey's brother in Doneraile,[232] while Colonel Gough got another from a 'committee man' who had turned informer.[233] A third copy was given supposedly by another informer to the authorities at Charleville.[234] David Nagle also swore a very similar oath.[235]

Table 2.1 Numbers of visits for money in the four baronies in the north of Cork[236]

	1821	*1822*	*1823*	*1824*	*Total*
Duhallow	1	2	2	2	7
Orrery & Kilmore		12	25	14	51
Fermoy		4	41	16	61
Condons & Clangibbon	2		17	2	21
Total	3	18	85	34	140

THE ROYAL UNITED IRISHMAN'S TEST
December 26, 1822.

1st, I do, in the awful presence of God, solemnly swear on the Holy Evangelist, to keep secret of my committee-man, and all those here present, until death.

2nd. That I will obey every lawful summons from my committee-man . . .

3rd. That I will not associate, join, aid, or assist or be present, if possible, at any one act, that might coincide or come within the limits of the present patriotic system, prevailing at present in Ireland, without the consent of my committee-man until death. . . .

4th. That if I hear of any boon brother, or loyal brethren that will violate or break through the above vow . . . without the consent of their committee-men . . . I am content to suffer the punishment due to such crime . . .

5th. That I will never see a brother or brother's wife in distress, without relieving them as far forth as I can . . .

6th. That I will not have a carnal knowledge of a brother's wife, or mother, when I know them to be so nearly connected, except by the awful sacrament of matrimony.

7th. That I will not rob, steal, or plunder, except fire, side-arms, or ammunition, or something belonging to them, but in time of an open rebellion.

8th. That I will join, aid, and assist to destroy all tyrants[,] kings' suppressors, and heretics not of the true Roman Catholic and Apostolic religion, until death. . . .

9th. That I will not go before judge or jury, court of enquiry, coroner's inquest, or any other trial whatsoever in life, so as that any member or members collectively, or individually, might suffer the slightest hurt or harm thereby.

10th. That I will not wrong any brother or brother's wife to the value of one shilling, without making restitution therein. . . .

11th. That I will not quarrel, brag, nor boast, of the strength of our confederates to any living human being, except to a brother; and that I will not quarrel nor fight, but against those who would do me or some of my royal brethren harm.

12th. That I will plant the Tree of Liberty in as many hearth [*sic*] as I can depend my life upon, and no others, of any rank on earth, until death.

13th. That I will fight knee-deep in Orange or any other heretic's blood. That the crying of children, the moaning of women, or the groaning of men shall never terrify or undaunt me without fighting for the long promised liberty of the Roman Catholic and Apostolic Church. . . .

14th. That I will not hint, dint, write, post, engrave, cut, paint, nor print, in any one form or shape whatsoever in life, so as to give any information against any of my loyal brethren, or break any of my lawful vows until death.

This oath has several features deserving attention. While phrases showing a strong Catholic identity are used, there is no reference to agrarian questions. 'Rebellion' or 'United Irishman' standing side by side with 'royal' seems strange, but the word 'royal' may have been used in order to dignify the organisation in the same way as Captain Rock's 'proclamations' were dressed in official rhetoric. Perhaps the most striking is the power which a committee man assumed over other members. Nagle supplemented it by stating that every leader or captain was sworn to obey a committee man.[237] The authority of a committee man is an important point, considering the significance attacked to 'captain' in the tradition of rural disturbances in Ireland. It seems that it was in the late 1790s that Cork first saw the establishment of an underground network of parish committees of agrarian disturbances.[238] However, two decades separated the late 1790s and the early 1820s. (Nagle and Hickey were young men.) How did the disturbers of the 1820s come to have a committee-based organisation?

Information given by John Hurien, a Rockite from Milford, provides a clue.[239] Hurien joined the attacks on barrack houses in Liscarroll and the police barracks in Churchtown mentioned above. According to him, there appeared around 1819 near Milford a Whiteboy organisation for the purpose of lowering the prices of potato and milk for 'poor people in distress'. Their oath was simply to keep secret and be ready when called on. After the Rockite disturbances broke out in Limerick, a man said to be from near Newcastle came and administered the following oaths to Hurien, viz., 'to be ready and willing when called on, nor to see a brother or brother's wife in distress, not to rob, steal or plunder except arms and ammunition, not to wrong a brother and brother's wife to the value of a shilling worth, not to deal with a Protestant to the value of something trifling'. These phrases were in substance also seen in 'the Royal United Irishman's Test', which suggests that the organisations at Milford and Mallow functioned under the same structure. In fact, when a 'committee' meeting held in a pub near Milford was raided by the authorities in June 1823, fifteen men including painters, tailors, farmers and servant boys were attending from various places of Cork and Limerick, one of whom had a letter 'purporting to be from Mallow committee'.[240]

Hurien's information suggests that the organisational structure of Cork Rockites was brought in from County Limerick, which fits in with the general picture of the origins of Rockite disturbances described so far in this book. Nagle also stated that he was sworn to his Rockite organisation by a man from County Limerick, that a central committee existed in Newcastle and that orders were given from thence to Cork committees.[241] Newenham, the magistrate who interrogated Hickey, testified that one of the oaths used in Hickey's organisation originated from Newcastle.[242]

Considering the fact that it was Dublin Ribbonmen who originally introduced an organisational structure into County Limerick, it seems safe to argue that the underground network of Cork Rockites centring on the Mallow committee was a graft of Ribbon organisational structure, via Limerick Rockites, on local Whiteboy organisations. As a result, 'in many cases,

Captain Rock's men became Ribbonmen', as was testified both by Major Warburton and a judge who presided over special sessions in Cork.[243] An informant corroborated this when he stated: when they were first introduced into an organisation, they swore to keep their secret and be ready when called on; at the next stage, they swore a more sophisticated 'Ribbonmen's oath'.[244] This grafting explains why a committee man, who was a key person in Ribbon organisations as was seen in the 'General Regulations for the Patriotic Association', could assume a superior power over a captain, who was essentially a Whiteboy character.

Their common organisational structure apart, whether the Cork Rockites and Dublin Ribbonmen were connected in any practical and meaningful way is not clear. Cork Rockites kept, at least in their minds, some communication with Dublin. Several notices, which appeared in Doneraile and Kildorrery after the Mallow committee session was held, had 'Dublin' as a signature.[245] Hickey stated that all catechisms and directions were sent from Dublin where the head committee lay.[246] Nagle also stated that the 'chief committee' at Newcastle kept regular communication with Dublin. He also gave the names of the two men who carried on the correspondence of the Mallow committee with the Dublin and Newcastle committees.[247] However, it is possible that Nagle and others only imagined that they had a Dublin connection. Either Nagle or Hickey did not provide any names of those on the Newcastle or the Dublin committees, while the two men whom Nagle mentioned as individuals responsible for liaison did not appear in the information supplied by spies in Dublin. What seems certain, however, is that in order to commit themselves to what in retrospect seems a wild idea of a general rising occasioning a social revolution, Rockites had to believe that they were connected with Dublin as part of a national network of organisations.

The end of the Rockite disturbances in Cork

The Rockite organisations in Cork collapsed before they could launch a general rising. By the end of 1823, Rockites as Ribbonmen-Whiteboys no longer existed. After 1824 only sporadic outbursts of violence were to be seen and these were reacting to particular agrarian issues in certain localities.

Although Rockites developed a network of underground organisations, which their eighteenth-century predecessors did not have, such organisations were in practice almost always penetrated by spies and informers.[248] Proceedings of a Rockite committee near Charleville, for instance, were leaked to the authorities,[249] and Colonel Gough could make a list of 170 Rockites based on information from his spies.[250] The severest blow was, however, the defection of renowned leaders.[251]

When Nagle turned approver, 'most respectable farmers . . . have come forward and acknowledged the part they have acted, or as they say were obliged to act'.[252] Although they declared to the authorities that they would now exert themselves to induce their labourers to give up their arms,[253] Nagle's information led to the arrest of twenty-five men.[254] Before that happened, Dundon's turning informer created a panic in Fermoy barony,[255] where twenty-one men absconded and fifty men were arrested.[256]

In addition, agricultural prices began to rise in 1823, and that marked an end to the worst period for market producers. In June 1824, it was reported from County Cork that 'Within my recollection, I never saw the Cos. Cork, Clare, Limerick, or Tipperary in a more flourishing, or in a state of yielding to the tenants an opportunity of paying their rents.'[257] Farmers now saw no point in running the risk of assisting or becoming Rockites for the purpose of coping with economic hardship. The improvement of their conditions had, of course, beneficial effects on those of their labourers.

In his report to the British government in January 1824, the Irish Lord Lieutenant could write that 'There has been a gradual progress towards amendment, in every circumstance, connected with the restoration of order, and the due administration of the law.'[258] Thus, the Rockites were defeated by the authorities in less than three years. Nevertheless, what is truly striking about the Rockites is their belief in radical political ideas. How did the Rockites develop these? Chapter 3 seeks to deal with that question.

Acknowledgments

Parts of this chapter were originally published in "The Rockite movement in County Cork in the early 1820s," *Irish Historical Studies*, vol. xxxiii, no. 131, May 2003, pp. 278–296.

Notes

1 James S. Donnelly Jr, *Captain Rock: the Irish agrarian rebellion of 1821–24* (Cork: The Collins Press, 2009), chap. 1.
2 Major Going to W. Gregory, 23 Dec. 1820, NAI, SOC, 2185/48 ; R. O. C. Newenham to C. Grant, 28 Dec. 1820, SOC, 2185/50.
3 Information of J. Hickey, 16 Sept. 1820, SOC, box 169.
4 F. Waldron to Gregory, 25 Aug. 1815, SOC, 1713/12.
5 J. Wills to Grant, 6 Feb. 1820, SOC, 2176/9.
6 Not only from Dublin but from Kildare and Limerick, the authorities received information 'corresponding in the minutest particulars, as to the place & time of . . . meeting'. Lord Talbot to Lord Sidmouth, 4 Nov. 1821, TNA, HO 100/202/9.
7 Anon., *Report of the trial of Michael Keenan for administering an unlawful oath* (Dublin: J. Exshaw, 1822), pp. 17–18.
8 Diary of Major Sirr, 9 Dec. 1821, Trinity College Dublin, Sirr Papers, 869/3.
9 *Report of the trial of Michael Keenan*, pp. 41–48.
10 J. Chritchly to Gregory, 8 Mar. 1822, SOC, 2368/21.
11 M. Martin to Brigade Major Croker, 24 May 1823, SOC, 2341/29. The magistrate could send only a part of the copy, because the suspected person tried to swallow the paper. Martin to H. Goulburn, 2 July 1823, SOC, 2341/33. The remaining part was later recovered and published in *Limerick Chronicle*, 16 Apr. 1823.

12 Boyd to R. Peel, 9 June 1823, Surrey History Centre, Goulburn Papers, 304/A1/1.
13 Rev. J. Pennefather to Grant, 13 Dec. 1821, NAI, CSORP, box 636.
14 There is another copy in CSORP, box 636, but nothing is attached to this copy.
15 Evidence of Major Warburton, 20 May 1824, BPP, Select committee to inquire into disturbances in Ireland, minutes of evidence, 1825 (20) VII. 1, p. 136; Evidence of the same, 26 May 1824, Select Committee of House of Lords on nature and extent of disturbances in Ireland, minutes of evidence, 1825 (200) VII. 501, pp. 84–85; Information of Hickey, 16 Sept. 1820, SOC, box 169.
16 British PPP, Select committee to inquire into the state of Ireland since 1835 in respect to crime and outrage, report and evidence, 1839 (486) XI.1, XII.1, questions (2301), (2314), (4022), (4380), (4601–4603).
17 O. O'Neill to Peel, 6 Feb. 1816, SOC, 1765/61.
18 J. H. Payton to Grant, 14 Oct. 1819, SOC, 2072/2.
19 Constable Armstrong to –, no date, SOC, box 169.
20 Major Warburton to Gregory, 15 Oct. 1821, CSORP, box 637; *Limerick Chronicle*, 17 Oct. 1821.
21 Major Going to Gregory, 16 Aug. 1821, CSORP, box 633; *Limerick Chronicle*, 18 Aug. 1821.
22 Major Going to Gregory, 18 Aug. 1821, CSORP, box 633; Majors Willcocks and Warburton to —, 10 Oct. 1821, CSORP, box 630; Evidence of Major Willcocks, 21 May 1824, Select committee . . . 1825 (200) VII. 501, pp. 49–50; Stanley H. Palmer, *Police and protest in England and Ireland 1780–1850* (Cambridge: Cambridge University Press, 1988), pp. 223–224.
23 *Limerick Chronicle*, 15 Mar. 1823; *Cork Constitution*, 26 Mar. 1824; R. Peppard to Goulburn, 7 Dec. 1824, CSORP, 1824/10438.
24 Diary of Major Sirr, 21, 27 Oct. 1821.
25 Diary of Major Sirr, 11 Nov. 1821. Dublin Castle ordered the Limerick police to conduct an investigation about 'Henry O'Brien', who was a servant employed by [P]uthill in Cappa in County Limerick. Grant to Major Willcocks, 15 Nov. 1821, Emory University, Gregory Papers, 624/13/8.
26 It was reported through spies in Dublin that 'Pat Bourke', 'captain of a boat' from Limerick attended a committee in February 1821. Diary of Major Sirr, 12 February 1821. Major Warburton, police officer who sent spies into the organisation in Limerick City, sent an urgent enquiry to Dublin Castle about 'Patrick Bourke', 'master of a boat' which belonged to pier no. 681. Major Warburton to Grant, 12, 24 Nov. 1821, CSORP, box 637. One more case of corroboration can be cited. Spies in Dublin communicated that Michael Power of Lisbane, son to William Power near Shanagolden, a rich farmer was a leading man. Diary of Major Sirr, 11 Nov. 1821. While Shanagolden was where Condons's catechism cited above was found, it was in the house of William Power, a rich farmer near Shanagolden, where two men were hid, who were involved in the murder of Major Hare near Rathkeale in January 1822. T. Keily to Gregory, 22 Apr. 1823, SOC, 2517/21; *Limerick Chronicle*, 26 Apr., 23 July 1823.
27 M. R. Beames, 'The Ribbon societies: lower-class nationalism in pre-Famine Ireland', in C. H. E. Philpin ed., *Nationalism and popular protest in Ireland* (Cambridge: Cambridge University Press, 1987), pp. 246–247; Jennifer Kelly, *'The downfall of Hagan': Sligo Ribbonism in 1842* (Dublin: Four Courts Press, 2008), p. 42.
28 Beames, 'The Ribbon societies', pp. 247–249.
29 John Cussen, who was tried with Shaughnessy, was also descried as a blacksmith. *Cork Morning Intelligencer*, 22 Apr. 1822.
30 Marianne Elliott, *Partners in revolution: the United Irishmen and France* (New Haven and London: Yale University Press, 1982), pp. 342, 355–356; Tom

Garvin, 'Defenders, Ribbonmen and others: underground political networks in pre-Famine Ireland', in Philpin ed., *Nationalism and popular protest in Ireland*, pp. 229–232. The Ribbonmen had non-political functions as well. For instance, some of the Ribbon societies in Leinster functioned as labour leagues, while in Connacht the main motive to join the Ribbonmen was to obtain opportunities for sociability and social advancement through membership as well as to oppose local Orangemen. John Belchem, '"Freedom and friendship to Ireland": Ribbonism in early nineteenth-century Liverpool', *International Review of Social History*, vol. xxxix, no. 1, 1994, pp. 35–36; Kelly, '*The downfall of Hagan*', pp. 48–49.

31 Marianne Elliott, 'The origins and transformation of early Irish republicanism', *International Review of Social History*, vol. xxiii, no. 3, 1978, pp. 420–421; *idem*, *Partners in revolution*, p. 42; Thomas Bartlett, 'Select documents XXXVIII: Defenders and Defenderism in 1795', *Irish Historical Studies*, vol. xxiv, no. 95, 1984–85, p. 377.

32 T. Crofton Croker, *Researches in the south of Ireland, illustrative of the scenery, architectural remains, and the manners and superstitions of the peasantry: with an appendix, containing a private narrative of the rebellion of 1798* (London: John Murray, 1824), p. 15.

33 Major Warburton to Grant, 24 Nov. 1821, CSORP, box 637; Evidence of Major Willcocks, 21 May 1824, Select committee . . . 1825 (200) VII. 501, p. 59; Evidence of Major Warburton, 26 May 1824, *ibid.*, pp. 84–85.

34 Diary of Major Sirr, 5 Nov. 1821.

35 Diary of Major Sirr, 27 Oct. 1821. Cf. *Report of the trial of Michael Keenan*, p. 10.

36 Diary of Major Sirr, 5, 11, 17 Nov. 1821.

37 Major Warburton to Goulburn, 2 Dec. 1822, SOC, 2341/48.

38 Brigade Major Mahony to Peel, 29 Dec. 1814, SOC, 1556/40; same to same, 9 Jan. 1815, SOC, 1716/2.

39 Major Going to Grant, 19 Nov. 1819, SOC, 2185/51; *Cork Morning Intelligencer*, 18 Oct. 1821.

40 *Dublin Evening Post*, 9 Oct. 1821; E. Harrison to Grant, 18 Dec. 1821, CSORP, box 633; A. Hoskins to the Lord Chancellor, 19 Jan. 1820, SOC, 2185/51.

41 Rev. W. Ashe to Major Going, 8 Nov. 1819, SOC, 2185/51; Captain Turvesville to Major General Aylmer, 8 Jan. 1820, SOC, 2185/51; Grant to H. Bateman, 19 Jan. 1820, NAI, Private Official Correspondence, letterbook 421.

42 Gregory to Grant, no date, SOC, 2185/51; Majors Warburton and Willcocks to Grant, 23 Oct. 1821, HO 100/202/25.

43 *Cork Constitution*, 5 Aug. 1822; Evidence of M. Barrington, 10 May 1825, BPP, Select committee to inquire into state of Ireland with reference to disturbances, 1825 (129) VIII. 1, p. 573.

44 *Ibid.*

45 Major Vokes to Goulburn, 3 Oct. 1825, SOC, 2728/39.

46 W. Allen to Grant, 22 Aug. 1821, CSORP, box 630; Rev. Chester to Grant, 26 Oct. 1821, CSORP, box 631.

47 Rev. T. Allen to –, 20 Oct. 1821, CSORP, box 633; W. Allen to Grant, 25 Oct. 1821, SOC, 2293/13; C. Crone to Gregory, 29 Oct. 1821, SOC, 2293/15.

48 Brigade Major Croker to Grant, 29 Mar. 1821, CSORP, box 638.

49 G. Nagle to –, 17 Jan. 1822, SOC, 2342/45; Croker, *Researches in the south of Ireland*, p. 221. Mackenzie gave a long account about John Cussen, a son of a bankrupt middleman in County Limerick. Cussen allegedly made a confession to Mackenzie that he had acted as a Captain Rock. R. Shelton Mackenzie, *Bits of Blarney* (New York: Redfield, 1954), pp. 151–230.

50 J. Anderson to –, 6 Nov. 1821, CSORP, box 630; Rev. M. Purcell to –, 6 Nov. 1821, CSORP, box 636; *Cork Morning Intelligencer*, 10 Nov. 1821; *Limerick Chronicle*, 14 Nov. 1821.
51 R. Aldworth to Gregory, 16 Oct. 1821, SOC, 2293/10.
52 C. O'Leary to –, 16 Oct. 1821, SOC, 2293/8.
53 Rev. J. E. Orpen to Gregory, 18 Oct. 1821, SOC, 2293/12.
54 Major Willcocks to Gregory, 26 Apr. 1822, SOC, 2352/35.
55 Compiled from *Cork Constitution*, *Cork Morning Intelligencer*, *Limerick Chronicle*, SOC and CSORP.
56 *Limerick Chronicle*, 22 Sept. 1821.
57 W. Furlong to Gregory, 19 Oct. 1821, CSORP, box 632.
58 Major General Lambert to Lt. Col. Sorell, 9 Oct. 1821, SOC, 2296/18.
59 Furlong to Gregory, 19 Oct. 1821, CSORP, box 632.
60 Brigade Major Croker to Gregory, 6 Oct. 1821, CSORP, box 631.
61 G. Bruce to –, 7 Nov. 1821, SOC, 2293/20.
62 Major Warburton to Gregory, 7 Oct. 1821, CSORP, box 637.
63 Grant to Hoskins, 14 Nov. 1821, CSORP, box 633.
64 Grant to Major Going, 13 Nov. 1820, Private Official Correspondence, letter-book 421; Grant to Hoskins, 14, 30 Nov. 1821, CSORP, box 633; Major Willcocks to Grant, 27 Nov. 1821, CSORP, box 637
65 Gregory to Brigade Major Croker, 11 Oct. 1821, CSORP, box 632; [?Grant] to D. C. O'Grady, [27] Oct. 1822, NAI, Chief Secretary's Office Official Papers, series II, 535/34.
66 *Limerick Chronicle*, 3, 6, 10 and 13 Oct. 1821. Shaughnessy was later transferred to Cork penitentiary in November. *Ibid.*, 21 Nov. 1821. There is no evidence of his execution.
67 Palmer, *Police and protest in England and Ireland 1780–1850*, pp. 204–205, 212.
68 Majors Warburton and Willcocks to Grant, 23 Oct. 1821, HO 100/202/25.
69 Grant to Lord Sidmouth, 8 Nov. 1821, HO 100/200/47–48.
70 Major Stewart to Gregory, 20 Oct. 1821, CSORP, box 636.
71 CSORP, box 634; Gregory to Major Stewart, 23 Oct. 1821, CSORP, box 634; Major Stewart to Grant, 27 Oct. 1821, CSORP, box 634.
72 W. Allen to –, 22 Jan. 1822, SOC, 2342/58; *Cork Morning Intelligencer*, 9 Feb. 1822. Another man arrested also in Duhallow had a catechism which had the following phrases 'What is the distance between the sun & moon[?] A. A square foot, an Irish heart in its full bloom. Q. Where do you stand? A. I stand straight, on a crooked line on a four road cross.' Information of T. McCarthy, 19 Jan. 1822, SOC, box 170; *Waterford Chronicle*, 7 Feb. 1822.
73 Rev. R. Kirchhoffer to Goulburn, 10 Jan. 1822, SOC, 2342/17; *Cork Morning Intelligencer*, 10 Jan., 21 Feb. 1822; Information of P. Leary, 13 Jan. 1822, SOC, box 170.
74 Major Carter to –, 16 Jan. 1822, SOC, 2342/38.
75 T. Hunt to Gregory, 16 Dec. 1821, CSORP, box 633; Information of J. Slattery, 22 Mar. 1822, SOC, 2355/60; Evidence of W. H. W. Newenham, 11 June 1824, Select committee . . . 1825 (200) VII. 501, p. 185.
76 Catechism, no date, National Army Museum, Gough Papers, 8303/105/232. It is written on the back of this document: 'given by Hickey'.
77 Lt. Col. Sorell to Major General Lambert, 17 Oct. 1821, National Library of Ireland, Kilmainham Papers, 1155/335–337.
78 Major General Lambert to Lt. Col. Sorell, 9 Oct. 1821, SOC, 2296/18; *Limerick Chronicle*, 10 Oct. 1821; Major Stewart to Gregory, 9 Oct. 1821, CSORP, box 636.
79 Magistrates to Lt. Col. Brown, 20 Aug. 1821, SOC, 2296/13; Major Going to Gregory, 30 July 1821, CSORP, box 636; Major General Lambert to Lt. Col.

Sorell, 9 Oct. 1821, SOC, 2296/18; Major Stewart to Gregory, 9 Oct. 1821, CSORP, box 636; *Limerick Chronicle*, 10 Oct. 1821.

80 G. Blennerhassett to –, 29 Sept. 1821, SOC, 2295/7; Major General Lambert to Lt. Col. Sorell, 9 Oct. 1821, SOC, 2296/18.

81 Major Stewart to Gregory, 9 Oct. 1821, CSORP, box 636; *Limerick Chronicle*, 10 Oct. 1821.

82 BPP, Return of number of persons indicted and tried: at assizes, and special commissions in Ireland, 1816–23, 1823 (305) (306) XVI. 625, 639. How many of them were actually executed is not known.

83 Major Willcocks to Gregory, 22 Dec. 1821, CSORP, box 637.

84 *Limerick Chronicle*, 10 July 1822.

85 Major Willcocks to Gregory, 6 Jan. 1822, SOC, 2350/9; same to same, 13 Jan. 1822, SOC, 2350/14.

86 Col. Thornton to Lt. Col. Sorell, 20 Mar. 1822, SOC, 2351/49; same to same, 4 Apr. 1822, SOC, 2352/6; *Limerick Chronicle*, 6, 10 Apr. 1822.

87 Col. Thornton to Lt. Col. Sorell, 13 Mar. 1822, SOC, 2351/45; Major Willcocks to Gregory, 16 Mar. 1822, SOC, 2351/39.

88 Col. Thornton to Lt. Col. Sorell, 22 Apr. 1822, SOC, 2352/29.

89 Major Willcocks to Gregory, 22 Apr. 1822, SOC, 2352/28. The total number of death sentences was forty-five, if those convicted for such 'ordinary' crimes as rape were included. Major Willcocks to Gregory, 23 Apr. 1822, SOC, 2352/31. The figure makes a contrast to that of the spring assizes in 1776, when Whiteboyism was raging in Tipperary, Kilkenny, Carlow and Queen's County. At those assizes, twenty-six men in all were capitally convicted. Maurice J. Bric, 'The Whiteboy movement in Tipperary, 1760–80', in William Nolan in association with Thomas G. McGrath eds., *Tipperary: history and society: interdisciplinary essays on the history of an Irish county* (Dublin: Geography Publications, 1985), p. 167.

90 E.g., Col. Thornton to Lt. Col. Sorell, 12 May 1822, SOC, 2353/12.

91 Col. Thornton to Lt. Col. Sorell, 27 May 1822, SOC, 2353/22.

92 Knight of Kerry to Col. Thornton, 7 May 1822, SOC, 2353/11.

93 BPP, Return of persons tried in counties in Ireland under Insurrection Act, 1823, 1823 (311) XVI. 687.

94 Grant to Major General Aylmer, 16 Nov. 1821, SOC, 2293/27.

95 Rev. Purcell to –, 3 Nov. 1821, SOC, 2293/17.

96 A. Batwell to Major Carter, 17 Nov. 1821, SOC, 2345/32; Major Carter to Gregory, 21 Nov. 1821, *ibid.*

97 Batwell to Major Carter, 17 Nov. 1821, SOC, 2345/32; Major Carter to Gregory, 21 Nov. 1821, *ibid.*

98 C. McCarthy to J. Purcell, 19 Dec. 1821, Cork City and County Archives, Ryan Purcell Papers, U 139, box 41.

99 Major General Aylmer to Lt. Col. Sorell, 29 Nov. 1821, SOC, 2293/31.

100 Col. Straton to the Adjutant General, 17 Jan. 1822, SOC, 2342/48.

101 Rev. Chester to –, 19 Jan. 1822, SOC, 2342/50. Underlines are original.

102 E.g. Rev. Purcell to –, 3 Nov. 1821, SOC, 2293/17.

103 Major General Aylmer to Lt. Col. Sorell, 16 Dec. 1821, SOC, 2293/40.

104 Ian d'Alton, *Protestant society and politics in Cork 1812–1844* (Cork: Cork University Press, 1980), pp. 9, 171.

105 Brigade Major Mahony to Peel, 10 Jan. 1817, SOC, 1835/2. See also Allan Blackstock, *Loyalism in Ireland 1789–1829* (Woodbridge: The Boydell Press, 2007), pp. 139–140.

106 Lt. Col. Sorell to – 7 July 1821, SOC, 2293/6; *Cork Morning Intelligencer*, 26, 28 July, 6 Oct. 1821; Jervois to Grant, 1 Oct. 1821, CSORP, box 634; Evidence of J. R. Elmore, 16 June 1824, Select committee . . . 1825 (20), VII. 1, p. 418.

107 – to –, 3 July 1821, CSORP, box 632.
108 *Cork Morning Intelligencer*, 10 July 1821; Evidence of Elmore, 16 June 1824, Select committee . . . 1825 (20), VII. 1, p. 418.
109 *Cork Morning Intelligencer*, 24 July 1821.
110 Provost of Bandon to Gregory, 17 Dec. 1821, SOC, 2293/38.
111 Provost of Bandon to Gregory, 17 Dec. 1821, SOC, 2293/38; same to same, 19 Dec. 1821, SOC, 2293/39.
112 Provost of Bandon to Gregory, 19 Dec. 1821, SOC, 2293/39; Lt. Col. Sorell to Major General Lambert, 29 Dec. 1821, Kilmainham Papers, 1155/401; same to same, 20 Jan. 1822, Kilmainham Papers, 1155/412.
113 Provost of Bandon to Gregory, 19 Dec. 1821, SOC, 2293/39; BPP, Return of number of troops or corps of effective yeomanry and volunteers in Ireland, 1820, 1821 (306) XIX. 177, p. 4.
114 E. Newman to Gregory, 9 Jan. 1822, SOC, 2342/11; A. Bernard to Major General Lambert, 10 Jan. 1822, SOC, 2342/26; *Cork Morning Intelligencer*, 10, 12, 15 Jan. 1822; Lord Carbery to –, 15 Jan. 1822, SOC, 2342/33; Lord Kingston to Goulburn, 20 Jan. 1822, SOC, 2342/52; *Waterford Mirror*, 23 Jan. 1822.
115 Lord Bantry to Goulburn, 13 Jan. 1822, SOC, box 170; *Cork Morning Intelligencer*, 15 Jan. 1822.
116 Whooley describes but does not analyse them. Finbarr Whooley, 'The Rockite movement in north Cork 1820–25', unpublished M. A. thesis, University College, Cork, 1986, pp. 33–35. Donnelly mentions the engagements only briefly. Donnelly, *Captain Rock: the Irish agrarian rebellion of 1821–24*, pp. 68–71. R. J. Bennett, 'The rising of 1822', *Ireland's Own*, 6 Jan. 1940 is an account on the battle of Keimaneigh.
117 *Cork Morning Intelligencer*, 26 Jan. 1822.
118 M. O'Sullivan to J. Browne, 24 Jan. 1822, SOC, box 170.
119 Major Carthew to Major General Lambert, 21 Jan. 1822, SOC, 2343/5. Italics are original.
120 O'Sullivan to Browne, 24 Jan. 1824, SOC, box 176; J. Gillman to Goulburn, 25 Jan. 1822, SOC, 2343/12; R. H. Eyre to – 13 June 1825, CSORP, box 1126.
121 Brian Brennan, *Máire Bhuí Ní Laoire: a poet of her people* (Cork: The Collins Press, 2000), pp. 34, 40–42.
122 Lord Bantry to Goulburn, 22 Jan. 1822, SOC, 2342/60; Major General Lambert to Lt. Col. Sorell, 24 Jan. 1822, SOC, 2343/13; O'Sullivan to Browne, 24 Jan. 1822, SOC, box 170. Author of 'A tour in Connaught' (Caesar Otway), *Sketches in Ireland: descriptive of interesting portions of the counties of Donegal, Cork, and Kerry* (second edition, Dublin: W. Curry Jr., and Co., 1839), pp. 261–273 is a semi-fictional account of the battle.
123 *Cork Morning Intelligencer*, 7 Feb. 1822.
124 Major Carthew to Major General Lambert, 21 Jan. 1822, SOC, 2343/5.
125 Major General Lambert to Lt. Col. Sorell, 22 Jan. 1822, SOC, 2343/5.
126 Browne to Gregory, 25 Jan. 1822, SOC, box 170; Major General Lambert to Lt. Col. Sorell, 31 Jan. 1822, SOC, 2343/41. Browne seems to have been not an alarmist but an active magistrate. W. Allen to Major Carter, 25 Jan. 1822, SOC, 2343/25.
127 Lord Wellesley to Peel, 29 Jan. 1822, HO 100/203/152–157.
128 R. P. Mahony to Gregory, 23 Jan. 1822, SOC, 2348/20.
129 Lt. Col. Mitchell to Major General Lambert, 24 Jan. 1822, SOC, 2343/5.
130 *Cork Morning Intelligencer*, 19 Feb. 1822.
131 R. Day to C. Tod, 26 Jan. 1822, SOC, 2348/24; [Y]. Busteed to [Sir H. Lees], 26 Jan. 1822, SOC, 2348/25; Berkelman to C. D. Oliver, 26 Jan. 1822, SOC, 2348/26.

132 Lt. Col. Mitchell to Major General Lambert, 24 Jan. 1822, SOC, 2343/5.
133 *Cork Morning Intelligencer*, 26, 29 Jan. 1822; *Limerick Chronicle*, 26, 30 Jan. 1822; *Saunders's Newsletters*, 28 Jan. 1822; *Dublin Evening Post*, 29, 31 Jan. 1822.
134 *Dublin Evening Post*, 29 Jan. 1822.
135 BPP, Abstract of answers and returns pursuant to act for taking account of population of Ireland; enumeration abstract, 1824 (577) XXII. 411, pp. 164–165.
136 Major Darcy to Col. Broke, 24 Jan. 1821, SOC, 2343/23.
137 *Dublin Evening Post*, 31 Jan. 1822. See also E. McCarty to Goulburn, 25 Jan. 1822, SOC, 2343/8.
138 A. Bernard and Lord Carbery to Major General Lambert, 25 Jan. 1822, SOC, 2343/23.
139 Lt. Col. Mitchell to Col. Broke, 25 Jan. 1822, SOC, 2343/23. See also *Dublin Evening Post*, 31 Jan. 1822.
140 Day to Tod, 26 Jan. 1822, SOC, 2348/24; Oliver to Goulburn, 27 Jan. 1822, SOC, 2348/26; Affidavit of B. Maguire[McGuire], *Limerick Chronicle*, 9, 16 Feb. 1822, 18 Aug. 1824; *Cork Constitution*, 14 Aug. 1822.
141 *Dublin Evening Post*, 31 Jan. 1822.
142 Rev. Orpen to –, 25 Jan. 1822, SOC, 2343/6.
143 Captain [Keappock] to Col. Gough, 24 Jan. 1822, Gough Papers, 8303/105/262.
144 Captain Keappock to Col. Gough, 25 Jan. 1822, SOC, 2343/31. See also W. Allen to Col. Straton, 26 Jan. 1822, SOC, 2343/42.
145 *Limerick Chronicle*, 30 Jan., 2 Feb. 1822.
146 *Cork Morning Intelligencer*, 26 Feb. 1822.
147 *Cork Morning Intelligencer*, 31 Jan. 1822. It was reported in a letter from Buttevant that the bodies of ten men who had been shot dead were left that night in a bog-hole near the place, until the nights became moonlight. *Limerick Chronicle*, 13 Feb. 1822.
148 *Waterford Mirror*, 9 Feb. 1822.
149 There were other engagements, though smaller ones, on the 25th. J. Lumsden to Major Carter, 25 Jan. 1822, SOC, 2343/11; Captain Stephenson to Major General Lambert, 26 Jan. 1822, SOC, 2343/23; *Dublin Evening Post*, 29 Jan. 1822.
150 *Limerick News*, 4 Mar. 1822. This clergyman was not trying to shift the responsibility to outsiders. He identified some of those who had been on the spot.
151 Croker, *Researches in the south of Ireland*, p. 221.
152 *Waterford Mirror*, 17 Aug. 1822; Barrington to Gregory, 8 Aug. 1822, SOC, 2349/51.
153 *Saunders's Newsletters*, 6 Mar. 1822.
154 *Correspondent*, 30 Jan. 1822.
155 Information by M. Brien, 18 Jan. 1822, SOC, box 170.
156 Major Carter to Gregory, 18 Feb. 1822, SOC, 2344/46. This is corroborated by the trial of Cotter. *Chute's Western Herald*, 18 Aug. 1824.
157 Major Carter to Gregory, 8 June 1824, SOC, 2615/38; same to same, 13 Aug. 1824, SOC, 2616/12. This judgement was shared by Col. Gough, the military commander of the north of County Cork. Major Carter to Gregory, 18 Feb. 1822, SOC, 2344/46.
158 Major Carter to Goulburn, 15 July 1824, SOC, 2615/57; E. Ellis to Goulburn, 16 July 1824, SOC, 2615/64; Major Carter to Gregory, 21 Aug. 1824, SOC, 2616/20.
159 *Dublin Evening Post*, 5 Feb. 1822.
160 Major General Lambert to Lt. Col. Sorell, 31 Jan. 1822, HO 100/203/223.
161 J. D. Freeman to Gregory, 31 Mar. 1822, SOC, 2345/50; Gregory to Freeman, 4 Apr. 1822, Private Official Correspondence, letterbook 422.

162 J. Longfield to Goulburn, 21 Sept. 1823, SOC, 2515/23; O'Leary to –, 8 June 1824, SOC, 2615/37; Major Carter to Goulburn, 23 Jan. 1825, CSORP, 1825/11051.
163 F. Hewitt to –, 1 Jan. 1816, SOC, 1769/1; same to Gregory, 5 Feb. 1816, SOC, 1769/23.
164 Rev. Orpen to Gregory, 15 Oct. 1818, SOC, box 168; Lt. Col. Colleton to Major General Gordon, 27 Oct. 1818, SOC, 1958/9.
165 O'Leary to –, 16 Oct. 1821, SOC, 2293/8; Aldworth to –, 1 Nov. 1821, SOC, 2293/16.
166 Rev. Kirchhoffer to Peel, 9 Nov. 1815, SOC, 1715/38.
167 Major General Lambert to Lt Col. Sorell, 24 Dec. 1821, SOC, 2293/43.
168 Table shewing the distribution of the several corps under the command of Major General Lord Aylmer, Buttevant, 23 Nov. 1821, SOC, 2293/30.
169 *Cork Morning Intelligencer*, 29 Jan. 1822. The officer later said at court that he led 100 men. *Ibid.*, 21 Feb. 1822.
170 Evidence of W. Wrixon Becher, 1 June 1824, Select committee . . . 1825 (200) VII. 501, pp. 140–141.
171 Brigade Major Mahony to Goulburn, 25 Jan. 1822, SOC, 2343/9.
172 Rev. Orpen to [E.] Orpen, 2 Feb. 1822, SOC, 2344/8.
173 Lt. Col. Mitchell to Major General Lambert, 24 Jan. 1822, SOC, 2343/5.
174 Evidence of J. Keily, 21 Apr. 1824, BPP, Select committee of House of Lords to inquire into state of Ireland with reference to disturbances, minutes of evidence, 1825 (521) IX. 249, pp. 318–321.
175 A. Hill to Goulburn, 26 Jan. 1822, SOC, 2343/22. See also Lt. Col. Hill to Goulburn, 26 Jan. 1822, SOC, 2343/21.
176 *Waterford Mirror*, 2 Feb. 1822.
177 W. H. W. Newenham to –, 1 July 1823, SOC, 2514/1.
178 *Limerick Chronicle*, 30 Jan. 1822; *Cork Morning Intelligencer*, 31 Jan. 1822. See also Rev. R. Herbert to Gregory, 28 Jan. 1822, SOC, 2348/27.
179 *Limerick Chronicle*, 30 Jan. 1822.
180 T. Busteed to –, 26 Jan. 1822, SOC, 2348/25; *Dublin Evening Post*, 31 Jan. 1822.
181 Major Willcocks to Gregory, 25 Feb. 1822, SOC, 2350/82; G. Ray to Gregory, 28 Mar. 1822, SOC, 2349/25.
182 A similar semi-panic or scare was seen when cholera became widespread in Ireland in 1832. S. J. Connolly, 'The "blessed turf": cholera and popular panic in Ireland, June 1832', *Irish Historical Studies*, vol. xxiii, no. 91, 1983, esp. pp. 215–220.
183 Lt. Col. Hill to Goulburn, 26 Jan. 1822, SOC, 2343/21.
184 O'Leary to —, 1 Feb. 1822, SOC, 2344/6; *Dublin Evening Post*, 2, 9 Feb. 1822; *Waterford Mirror*, 2, 4 Feb. 1822; *Cork Morning Intelligencer*, 7 Feb. 1822; *Limerick Chronicle*, 20 Feb. 1822; J. Leader to J. Lloyd, 4 Mar. 1822, SOC, 2345/13.
185 Major Carter to Goulburn, 30 Jan. 1822, SOC, 2343/39; G. B. Lowe to Goulburn, 31 Jan. 1822, SOC, 2343/44; *Cork Morning Intelligencer*, 7 Feb. 1822; Confession of J. Walsh, 10, 11 Jan. 1824, SOC, 2618/4; Confession of the same, 13 Jan. 1824, SOC, 2614/13; Rev. Purcell to Goulburn, 6 Feb. 1822, SOC, 2344/14.
186 Major Carter to Goulburn, 1 Feb. 1822, SOC, 2344/3; *Cork Morning Intelligencer*, 5, 23 and 28 Feb. 1822.
187 Rev. Purcell to Goulburn, 1 Feb. 1822, SOC, 2344/2.
188 Crone to Goulburn, 3 Feb. 1822, SOC, 2344/13; *Cork Morning Intelligencer*, 7 Feb. 1822.
189 *Limerick Chronicle*, 6 Feb. 1822; Lt. Col. Sorell to Gregory, 6 Feb. 1822, SOC, 2344/15; Crone to Goulburn, 13 Feb. 1822, SOC, 2344/33.

190 *Cork Morning Intelligencer*, 21 Feb. 1822.
191 *Ibid.*, 9 Apr. 1822.
192 A. Batwell to Goulburn, 22 Feb. 1822, SOC, box 170. One of the Rockites allegedly declared that he would let the riflemen know they were Captain Rock's men. *Cork Morning Intelligencer*, 9 Apr. 1822.
193 *Cork Morning Intelligencer*, 16 Feb. 1822.
194 J. S. Townsend to Gregory, 23 Feb. 1822, SOC, 2344/58.
195 *Cork Morning Intelligencer*, 19, 21, 23, 26 Feb. 1822; *Saunders's Newsletters*, 21, 22, 23 Feb. 1822.
196 *Cork Morning Intelligencer*, 28 Mar., 2 Apr. 1822.
197 Major Carter to Goulburn, 3 Sept. 1822, SOC, 2346/42.
198 Col. Gough to Lt. Col. Sorell, 20 Sept. 1822, SOC, 2346/52.
199 For instance, he sent four reports between 22nd and 27th of September Major Carter to Goulburn, 22 Sept. 1822, SOC, 2346/54; same to same, 23 Sept. 1822, SOC, 2346/58; same to same, 24 Sept. 1822, SOC, 2346/62; same to same, 27 Sept. 1822, SOC, 2346/70.
200 Lord Wellesley's note on SOC, 2346/62.
201 W. H. W. Newenham to –, 13 Apr. 1823, SOC, 2512/16.
202 Major Carter to Gregory, 17 Apr. 1823, NAI, Prisoners' Petitions, 1987; Lord Doneraile to –, 19 Apr. 1823, SOC, 2512/25.
203 Hickey's address, 17 Apr. 1823, SOC, 2512/25.
204 He conveyed this information to a Roman Catholic priest. Evidence of the Rev. O'Brien, 10 May 1825, Select committee . . . 1825 (129) VIII. 1, pp. 584–586. However, he refused to give information concerning his fellow Rockites to the authorities, saying that 'Would you have me become the prosecutor of the very men that I myself have deluded, and swear away the lives of those people that I have brought into this business [myself]'. *Ibid.* In fact, O'Brien testified that information given by Newenham about Hickey was not an exact account. However, what Hickey told O'Brien was not completely accurate, either. For instance, while Hickey told O'Brien that Doneraile and Mallow had no connection, his attendance at a committee at Mallow was confirmed by Nagle. In addition, Newenham testified that Hickey's information was corroborated by information from other sources. Newenham to –, 13 Apr. 1823, SOC, 2512/16; Evidence of W. H. W., 11, 14 June 1824, Select committee . . . 1825 (200) VII. 501, p. 184.
205 Major Carter to Gregory, 21 Mar. 1823, HO 100/208/91–96; Lord Doneraile to –, 2 Apr. 1823, SOC, 2512/3; Col. Arbuthnot to Lt. Col. Finch, 2 Apr. 1823, SOC, 2512/3.
206 Newenham to –, 13 Apr. 1823, SOC, 2512/16; Evidence of W. H. W. Newenham, 11, 14 June 1824, Select committee . . . 1825 (200) VII. 501, pp. 182–184.
207 Confession of Nagle, [23] Aug. 1823, SOC, 2514/55; Confession of Nagle, 25 Aug. 1823, Gough Papers, 8303/105/387; 'Extract from the confession of David Nagle taken before Lt. Col. Hill', Jan. 1823 [1824], Gough Papers, 8303/105/335; information of Nagle, no date, SOC, 2614/1; Confession of Nagle, 4 July 1824, SOC, 2615/23. SOC, 2514/55 and Gough Papers, 8303/105/387 are long documents.
208 Lord Doneraile to M. Blacker, 22 Apr. 1825, CSORP, 1825/11210.
209 Col. Gough to Lt. Col. Finch, 24 Feb. 1824, SOC, 2614/42; same to same, 3 May 1824, SOC, 2615/21; A certificate on Nagle and his conduct, 2 Oct. 1824, CSORP, 1824/10851. Major Carter obtained information from Patrick Kelleher for the purpose of corroborating Nagle's information. Kelleher named nine men who attended a committee at Mallow in Apr. 1823, four of whom can be identified in Nagle's information. Information of P. Kelleher, 26 Sept. 1823, SOC, 2515/35.

210 *Cork Constitution*, 23 Aug. 1822; J. Connery to Johnston, 5 June 1822, SOC, 2345/77.
211 'Extract from the confession of David Nagle taken before Lt. Col. Hill', Jan. 1823 [1824], Gough Papers, 8303/105/335.
212 Statement and further statement of P. Daly, [12 Feb. 1824], Gough Papers, 8303/105/334.
213 'Extract from the confession of David Nagle taken before Lt. Col. Hill', Jan. 1823 [1824], Gough Papers, 8303/105/335; Confession of Nagle, [23] Aug. 1823, SOC, 2514/55.
214 Confession of Nagle, 25 Aug. 1823, Gough Papers, 8303/105/387.
215 'Voluntary confession of William Thornhill of Carker in Doneraile', 18 July 1823, Gough Papers, 8303/105/132.
216 T. Doolan to Gregory, 1 May 1823, SOC, 2517/25; *Cork Constitution*, 2 May 1823; *Limerick Chronicle*, 3, 21 May 1823.
217 Col. Arbuthnot to Lt. Col. Finch, 3 May 1823, SOC, 2513/3; *Cork Morning Intelligencer*, 3 May 1823. This day's *Cork Morning Intelligencer* is enclosed in SOC, 2513/2.
218 *Cork Constitution*, 22, 26 Mar. 1824; *Limerick Chronicle*, 24 Mar. 1824.
219 Lord Ennismore to Gregory, 25 June 1823, SOC, 2513/83.
220 'Report of John Dundon to Lt. Colonel Hill Sept. 1823. Relative to the burning of Mr. Hill's haggard at Graig, etc.', no date, Gough Papers, 8303/105/501. Nagle's and Dundon's information agreed on the name, birthplace and occupation of this Griffin.
221 'Extract from the confession of David Nagle taken before Lt. Col. Hill', Jan. 1823 [1824], Gough Papers, 8303/105/335.
222 Confession of Nagle, [23] Aug. 1823, SOC, 2514/55. A pike illustration can be seen in another of his confession. Confession of Nagle, 25 Aug. 1823, Gough Papers, 8303/105/387.
223 'Extract from the confession of David Nagle taken before Lt. Col. Hill', Jan. 1823 [1824], Gough Papers, 8303/105/335.
224 'Report of John Dundon to Lt. Colonel Hill Sept. 1823. Relative to the burning of Mr. Hill's haggard at Graig, etc.', no date, Gough Papers, 8303/105/501. Dundon stated the same thing on another occasion. Col. Arbuthnot to Lt. Col. Finch, 24 June 1823, SOC, 2513/79; Lord Ennismore to Gregory, 25 June 1823, SOC, 2513/83.
225 Col. Gough to Lt. Col. Finch, 21 Feb. 1823, Gough Papers, 8303/105/135.
226 E.g., James Kelly, ' "We were all to have been massacred": Irish Protestants and the experience of rebellion', in Thomas Bartlett, David Dickson, Dáire Keogh and Kevin Whelan eds., *1798: a bicentenary perspective* (Dublin: Four Courts Press, 2003), pp. 313–316.
227 Confession of Nagle, 25 Aug. 1823, Gough Papers, 8303/105/387.
228 Information of Nagle, no date, SOC, 2614/1.
229 Major Carter to Gregory, 8 Mar. 1823, SOC, 2511/43; *Cork Constitution*, 4 Apr. 1823. When pike heads were found near Rathkeale in County Limerick in July 1823, the authorities judged that they were not for an actual rising but for monetary emolument, i.e. a fabrication by a paid informer. One of the grounds for that judgement was that these pikes were different from those manufactured in Doneraile. G. Blennerhassett to Gregory, 10 July 1823, SOC, 2517/48; *Limerick Chronicle*, 12 July 1823; Major Drought to Gregory, 19 July 1823, SOC, 2517/53; Major Warburton to Gregory, 19 July 1823, SOC, 2517/54; Major Willcocks to Gregory, 19 July 1823, SOC, 2517/55.
230 Confession of Nagle, [23] Aug. 1823, SOC, 2514/55.

231 There is some information that committees existed in County Limerick as well. *Limerick Chronicle*, 16, 30 Mar., 6 Apr. 1822; *Limerick News*, 4 Apr. 1822; Col. Thornton to Lt. Col. Sorell, 14 Mar. 1822, SOC, 2351/38; same to same, 15 Mar. 1822, SOC, 2351/40; Major Willcocks to Goulburn, 3 Oct. 1822, SOC, 2354/31.
232 Major Carter to Gregory, 21 Mar. 1823, HO 100/208/91.
233 Col. Gough to Lt. Col. Finch, 5 Mar. 1823, SOC, 2511/41.
234 Major Maxwell to Gregory, 28 Feb. 1823, SOC, 2511/37.
235 'The Irish United mans Test', given by David Nagle, no date, Gough Papers, 8303/105/336. See also Confession of Nagle, [23] Aug. 1823, SOC, 2514/55.
236 In order to make a distinction from mere robbery, those cases in which other things than money were taken are excluded.
237 'Extract from the confession of David Nagle taken before Lt. Col. Hill', Jan. 1823 [1824], Gough Papers, 8303/105/335; Confession of Nagle, [23] Aug. 1823, SOC, 2514/55.
238 David Dickson, *Old world colony: Cork and south Munster 1630–1830* (Cork: Cork University Press, 2005), p. 464.
239 Information of Hurien, 22 July 1823, SOC, 2513/74. For this informant, W. H. W. Newenham to –, 25 June 1823, SOC, 2513/82; same to –, 1 July 1823, SOC, 2514/1.
240 *Cork Constitution*, 9 June 1823; *Cork Mercantile Chronicle*, 9 June 1823; Major Maxwell to Sergeant Torrens, 11 July 1823, SOC, 2514/14.
241 Confession of Nagle, [23] Aug. 1823, SOC, 2514/55; 'Extract from the confession of David Nagle taken before Lt. Col. Hill', Jan. 1823 [1824], Gough Papers, 8303/105/335.
242 Evidence of W. H. W. Newenham, Select committee. . . (200) VII. 501, pp. 184–185.
243 Evidence of Major Warburton, 20 May 1824, Select committee . . . 1825 (20) VII. 1, p. 137; Evidence of the same, 26 May 1824, Select committee . . . 1825 (200) VII. 501, p. 92; Evidence of J. Lloyd, 28 May 1824, *ibid.*, p. 118.
244 Evidence of J. Moynehan, *Cork Constitution*, 14 Apr. 1824.
245 SOC, 2512/29, 2512/33, 2614/30, 2615/47, 2616/38.
246 W. H. W. Newenham to –, 13 Apr. 1823, SOC, 2512/16; Evidence of the same, 11, 14 June 1824, Select committee . . . 1825 (200) VII. 501, pp. 182–184. This is corroborated by Newenham, who had another source of information. *Ibid.*, pp. 184–185. See also E. Newson to Goulburn, 20 Jan. 1822, SOC, 2345/19.
247 'Extract from the confession of David Nagle taken before Lt. Col. Hill', Jan. 1823[1824], Gough Papers, 8303/105/335. One of these two men was mentioned by Dundon as well. 'Report of John Dundon to Lt. Colonel Hill Sept. 1823. Relative to the burning of Mr. Hill's haggard at Graig, etc.', no date, Gough Papers, 8303/105/501.
248 Frank Ongley Darvall, *Popular disturbances and public order in regency England: being an account of the Luddite and other disorders in England during the years 1811–1817 and of the attitude and activity of the authorities* (reprint, London: William Clowes and Sons, 1969), chap. 14; Malcom I. Thomis and Peter Holt, *Threats of revolution in Britain 1789–1848* (London: Macmillan, 1977), p. 70.
249 Major Maxwell to Col. Gough, 4 Mar. 1823, Gough Papers, 8303/105/400. Folder 2.10 in Gough Papers contain memoranda from spies used by Colonel Gough.
250 'A list of the disturbers of the parish of Burnforth', no date, Gough Papers, 8303/105/522.

251 Blacker to Gregory, 12 July 1823, SOC, 2514/15.
252 Col. Gough to Lt. Col. Finch, 24 May 1824, SOC, 2615/28.
253 Major Carter to Gregory, 8 May 1824, SOC, 2615/23.
254 *Ibid.*
255 Major Carter to Gregory, 24 June 1823, SOC, 2513/80.
256 Col. Arbuthnot to Lt. Col. Finch, 23 June 1823, SOC, 2513/79; same to same, 27 June 1823, SOC, 2513/86; same to same, 30 June 1823, SOC, 2513/89; same to same, 6 July 1823, SOC, 2514/8. Dundon gave information without any offer of emoluments. Lt. Col. Finch to Gregory, 21 July 1823, SOC, 2514/24. He also wrote letters to his former comrades telling them to give up their arms. Col. Arbuthnot to Lt. Col. Finch, 23 June 1823, SOC, 2513/79. The information given by Hurien led to the arrest of sixteen men, though he may not have been one of the captains. W. H. W. Newenham to –, 25 June 1823, SOC, 2513/82; same to –, 1 July 1823, SOC, 2514/1; Col. Gough to Lt. Col. Finch, 28 June 1823, SOC, 2513/90.
257 Brigade Major Croker to Gregory, 28 June 1824, SOC, 2627/9.
258 Lord Wellesley to Peel, 28 Jan. 1824, HO 100/210/13–19.

3 Rockites' political world

Anti-Protestant mentality

Rockites used violently sectarian words. Evidence shows that such words were not aimed at obnoxious individuals in a locality who happened to be Protestants, but Protestants in general in the island. The Protestants of Munster of course did not constitute a monolithic body by any means. There were several divergences between rural and urban Protestants as well as between large landowners and small farmers, not to mention the Protestant dissenters.[1] However, in the highly sectarianised mindset of the Rockites, 'Protestants' meant everything Protestant in the island. In February 1822, the following notice appeared near Listowel in Kerry:

> **Corporation of Dublin**
> Beware – give us no more of your firebrand toasts, or, by the powers of Moll Kelly, you shall feel the effects of my wrath[.] I give you fair warning of the fate that awaits you, if you dare to disobey my orders.
>
> You shall neither be shot, hanged or beheaded, for such would be too manly a death for you. But your fate has been thus decided on in council. I will have some of *Lady Rock's* Amazons sent to stitch you up at one end; and, by the same mighty powers, you shall be crammed with turtle mad madeira at the other till you burst.
>
> . . . and now you know your doom, if you do not desist, and obey the commands of ROCK,
> Marshal Commandant.
> Given at our head quarters,
> *The Commons of Rathkeale*.[2]

The toast in question was the toast of 'the glorious and immortal memory of King William', which was proposed at dinners on official occasions as the standard toast of the corporation. The toast of itself was part of the well-established practice of post-dinner toasts. However, because the Williamite symbols in general were increasingly identified with the Orange Order, Catholics commonly regarded the toast as an anti-Catholic practice.[3]

A more openly antagonistic expression could be used. As has been seen above, Rockite oaths often included articles to avoid trading with Protestants or even to 'fight knee-deep in Orange or any other heretic's blood.' The following notice in December 1821 in County Cork is another example:

> We the honorable parliament of Ireland do offer a reward of 50 pounds to any person or persons that will kill a Protestant general, justice a peace, or a member of parliament[,] 30 pounds to any person or persons that will kill a soldier or a police and take away his arms, and 20 pounds to any person or person that will kill a Protestant, rich or poor, big or little – Signed by our Catholic General at Limerick, the 4th of December 1821[.]
> long life to him.[4]

Not only in words but in actions Rockites showed their anti-Protestant stance. During the attack on Glenasheen in County Limerick, planned and carried by Doneraile Rockites, they allegedly mentioned 'a Protestant Devil' and cried that not one should be spared.[5] Rockites even set fire to Protestant churches. In September 1823, the large church at Whitechurch near Cork City was set on fire.[6] In Counties Kerry and Limerick too, churches were burnt.[7] While setting fire to church buildings was itself an unprecedented conduct in the history of rural disturbances in Ireland,[8] the fact that the Bible and prayer books were burnt or that the communion table was carried away suggests that Protestantism as such was targeted.

This violently anti-Protestant stance was a unique phenomenon in the history of rural disturbances in Munster. Eighteenth-century Whiteboyism was never, at any stage, a confessional movement inspired or maintained by the slogans or organisation of Irish Catholicism.[9] The Rightboy disturbances in County Cork in the 1780s had Protestant gentry among their leaders, while Rightboys were not only opposed to tithe but also priests' dues which pitted them against the Catholic Church.[10] In the 1790s, when the United Irishmen spread their network of organisations in the rural areas in County Cork, their oath contained a provision that 'I do voluntarily declare that I will endeavour to promote a brotherhood of affection & union amongst Irishmen of every religious persuasion'.[11]

What brought about Rockite sectarianism was, first of all, the political and social context of the early nineteenth century. There had been, of course, liberal Protestants since the late eighteenth century who favoured removing the Catholic legal disabilities laid down in the Penal Laws, as well as Catholics who expressed their loyalty to the Hanoverian dynasty, having cast away their older Jacobite sympathies.[12] And yet, the middle ground was becoming less and less visible in the overall polarisation occurring in the early nineteenth century. On the side of the Protestants, there were those conservative Protestants, not small in number, who thought that enough had been already conceded to the Catholics and took a defensive attitude against them. As a result, most members of the established church found a new purpose in a state which was now refusing to grant full Catholic Emancipation.[13] On the Catholic side, their sense of alienation must have been strengthened by their practical exclusion from legally accessible status and posts in the Irish state. While there were 2,459 public positions in Ireland in 1823, only 106 of them were held by Catholics.[14]

Furthermore, Ireland was, independent of the Catholic question, experiencing the emergence of the sectarianism which was to affect all levels of society after 1820.[15] The early nineteenth century was an age of revival for both the Church of Ireland and Catholic Church.[16] In County Cork, while the Church of Ireland constructed about twenty new churches in the diocese of Cloyne and the same number in Cork and Ross between 1787 and 1832, in terms of organisation, discipline, material resources and lay involvement, the local Catholic Church was in better shape by 1815 than it had been at any time since the sixteenth century. Backed by such developments, a new rhetoric was deployed to defend the independence of the Catholic Church and endow it with a sense of a struggle between a state-supported church and a popular 'national' church.[17] In addition, a new element, the Evangelical movement, disturbed the existing denominational relationships.

The Evangelical movement appeared in Ireland in about 1805.[18] Evangelicals found it their duty to save the 'deluded' Irish peasantry from the Catholic Church and to awaken in their breasts the 'true' faith.[19] The chief weapon of Evangelicals was the Bible. The Hibernian Bible Society, a sister organisation of the English Society, was the largest Evangelical organisation in Ireland: it claimed that it had established 480 schools for reading the Bible and that it had distributed almost one million copies of the Bible by 1828.[20] In County Cork, the Youghal Bible Society, a minor branch, distributed 2025 Bibles and testaments between 1813 and 1821,[21] and the Cork Auxiliary Bible Society had 140 Bible institutions in the county by 1828.[22]

The Evangelicals' aggressive stance was of course countered by the Catholic side. When the Cork branch of the Hibernian Bible Society established a school near Castlemagner, the parish priest threatened the severest censure on any parents who should send their children to the school, declaring that the schools were part of a system carried on by the Protestants for 400 years, to draw Catholics to heresy, which had commenced with the hanging of many priests, and now was taking the shape of relief and charity.[23] This case was by no means an exception, with the Catholic clergy seeing the retention of elementary schooling within their sphere of influence as a vital strategic interest. At the same time, their new assertiveness and display of discipline over their flocks only enhanced Protestant distaste for the Catholic Church as an institution.[24]

That said, the rise of sectarianism was not of itself sufficient to explain Rockite thought. To massacre Protestants meant not only to eliminate another confessional group from the country, but to establish a completely new order of things since Protestants had a virtual monopoly in land and state. To pursue such a wild objective needed in itself some sort of strong instigating force. In addition, Rockites had to face two major impediments, both physical and moral: while they had to face a greater possibility of repression from the strengthened authorities than their predecessors had experienced (Chapter 4), they also faced a stronger censure from their own church. In other words, although the Rockites' anti-Protestant stance could unite men various as agricultural labourers and rich millers to act together as disturbers, 'the Catholic' were not monolithic.

Since the eighteenth century the Catholic Church had condemned the Whiteboys as disturbers of law and order.[25] After the decade of the revolution of the 1790s, the Catholic Church had even more reason to be critical of disturbers. In addition, the Irish Catholic Church in the early nineteenth century had a powerful mouthpiece in the person of Bishop Doyle, the most renowned prelate of the day, who published a pastoral address of unqualified condemnation in November 1822:

> And first, who are those who would undertake to subvert the laws and constitution of this country? Persons without money, without education, without arms, without counsel, without discipline, without a leader; kept together by a bond of iniquity, which it is a duty to violate, and a crime to observe. Men destitute of religion, and abandoned to the most frightful passions; having blasphemy in their mouths, and their hands filled with rapine, and oftentimes with blood. Can such as these regenerate a country, and make her free and happy? . . . Atone, dearly beloved . . . for the injuries you have done your neighbour, your country, and your God. Wipe away, by your peaceable demeanour for the time to come, that foul stain which your conduct has . . . already cast upon your religion![26]

While Dublin Castle had 300,000 copies of this address printed and distributed throughout the country,[27] the commander of the forces in Munster district also distributed copies, which allegedly 'produced a very powerful and happy effect on the minds of the people.'[28] It seems that such a moral reproach had as deep an impact upon the minds of Rockites as the fear of repression. The Rockite John Hickey observed to Newenham, a magistrate:

> Newenham – You perceive by what happened to your hand . . . that the visitation of God was upon you?
> Hickey – It struck me so the moment it happened. The moment it occurred, I knew this would be my fate.[29]

On the occasion of his execution, Hickey exclaimed to the public, 'Take warning by my fate, you see what I am brought to[.] Abandon the abominable system that is now in this part of the country'.[30] It is true that he uttered his admonition because he had been urged to do so by Colonel Gough, to whom Hickey felt obliged.[31] However, he wrote in a private letter addressed to his brother the day before the execution that 'I hope that my example will preserve many men from destruction which is lighting on their head and if not prevented in time will bring ruin on the country'.[32]

Nevertheless, Hickey's apparent vacillation and conversion showed, paradoxically, the force of the notion which haunted Rockites. In other words, Rockites committed themselves to a highly dangerous and 'immoral' movement, because they were driven by a powerful notion. Several accounts were sent to the authorities of the peculiar state of mind of the people in the early 1820s. Some of these have been drawn on in Chapters 1 and 2. In County Cork a warning was sent to Colonel Gough that 'I perceived a great change in the manners and dispositions of the peasantry which I considered a forerunner of something worse . . . My apprehensions and forebodings have now begun to be realized'.[33] A magistrate in County Limerick sent a report to the Dublin administration that there was a great change in the manners of the lower orders and that a woman told a lady in Limerick City, 'she would not be long in possession of her fine clothes.'[34] What brought about this 'great change in the manners and dispositions' of the people?

Pastorini's prophecy

Catholics in Ireland in the early 1820s had a conviction that something extraordinary was going to happen shortly. Croker, the folklorist cited above, who purchased about 400 popular ballads randomly in the south of Ireland in 1821, found 'a rebellious tendency' among more than a third of them. What particularly attracted his attention were the following verses:

> You, sons of poor Erin, therefore don't fail
> From Cork to Kinsale, and off to Cape Clear,
> Come excite your parties, its [*sic*] no time to bewail,
> Tho' bad alterations we've plenty this year;
> Now the year 21 is drawing in by degrees
> In the year 22 the locusts will weep;
> But in the year 23 we'll begin to reap . . .
> Good people, take courage, don't perish in fright,
> For notes will be nothing in the year 1825. . . .[35]

The 'locusts' meant Protestants. A piece of doggerel, which also foretold that some great change would happen in the early 1820s, was found in Cork:

> Eighteen hundred and twenty one
> Great tumults are begun,
> Eighteen hundred and twenty three
> Dreadful wars by land and sea,
> Eighteen hundred and twenty five
> Not a Protestant left alive . . .

The above poetry was printed and, according to a magistrate, was 'industriously and with the greatest secrecy circulated among the lower orders who plac[ed] implicit confidence in its contents.'[36]

It is fairly clear, thanks to the study by Donnelly, that the origin of these pieces of popular literature lay in a prophecy predicting the annihilation of Protestantism on earth in the year 1825, which had wide circulation in the whole of Ireland.[37] The prophecy in turn was based on Pastorini's *General History of the Christian Church*. 'Pastorini' was in fact a pen name of Charles Walmesley, an apostolic vicariate of the Roman Catholic Church in the western district of England, who tried to offer an interpretation of the Book of Revelation in the following passages of his book:

> *But it was given unto them*, the locusts, *that they should torment them five months*. . . .
>
> It is said, this torture was to last *five months*. Here the Almighty prescribes a term to that great severity, the Protestants were permitted to exercise against the true servants of God. This term is five months, or 150 days, giving 30 days to every month . . . But it is to be observed, that days in the prophetic style are sometimes used for years. . . . If then the 150 years be counted from the year 1525, about which time those violences began to take place, they will bring us to the year 1675. . . .
>
> . . . here begins a new period of *five months* or 150 years. . . . The distinction of two periods, each of 150 years, being thus stated; as the first began with the Reformation about the year 1525 and expired at 1675, the second will reach to 1825. . . . In the preceding period they were allowed *to torment mankind*, v. 5.; but in the present period it is said, *their power is to hurt mankind*. . . .
>
> V. 12. *One wo is past*. The period of 300 years assigned to the power of locusts, being expired, St. John then adds: *One wo is past*. . . .
>
> In fine, we saw in the first trumpet the Roman Emperors persecuting the Christian religion; and the first vial was poured upon them. In the second trumpet we saw the Arians rebelling against the Church; and the second vial was poured upon them. In the third trumpet we saw the Roman Empire declining on account of it's [*sic*] idolatry and enmity to Christianity; and the third vial was poured upon it, to extinguish it. In the fourth trumpet we saw the revolt of Greeks against the Church; and the fourth vial punished them. In the fifth trumpet we see the Protestants revolting against the Church; upon whom then must the fifth vial fall? . . .[38]

In the early 1820s many warnings were sent to Dublin Castle about the grip of 'Pastorini's prophecy' upon the minds of the people. According to an anonymous writer in County Limerick, a frieze-coated man said to him that 'you know, Sir, it must be so; the prophecies must be fulfilled; Pastorini was no liar', while another man said, 'I w[oul]d believe Pastorini sooner than the

Bible, the date of the Protests[tants] is out.'[39] From Limerick City another writer observed that 'this vol. is as much read, commented on, carried from house to house, as Pain's Age of Reason was a few years ago. The body of Catholics talk as freely of the description . . . as upon any common article of life. . . . I know it as a fact, that they have told some of the Protestants [that] they have no right to their lands; that they must soon leave them, [and] that the time is just at hand.'[40]

That prophecy with its grip on the minds of Catholics was ominous to Protestants, who feared that, however ill-founded the prophecy may have been, Catholics who believed in it might become increasingly violent in their actions as the alleged year of its fulfilment approached. A Protestant sent a warning to a newspaper, 'What then must be the effect, on minds so prepared, of a persuasion that an exterminating evil will take place in 1825, and that Popery will then triumph in the ruin of Protestants'.[41] This kind of warning in general can be often exaggerated. However, it is remarkable in the case of Ireland in the 1820s that not only Protestants who had good reason to be frightened but well-disposed Catholics were warning Protestants that 'we are not to be trusted'. A magistrate in Cork reported that an old servant on his death bed told his master 'to take care of himself, to keep his sons at home and not let them go about the country, for . . . the very devil has got amongst the people, and they are determined to murder and destroy every Protestant in the country'.[42] The reliability of this magistrate was confirmed by a Dublin Castle official who observed that 'I have known Barry for many years, he is a sensible man, and not easily frightened.'[43]

Most importantly, the Rockites themselves were under the influence of Pastorini's prophecy. John Dundon, a Cork Captain Rock, stated that Pastorini had made a strong impression on their minds and that they fully expected that the prophecy would be fulfilled.[44] John Hurien, a Rockite from Milford also stated that 'they faithfully believed the prophecies as related by Pastorini'.[45] It seems possible that the name Rock itself was based on the prophecy.[46] Patrick Dillane, the first Captain Rock, was 'baptised' by a school master as Captain Rock. It might have been that the master on that occasion used the *General History of the Christian Church* which contained the following phrases:

> How different is the government and proceeding of the Catholic Church! Founded on the *Rock* which is Christ, and governed by him according to his promise, she is always uniform and unanimous in her doctrine.[47]

In any event, it was because of their expectation of the intervention of supernatural force on their side that Rockites could commit themselves to such a wild idea of 'the total upset of the established order of things'. In other words, Rockites were planning to take advantage of, and to assist by a general rising, the anticipated annihilation of Protestantism. In this respect, Rockites were not self-reliant revolutionaries. What was more, the fact that Rockites believed in the prophecy meant that they had to wait until the time came. This may help to explain why they did not launch the often-mentioned general rising before their movements were suppressed. In that sense, Pastorini's prophecy, while providing the Rockites with a strong urge, also worked as a restraint on their activities.

The above restraint is a common one among social movements entertaining millenarian beliefs. If further generalisation is attempted, it is easy to identify irrationality in popular mentality, but it is also easy to see the truth in Hobsbawm's words: 'Men can live without justice, and generally must, but they cannot live without hope'.[48] What is important to those living under hardship is not the rationality of a notion but the possibility it offered of making tomorrow better than today. This is why millenarian prophecies in general can have a powerful appeal which provides a vision of better future by predicting that something supernatural will happen shortly to bring about a radical change to the present world, and to supersede it with a new and heavenly one to last a thousand years.[49]

That said, the argument for Pastorini's grasp over the minds of Irish Catholics in the early 1820s needs to be proven. In the first place, it should be confirmed that prophecies in various forms were so widespread, at least in popular literature, among Irish Catholics in the eighteenth century that such prophecies might be considered as constituting the chief element in their popular culture.[50] However, there does not seem to have been so dramatic a surge of millenarian sentiment in the eighteenth century as in the 1820s. Why could Pastorini's prophecy in particular have such a large and seemingly 'real' influence?

It may seem odd, at first glance, that Pastorini's prophecy could be influential at all. While it was a relatively new prophecy to Irish Catholics who had been long familiar with such prophecies as those ascribed to St Colum Cille, it differed from these more traditional prophecies in that it was based on the Book of Revelation.[51] The *General History of the Christian Church* was written by an English Catholic bishop living on the continent who intended to show 'that the Apocalypse could be explained with as much reason against Protestants as some Protestant or Protestants have explained it against Catholics'.[52] Accordingly, while Pastorini's book was well known, being translated into several languages,[53] it was a long and pseudo-scholarly book, not easy for common people to assimilate. It was natural that copies of it tended to be found in the libraries of Protestant gentlemen.[54]

Historians have made several points to show how Pastorini's prophecy could overcome its disadvantages and become influential. First, the early 1820s were a time of particular hardship in rural Ireland as was shown in Chapter 1.[55] Secondly, unlike other prophecies in Ireland, it had 'official' support. According to one historian, while the book, first appearing in 1771, went through ten editions in Ireland between 1790 and 1821, its publication was at one time encouraged by the British government. The government attempted to detach Irish Catholics from 'godless' France and its subversive ally the United Irishmen by adding to the text phrases describing revolutionary France as the agent of Satan which attacked the Pope. However, the book appeared in a radically different way in the context of the heightened sectarianism of the 1820s, when the passages which predicted the triumph of Catholicism were extracted from the book and reproduced in numerous pamphlets.[56]

This fact leads to the third point. Pastorini's prophecy was probably not widely read in the 1820s in the difficult *General History* but in tracts or ballads which either cited relevant passages from the book or sometimes rearranged them. These abridged versions for a popular audience were printed and circulated by publishers in Dublin, Cork and Limerick Cities.[57]

It might be added that another of Pastorini's advantages was that it had a fixed date of fulfilment. Although it may seem self-evident that the approach of the year 1825 should bring about an increase in influence of the prophecy, it should be remembered here that the other prophecies which had circulated before it were not so specific about the timing of their fulfilment.

Notwithstanding the above points, there still remains a problem about the influence of Pastorini's prophecy. *The General History* was vague enough to allow radically different interpretations. It might even be argued that this kind of vagueness is a common feature of millenarian prophecies. In short, it is difficult to attribute this or that element of Rockite political notions solely to Pastorini's prophecy. Hickey mentioned their expectation of assistance from France, while Hurien provided the following image of Rockites' encounter with the army: 'though they may be beat back twice or thrice by the army, yet when, having turned, they will meet a man in the way who comes from heaven, he having sprinkled them with holy water, they will turn round again, and the army will fly before them, though they (the Whiteboys) should fold up but straws'.[58] Neither Hickey's expectation nor Hurien's image can be found in Pastorini's work.

Many of the elements in the Rockites' political notions were derived from sources other than Pastorini; his prophecy with its surge of sentiment offered a general framework, within which Rockites developed their images of deliverance from hardship and of construction of a new and better world.[59]

Expectation of foreign assistance and the legacy of Jacobitism

While Hurien's image was probably based on a common literal motif of eighteenth-century Ireland, of a heroic liberator coming to the aid of the native population and leading them in a final battle in which the old order is restored,[60] eighteenth-century Irish literature had another important motif, that is, foreign assistance, particularly from France or Spain.[61] Whether Hickey's expectation belonged to this tradition or not is considered below. Here it deserves to be mentioned that such motifs were reflected in another prophecy, which had, next to Pastorini's, a wide influence in the early nineteenth century, that is, the prophecy ascribed to St Colum Cille, an Irish saint of the sixth century.

According to an observer in County Limerick, St Colum Cille's prophecy was believed to foretell that in a future war the children of God were to be defeated with great loss in the first two battles, but that before the third, on their march, they were to meet with a white horse, and that they were then to become victorious and to chase the locusts into the north. It was further prophesied that two brothers, McDonnells by name, were to come to the relief of Ireland with their fleets, one of whom was to land in the north, the other in the west; when all was over, the Spaniards were to settle a kind of government; Ireland was to be thenceforth to be their possession.[62]

A somewhat different version of St Colum Cille's prophecy was heard in County Cork, where it had 'a very great effect' on the minds of the people. The magistrate who arrested "Captain" David Nagle testified that:

> I was passing through one of my own fields, and heard some persons talking. I found my own mason reading to my gardener. . . . I ascertained from the gardener that it was the very same prophecy that I had a copy before. Those were the prophecies of Clumb Kill. . . . They point to a period when the Irish power is to be predominant, and the English to be annihilated. The Marquis of Abercorn is to be the great champion of the English cause, and General O'Donnell is to appear on the Irish side.[63]

This O'Donnell seems to have been Marquess O'Donnell, an Irish-born officer serving in the Spanish army who came to the relief of the Catholics a few days after the Battle of the Boyne. Thus, the motifs of a heroic liberator and foreign assistance reflected in Hurien's image or the prophecy of St Colum Cille were closely mixed together with Jacobite expectations.

Geographical closeness to the continent and historical incidents made Munster, particularly County Cork, familiar to Jacobitism. In 1689 a French fleet had come to Bantry Bay, where they fought an engagement with an English fleet. The battle took place immediately after the landing of James II, backed by Louis XIV's France, in Kinsale. After the final surrender of the Jacobites in 1691, Jacobitism did not become a completely dead notion, and the French and the Spanish connections were maintained in the form of recruitment of Irish Catholic soldiers from the south of Ireland into the French and Spanish armies, the peak of which was in the 1720s and 1730s.[64] Attacking Ireland remained a military option in French strategy until Napoleonic times.[65] Accordingly, expectations of deliverance by a French or Spanish army were often expressed in the form of ballads or prophecy in Munster in the eighteenth century.[66] At least fifty poets were associated with Muskerry barony in the period, a substantial part of whose literary output had references to the Jacobite court in exile and to their royal patrons in France and Spain.[67]

Jacobite rhetoric could be found not only in prophecies or ballads but in Rockite notices, as in January 1822 in a notice in Fermoy barony:

> I John Rock but my Christian name is James Stewart son of Charles Stewart [while] he was son of James Stewart king of England, Ireland & Scotland[,] do inform you that any person that will not take arms will looze what they have in this nation and their lives two [*sic*][.] I am aided by the king[s] of France Spain and the rest of [the] Catholic powers of Europe[.] . . . there is thirty thousand men coming from Spain, and France will maintain war with England[.] There is but 5000 arm[ed] hereticks in this nation . . .[68]

A rumour that a Spanish army would land in Ireland in late August corresponding to that notice was spreading in the summer of that year in County Cork.[69]

That said, it would be simplistic to conclude that the Cork Rockites were descendants of Jacobites. Jacobite rhetoric was actually rather unusual in the whole body of known Rockite discourse. Even in the eighteenth century, it is quite possible that the Jacobite discourse abundant in Munster was no more than a literary style without the backing of reality.[70] While nothing happened in Ireland either in 1715 or 1745, Rome conceded, on the occasion of the death of 'James III & VII' in 1766, that the house of Hanover was the rightful dynasty of Great Britain and Ireland. When 'Charles III' died in 1778, a large number of propertied Catholics in and around Cork took the oath of allegiance to the house of Hanover.[71] In short, Jacobite rhetoric in the early nineteenth century seems to have signified no more than an outdated style in which hopes for the remedy of social and political discontents could be expressed.

What about Hickey's expectation of French assistance? There is evidence to show that when he mentioned French assistance, it had a more direct source of inspiration than the traditional Jacobite discourse. Ireland in the 1820s, particularly County Cork, had a living memory of the coming of the French fleet in late 1796, with 13,000 soldiers to assist the revolutionary movement of the United Irishmen.[72] Bad weather prevented the troops from landing and the fleet eventually had to return to France. However, the inhabitants in County Cork went to look at the site in large numbers and the incident was vividly told in the county well into the twentieth century.[73] To contemporaries, it may have been the near fulfilment of the Jacobite hope and prophecies, but to the next generation living in the 1820s the moment was the beginning of another legend of Irish history.

Other Rockite references to French assistance were made in a more positive way than Hickey's somewhat casual mention. The oath found in Listowel in Kerry in November 1821 included a provision, 'I do further swear to help the French and my brothers in case of invasion.'[74] Another oath used near Tralee also had a phrase 'join the French'.[75] In addition, the Rockite image of a 'general rising' planned and to be launched by a network of underground organisations was not a legacy of Jacobitism but that of the revolutionary movement of the late 1790s. In fact, Rockites frequently styled themselves as descendants of the rebels of the 1790s, which, together with their millenarian belief and anti-Protestant stance, constituted the most important element in their political notions. If Rockites were not Jacobites in any meaningful way, they were Jacobin, at least in some of their discourse and image. The next thing, therefore, to consider is how they revived the discourse and image of the 1790s, which as a revolutionary decade created a major dividing point in the modern history of Ireland.

'John Rock, Commander in Chief of the United Irishmen'

Rockites revived the discourse and impression of the 1790s in various ways. In February 1822, a short time after the January engagements, the following proclamation appeared at Adare in County Limerick:

> General Rock, Commanding-in-Chief the army of Ireland, being desirous of organising, with as little delay as possible, an administrative power for the province of the County of Cork, directs as follows: – 1st. That every individual from the age of 16 to 40 inclusive, is required in the name of the Irish Republick, instantly to repair to the rebel camp, in order to march in mass against the common enemy, the tyrant of Ireland – the English, whose destruction alone can insure the independence and the welfare of the antient Hibernia.
>
> The General Commanding-[in]-Chief the army of Ireland,
> John Rock, K. C. B.
>
> All to march to M'Croom or Mallow with speed, the fate of the Palatines will be the fate of all who say [a tome] these bad times.[76]

This was a parody of the proclamation issued by the French general at the landing of his troops in County Mayo in 1798.[77]

French assistance was mentioned in other ways, possibly more seriously. It was rumoured in County Kerry that Captain Rock would return from France in May 1822,[78] while several notices were posted in County Limerick in February 1822 requiring people to be ready to meet Captain Rock on his return in May.[79] In County Cork a rebel 'captain' who had fled from Duhallow told an informer: 'Captain Rock, who is son to one O'Connor who went to France from this country formerly . . . promised to return precisely the 16th ultimo [May 1822]'.[80] An uprising in May 1822, in concert with the coming of French assistance, was mentioned in other instances in County Cork.[81] This 'O'Connor' was Arthur O'Connor, a major United Irish leader who was resident in France in the 1820s. Already in late 1821 a rumour was spread around Mallow that O'Connor was back in Ireland to promote disturbances.[82]

It was the Rockites around Mallow who were the most expressive in rhetoric reminiscent of the 1790s. They referred to themselves as the United Irishmen. Several notices with the signature 'John Rock, Commander in Chief of the United Irishmen' appeared in Doneraile and other places, one of which declared 'a gallow filled with radicals or a ship laden with White Boys cannot intimidate the heart of a true United Irishman, inflamed by the spirit of liberty'.[83] While the title of the oath of Mallow committee was 'The Royal United Irishman's Test', the oath found with David Nagle, a copy of which was given by another informer, contained the phrase 'when I was put up to this United Irishmans Oath'.[84] In addition, Hickey's catechism contained the following phrases:

> 4 What is that in your hand [?]
> a. It is an olive branch with 3 different colours
> 5 —— Where did it grow [?] ——
> [a.] It grew in America, blossomed in France & took root in Ireland,
> 6 —— Who comes there [?] ——
> a. A French governor . . .[85]

Considering the fact that no evidence suggests that the United Irish organisation survived in County Cork into the 1820s, how these various idioms and images reminiscent of the 1790s were transmitted to or revived in the 1820s needs some analysis. Three factors seem to have been at work. The first was the politicisation of the 1790s. Although County Cork (or Munster) was largely quiet in 1798, the United Irishmen had developed their organisations,[86] as a result of which the numbers who were sworn in as United Irishmen in the county in 1797–98 were 'extremely large'.[87] It may be remembered that such United Irish leaders of national fame as Thomas Addis Emmet, Arthur and Roger O'Connor, and Thomas Russell were all Cork men. It is probable that this politicisation did not end as a temporary phenomenon but left a legacy to succeeding generations, in consequence of which idioms reminiscent of the 1790s were familiar to those who did not experience the revolutionary movement of the 1790s themselves.

It needs to be mentioned here, however, that politicisation did not necessarily mean the full acceptance of the republican ideology or the nationalism of the United Irishmen itself. Rather, it was the fear of Orangemen which was the most powerful weapon for popular political mobilisation in Munster in the 1790s.[88] Hence, it is not very likely that Catholic people were driven by a desire to establish the non-sectarian, middle-class dominated republic conceived by the United Irishmen.[89] In any event, such sectarian (non-nationalistic) politicisation, alongside the past experience of French assistance, made the early nineteenth-century Catholics of the south susceptible to the ideology of the Ribbonmen, descendants of the Defenders who had envisaged a French-assisted Catholic rising against the Protestant establishment, as was seen in Chapter 2.[90] That was the second factor in the revival of idioms and conceptions of the 1790s. Hickey's catechism above was reportedly conveyed from Newcastle and Dublin by Ribbonmen.

Hence, another point to distinguish the Rockites from the United Irishmen was that the Rockites were not markedly nationalistic. They do not seem to have been concerned with such questions as dependence of Ireland or the predominance of English culture in Ireland. Rockites (and Ribbonmen) could even show sympathy for England and its people. They expected that on the occasion of an actual general rising in Ireland, assistance would come from England or a co-ordinated popular rising would be launched there.[91] Queen Caroline enjoyed a great popularity among Rockites and Ribbonmen.[92] The primary enemy of the Rockites was the Protestant establishment in the country, which Hickey's following reaction seems to have substantiated:

> Newenham —— If ever all persons now having property were swept away, you don't think England would allow you to hold the land?
> To this he was silent, but appeared as if he had not considered that part of the business.[93]

In any event, there remains another factor to be taken into consideration, and that is the uneven distribution of the idioms of the 1790s. The main activities of the United Irishmen in County Cork had been in the south of the county, with the sole significant rebel engagement with the military in the county fought in the north of Clonakilty in 1798.[94] Also, Ribbonmen had spread their network to various places in Munster. Nevertheless, it was in the region under the Mallow committee leadership where the usage of the idiom of the 1790s was the most conspicuous in the 1820s. Here attention should be paid to the peculiarities of Mallow and its surroundings, where the political divide created in the 1790s continued into the 1820s. This is the third factor in the revival of idioms and conceptions of the 1790s.

The divide was created by the conflict and skirmishes between the United Irishmen and the local authorities of Mallow. By the middle of 1797 a United Irish organisation was formed in Mallow,[95] against which the local authorities embodied two yeomanry corps.[96] The yeomanry, as a tool of the local authorities, could resort to severe measures of repression, against which the rebels made counterblows. For instance, the house of Sir James L. Cotter, captain of the Mallow Boyne Cavalry, one of the two Mallow yeomanry corps, was plundered of sixty arms by the rebels in early (March or April) 1798. It is possible that these arms were stored there for his yeomanry corps. While several other houses were also robbed of arms in the neighbourhood of Mallow, another yeomanry corps successfully retook most of the arms, killing one of the rebels and arresting three.[97] Soon afterwards the authorities in Cork began a counter-insurgency campaign of searching houses for arms, free-quartering and selective burning of houses.[98] This counter-insurgency operation was conducted chiefly in the south of the county, but the house of the main branch of the Catholic Nagle family was looted by yeomanry in May of the same year and the master of the family was arrested as a suspected rebel.[99]

Even after the commotion of 1798 had passed, the situation was far from tranquil. County Cork saw rural disturbances in the winter of 1798–99, whose scale of violence far surpassed that of the traditional Whiteboyism.[100] The situation around Mallow was particularly combustible. In May 1799 United Irishmen planned a raid on the town of Mallow, where the Royal Meath Militia was stationed. The plan was disclosed and failed, but in the following skirmish several lives were lost, and thereafter eight men were sentenced to death in the court martial held to deal with the conspiracy.[101] Because several soldiers of the Meath Militia were involved in the conspiracy, the commanding general had to remove the regiment of Meath Militia to Cork City.[102]

The conflict between the local authorities and actual and potential rebels continued well into the nineteenth century in local parliamentary politics. The effect of the Anglo-Irish Union of 1801 on the general political map of County Cork had made Mallow a special place in the north of the county. County Cork before the Union sent twenty-six MPs (including the two for the county) to parliament, which the Union drastically reduced to eight. In particular, the south of the county, Cork's politically most dynamic area since the days of the Volunteer movement and the United Irish movement,[103] experienced a heavy loss of seats, while in the north Mallow remained as the sole parliamentary borough. It is argued that while the interest of family and its influence seems to have been paramount in high and electoral politics in early nineteenth-century Cork in general,[104] there was a real disjuncture between the parliamentary game and the evolution of 'popular politics'.[105] However, Mallow seems to have been an exception to this general pattern. Elections in Mallow were accompanied by issues of national as well as local dimensions, with popular mobilisation of some scale.

The most influential family in Mallow was the Jephsons.[106] Denham Jephson, who was the former Captain of the other of the two yeomanry corps of Mallow,[107] served as a MP for Mallow between 1802 and 1812 and took an anti-Catholic stance in parliament.[108] He was succeeded by Cotter whose house had been attacked in 1798 and who also took a clear stance against removal of Catholic disabilities.[109] The 1818 parliamentary election was a turning point in the local politics of Mallow. During that campaign Cotter had to resign from the electoral contest when Cotter realised that William Wrixon Becher, his opponent, representing the Catholic interest had a bigger chance of winning the election.[110] The next election of 1820 turned out to be of still greater significance. Cotter retired from politics and was succeeded by Charles Denham Orlando Jephson, another of the Jephsons.[111] Although he expressed his sympathy towards Catholic Emancipation, it was for the purpose of regaining Mallow from the Catholic electors,[112] and his being backed by Henry Croker and John Longfield, both yeomanry officers and Tories,[113] meant he did not diverge from the Cotter line. Mallow had no corporation, with the result that the Jephsons and the Crokers, its proprietors, had direct influence on town politics.[114] However, Wrixon Becher had a powerful ally in the person of Daniel O'Connell who acted as his election agent,[115] and that must have enhanced the 'Catholic' and popular nature of Wrixon Becher's side. Wrixon Becher was again returned in 1820.[116] While the borough had about 500 voters, it is remarkable that four forty-shilling freeholders of the manor, in fact 'poor labourers', voted, against Jephson's direction and 'according to their conscience', for Wrixon Becher.[117]

The loyalist pressure on Catholic freeholders was expounded by O'Brien, the Catholic priest of Doneraile, who testified that 'I have myself witnessed the tears of those poor creatures, going to the county town to give their vote against what they called their consciences; meaning by that, that they were going to vote for persons who were hostile to Catholic emancipation, but who were [standing] in the interests of their landlords.'[118] The four men who did not betray their conscience at the Mallow election of 1820 were chaired together with Wrixon Becher in triumph after the poll. In the front of the procession were two flags, borne by two of those 'brave fellows'. A band, composed of the young men of the town, played 'Patrick's Day' and other popular national tunes. They were followed by Wrixon Becher's electors, two and two, with laurel branches in their hats, and white wands in their hands surmounted with green wreaths. The rear of the procession was brought up by 'a vast multitude'. When they arrived in the mainstreet, the doors and windows were literally 'choaked with spectators'.[119]

The 1820 election did not bring to an end the conflict between the two forces in the local politics of Mallow. The anti-Catholic side could demonstrate their force in another way by using their traditional instrument, the yeomanry. When a fair was held at Mallow in July 1821, a faction fighting was intended with allegedly five hundred people assembling on both sides. The fighting started in the evening, and was repeated the next day. Although faction fighting in general was essentially a kind of non-political 'recreation', the yeomanry was called out. While the nominal ground of the call was to preserve law and order, it seems that the occasion was used by the anti-Catholic side for the purpose of displaying their strength, as the yeomanry paraded in streets with arms in their hands. Soon afterwards, the gentlemen of Mallow held a meeting where they agreed that they should express their thanks to Jephson and Cotter. Although twenty-two men signed the agreement, Wrixon Becher, the MP, did not put his name to it.[120]

Thus, it seems natural that when the formidably anti-Protestant Rockites appeared in the region, the local authorities at Mallow found the yeomanry the most reliable force to defend themselves. When Dublin Castle responded to their appeal by placing the Mallow Boyne Cavalry on permanent duty,[121] it meant to Catholics as well as Rockites in the region the revival of the situation of the 1790s, more clearly so than in other regions because the division created around Mallow in the 1790s not only continued but remained strong into the 1820s. Hence, it seems also natural that Rockites in turn reacted by beginning to style themselves the United Irishmen, who had been the biggest challenge to the authorities in the 1790s.

This process of interaction between the disturbers and the authorities in the Mallow region was accurately summarised by Chief Secretary Goulburn, when he observed that 'Every body [almost] tells me that we are again to have the scenes of 1798 and that the proceedings in the Co. Cork correspond in every particular with what then occurred'.[122]

The Rockites and the Catholic question

One further thing remains to be considered in the discussion of the Rockites' political ideas, and that is their interest in the Catholic question. Already before the establishment of the Catholic Association in 1823 and its mass movement which began in 1824, popular mobilisation had been successfully launched by O'Connell in 1821. In the early months of that year, a Catholic relief bill introduced by William C. Plunket was passed in the Commons, which marked the first passage of a relief measure in the Commons since the Union. It was, however, defeated in the Lords. What made Plunket's bill a grave political issue of the day was its clause on 'securities', a royal veto over Catholic Episcopal appointments. Catholics as well as liberal Protestants were divided between vetoists and anti-vetoists, the latter of whom welcomed the ultimate failure of the bill.[123]

The veto question, emerging as a new political issue to Catholics in Ireland in 1808, deserves attention. By the European standard of the day, Irish Catholics may have been regarded as overreacting. State interferences in church matters were not uncommon, and the Papacy itself accepted the royal veto in principle.[124] In addition, while there was no established routine in the appointment of Irish Catholic bishops,[125] it often happened that the Catholic Church voluntarily refrained from nominating those clergymen who were considered to be unfavourable to the British crown.[126] It is this, paradoxically, that makes noteworthy the concern which Catholics showed over the veto question, since the veto episode indicates how the majority of politically-aware Catholics withheld from the state a last but crucial degree of legitimacy.[127]

It was O'Connell who was in the van of the anti-vetoists. He published the following letter in several of the Dublin newspapers, 'I have long known that Mr. Plunkett was a man of great and powerful ingenuity; but I did not think he had acuteness enough to frame so complete a snare for the Catholic religion. . . . If this bill passes, the Catholic religion could not survive it fifty years in Ireland.'[128] The division between vetoists and anti-vetoists and the accompanying agitation was intense in Munster.[129] During consideration of Plunket's bill in parliament, anti-vetoists held meetings in several places in Munster.[130] The meetings were reportedly dominated by the lower orders led by O'Connell.[131] At the meeting in Cork City, thanks were given to O'Connell instead of Plunket, while the following resolution was passed that 'we do for ourselves and our children protest against that bill passing into a law, as it would be more oppressive, penal, and afflictive to conscience and religion, than any statute of force in Ireland, during the blackest days of persecution and bigotry.'[132] About this meeting, the vetoist *Southern Reporter* observed:

> We learn from all quarters . . . that the meeting was one of the most uproarious that was ever held, and that one or two gentlemen who sought to deliver their opinions were assailed with such deafening cries as were never before sent forth . . . when it was moved to thank Mr. Plunkett, Sir John Newport, Sir Henry Parnell, and the other friends of Catholic freedom, an amendment was proposed – that there should be a *round of groans* given for these personages, which was carried with a burst of sound which shook the altar and the edifice.[133]

Needless to say, the Rockite disturbances were in many respects dimensionally different from the O'Connellite movement, the main weapon of which was the mobilisation of 'public opinion' by public meetings and print media. However, the agitation over the veto question appears to have had repercussions on the political thinking of the Rockites. As John Hickey observed, the Mallow committee Rockites had the Catholic emancipation as one of their objectives.[134] A Rockite catechism found in Shanagolden in County Limerick in the autumn of 1821 contained the following phrases:

> . . . veto . . . Plunket as their agent . . . Plunket[']s [rumination] and hellish observation and dismal consternation to the nation . . . we renounce his insinnuation . . . by consecration we ill [*sic*] plant an imansipation . . . what did he sea [*sic*] that the Romans would obtain the rights . . .[135]

It might be added that the Rockites' interest in the Catholic question went hand in hand with their adoration of O'Connell. O'Connell himself did not live outside the world of the Rockites or the Whiteboys. He even defended Rockite prisoners at court as a counsel.[136] For instance, he defended first Rockites in County Limerick who were tried for having 'visiting' the agent Hoskins's house near Newcastle.[137] O'Connell seems to have felt sympathies towards disturbers in general. He wrote in 1830:

> What a contrast between the Irish and English insurgents. The latter demand money and take provisions by force. The Whiteboys despised the money and, even where it was offered, have repeatedly refued it.[138]

O'Connell had established himself as 'The Counsellor' in the assizes of the Munster circuit well before the 1820s.[139] In 1818, a magistrate who had put three men into prison for illegal possession of a house reported from north

Cork that 'O'Connell now boasts that he will be their liberator at the next assizes'.[140] In fact, O'Connell was more than 'The Counsellor'. The Rockite catechism above placed O'Connell in line with other prophets:

> . . . the times being once complated as St John had revealed it[,] Columkill relates the same at a par[,] MCouliffe like an angel who rote [*sic*] by inspiration and O Connell the wise sage who oout [*sic*] equel them all in propisizeing . . .[141]

'MCouliffe' was Malachy MacAuliffe, a seventeenth-century Gaelic lord in Duhallow, who was believed to have left a verse prophecy on the future of the country.[142] While no other historical personality in Ireland would be the object of so rich a variety of folklore as O'Connell, a number of supernatural traits would be attributed to him.[143] This exultation meant that to the Catholic lower orders in general of pre-Famine Ireland the early nineteenth century was an age of Liberator O'Connell and 'Captain'.

The suppression of the Rockites coincided with the beginning of the mass agitation led by O'Connell and his Catholic Association, which swept Munster and Leinster in the latter half of the 1820s. It should be noted that County Cork was the biggest contributor, ahead of County Dublin, of the Catholic Rent, donation for Catholic Association.[144] However, there is evidence to suggest that some of the former Rockites in Cork were invigorated by the O'Connellite agitation. The police reported that former Rockites had come to regard their previous outbreaks as premature but preparatory to the general organisation developed by the Catholic Association.[145] It was also reported from Cork that many of the lower orders imagined that by paying the Catholic Rent they would certainly have Emancipation. In turn Emancipation would mean that they would be 'independent' and that the land of the country would be 'equally divided' among them.[146] Even at the height of the O'Connellite agitation, the world of the Rockites had not disappeared completely.

While some elements of the political thinking of the Rockites were thus closely interconnected with the local and national politics of early nineteenth-century Ireland, it can be recalled that the Catholic question, in particular, was not only an Irish question but also an issue in the early nineteenth-century politics of the United Kingdom. The next chapter tries to contextualise the Rockites in the overall political and governmental structures of early nineteenth-century Ireland and of the United Kingdom.

Acknowledgments

Parts of this chapter were originally published in "The Rockite movement in County Cork in the early 1820s," *Irish Historical Studies*, vol. xxxiii, no. 131, May 2003, pp. 278–296.

Notes

1 For County Cork, see Ian d'Alton, *Protestant society and politics in Cork 1812–1844* (Cork: Cork University Press, 1980), chap 1.
2 *Kerry Evening Post*, 13 Feb. 1822. This day's *Kerry Evening Post* is enclosed in NAI, SOC, 2348/53.
3 Shunsuke Katsuta, 'Conciliation, anti-Orange politics and the sectarian scare: Dublin politics of the early 1820s', *Dublin Historical Record*, vol. lxiv, no. 2, 2011, pp. 145–146.
4 W. C. Collins to H. Goulburn, 10 Dec. 1821, NAI, CSORP, box 631.
5 C. D. Oliver to W. Gregory, 1 May 1823, SOC, 2517/26; *Limerick Chronicle*, 3 May 1823.
6 J. McCarthy to Goulburn, 18 Sept. 1823, SOC, 2515/21; *Cork Constitution*, 19, 24 Sept. 1823; Rev. J. Hingston to Goulburn, 24 Sept. 1823, SOC, 2515/30.
7 For the case of Knockanae parish in Kerry, see S. Gallwey to Brigadier Major Mahony, 24 Nov. 1821, CSORP, box 635; J. Godfrey to C. Grant, 26 Nov. 1821, CSORP, box 633; *Cork Morning Intelligencer*, 29 Nov. 1821; E. Conyers to Grant, 1 Dec. 1821, CSORP, box 631; E. Fitzconyers to Goulburn, 4 Jan. 1822, SOC, 2348/12. For the case of Templenoe in Kerry, see Captain Mahony to Brigade Major Mahony, 6 Jan. 1822, SOC, 2348/3; *Cork Morning Intelligencer*, 12 Jan. 1822. For the case of Kileedy in Limerick, see *Limerick Chronicle*, 9, 13 Feb. 1822; Major Willcocks to Gregory, 10 Feb. 1822, SOC, 2350/54; – to E. Gerahty, 11 Feb. 1822, SOC, 2350/60; Memorial of Gerahty, 1 June 1822, CSORP, 1822/657; Information of P. Mulcahy, 6 Aug. 1823, SOC, 2517/64. The Incident was followed by the burning of the parish church of Caherconlish. Col. Thornton to Lt. Col. Sorell, 20 Feb. 1822, SOC, 2350/77; Rev. Madder to —, 21 Feb. 1822, SOC, 2350/73; *Limerick Chronicle*, 23 Feb. 1822; T. F. Maunsell to —, 28 Feb. 1822, SOC, 2350/94. A few days later the church at Athlacca in Limerick was further burnt, when about fifty men were firing shots and cheering as the fire blazed higher. C. O'Grady to —, 26 Feb. 1822, SOC, 2350/93; *Limerick Chronicle*, 27 Feb., 2 Mar. 1822.
8 James S. Donnelly Jr, *Captain Rock: the Irish agrarian rebellion of 1821–24* (Cork: The Collins Press, 2009), p. 136.
9 Maurice J. Bric, 'The Whiteboy movement in Tipperary, 1760–80', in William Nolan in association with Thomas G. McGrath eds., *Tipperary: history and society: interdisciplinary essays on the history of an Irish county* (Dublin: Geography Publications, 1985), p. 168.
10 James S. Donnelly Jr, 'The Rightboy movement 1785–8', *Studia Hibernica*, nos. 17/18, 1977–78, pp. 163–175; Maurice J. Bric, 'Priests, parsons and politics: the Rightboy protest in County Cork, 1785–1788', C. H. E. Philpin ed., *Nationalism and popular protest in Ireland* (Cambridge: Cambridge University Press, 1987), pp. 164–168, 172–174.
11 Lord Longueville to –, 11 Apr. 1797, NAI, Rebellion Papers, 620/29/222; Lord Bantry to –, 12 Apr. 1797, *ibid.*, 620/29/230.
12 James Kelly, 'The genesis of "Protestant Ascendancy": the Rightboy disturbances of the 1780s and their impact upon Protestant opinion', in Gerard O'Brien ed., *Parliament, politics and people: essays in eighteenth-century Irish history* (Dublin: Irish Academic Press, 1989), pp. 97–98.
13 David Dickson, *Old world colony: Cork and south Munster 1630–1830* (Cork: Cork University Press, 2005), pp. 476–477.
14 Speech of J. Hume, 25 June 1823, *Hansard's parliamentary debates*, second series, vol. 9, c. 1214–1215.
15 S. J. Connolly, 'Mass politics and sectarian conflict, 1823–30', in W. E. Vaughan ed., *A new history of Ireland V: Ireland under the Union, I 1801–70* (Oxford: Clarendon Press, 1989), p. 74.

16 Donald Harman Akenson, *The Church of Ireland: ecclesiastical reform and revolution, 1800–1885* (New Haven and London: Yale University Press, 1971), chap. 2; Desmond J. Keenan, *The Catholic church in nineteenth-century Ireland: a sociological study* (Dublin: Gill & Macmillan, 1983), pp. 114–118; Emmet Larkin, *The pastoral role of the Roman Catholic church in pre-Famine Ireland 1750–1850* (Dublin: Four Courts Press; Washington D. C.: The Catholic University of America Press, 2006), pp. 5–6; Nigel Yates, *The religious condition of Ireland 1770–1850* (Oxford: Oxford University Press, 2006), pp. 134–137, 146–152.

17 Dickson, *Old world colony*, p. 480.

18 Irene Whelan, *The Bible war in Ireland: the 'Second Reformation' and the polarisation of Protestant-Catholic relations, 1800–1840* (Madison, Wis.: University of Wisconsin Press, 2005), p. 62.

19 Desmond Bowen, *The Protestant crusade in Ireland, 1800–70: a study of Protestant-Catholic relations between the Act of Union and disestablishment* (Dublin: Gill & Macmillan; Montreal: McGill-Queen's University Press, 1978), pp. xii, 83; David Hempton and Myrtle Hill, *Evangelical Protestantism in Ulster society 1740–1890* (London: Routledge, 1992), pp. 81–82; Whelan, *The Bible war in Ireland*, pp. 140–141.

20 Stewart J. Brown, 'The new reformation movement in the Church of Ireland, 1801–1829', in *idem* and David W. Miller eds., *Piety and power in Ireland 1760–1960: essays in honour of Emmet Larkin* (Queen's University of Belfast: Institute of Irish Studies, Notre Dame, Indiana: University of Notre Dame Press, 2000), p. 189; Desmond Keenan, *Pre-Famine Ireland: social structure* (United States of America: Xlibris, 2000), p. 345; Whelan, *The Bible war in Ireland*, p. 68.

21 Minute Book of the Youghal Auxiliary Bible Society, 1813–25, NAI, MFA 12 (1). Cf. Note 51 of this chapter.

22 Minute Book of the Cork Auxiliary Bible Society, 1827–57, MFA12 (2).

23 J. R. Cotter to Goulburn, 12 Dec. 1822, CSORP, 1822/2480.

24 Dickson, *Old world colony*, p. 484.

25 Donnelly, 'The Rightboy movement 1785–8', pp. 167–170; Donal A Kerr, 'Priests, pikes and patriots: the Irish Catholic church and political violence from the Whiteboys to the Fenians', in Brown and Miller eds., *Piety and power in Ireland*, p. 18.

26 Evidence of the Archbishop of Dublin, 17 May 1825, BPP, Select committee to inquire into state of Ireland with reference to disturbances, minutes of evidence, 1825 (129) VIII. 1, pp. 667–672.

27 Maurice Colgan, 'Prophecy against reason: Ireland and the apocalypse', *British Journal for Eighteenth-Century Studies*, vol. viii, 1985, p. 214.

28 Evidence of the Archbishop of Dublin, 17 May 1825, Select committee . . . 1825 (129) VIII.1, p. 665; Evidence of Bishop Doyle, 16, 18 Mar. 1825, *ibid.*, p. 197.

29 W. H. W. Newenham to –, 13 Apr. 1823, SOC, 2512/16; Evidence of the same, 11, 14 June 1824, BPP, Select committee of House of Lords on nature and extent of disturbances in Ireland, minutes of evidence, 1825 (200) VII. 501, pp. 182–184. Hickey had lost his hand at the 'visit' at Norcott's house.

30 Hickey's address, 17 Apr. 1823, SOC, 2512/25.

31 Col. Gough to Lt. Col. Finch, 17 Apr. 1823, National Army Museum, Gough Papers, 8303/105/111.

32 Hickey's address, 17 Apr. 1823, SOC, 2512/25.

33 T. Wallis to Col. Gough, no date, Gough Papers, 8303/105/172.

34 [E.] Carte to –, 1 Nov. 1821, CSORP, box 631.

35 T. Crofton Croker, *Researches in the south of Ireland, illustrative of the scenery, architectural remains, and the manners and superstitions of the peasantry: with an appendix, containing a private narrative of the rebellion of 1798* (London: John Murray, 1824), pp. 329–330.

36 A. Batwell to Goulburn, 10 Feb. 1822, SOC, box 170. Colonel Gough also regarded it as influential. Col. Gough to Lt. Col. Finch, 11 Feb. 1823, SOC, 2511/27.
37 Donnelly, *Captain Rock: the Irish agrarian rebellion of 1821–24*, chap. 4, esp. pp. 122–123.
38 Sig. Pastorini, *The general history of the Christian church, from her birth to her final triumphant state in heaven: chiefly deduced from the apocalypse of St. John the apostle and evangelist, second edition, with a few additional remarks and elucidations, by the author* (London: J. P. Coghlan, 1798), pp. 207–209, 237–239, 252, 257–258. Italics are original.
39 'Indigator' to Goulburn, 29 Jan. 1822, SOC, 2350/30.
40 'Coltatius' to Gregory, 19 Dec. 1821, CSORP, box 630.
41 *The Irish Protestant, and faithful examiner*, vol. 1, no. 14, 16 Dec. 1822, p. 108; *Dublin Evening Mail*, 11, 13 and 16 June 1823.
42 Major General Barry to Col. Arbuthnot, 12 Apr. 1823, SOC, 2512/24.
43 Gregory to Goulburn, 16 Apr. 1823, Surrey History Centre, Goulburn Papers, 304/A1/15/06.
44 Col. Arbuthnot to Lt. Col. Finch, 24 June 1823, SOC, 2513/79.
45 Evidence of W. H. W. Newenham, 11, 14 June 1824, Select committee . . . 1825 (200) VII. 501, pp. 198–199.
46 'Coltatius' to Gregory, 19 Dec. 1821, CSORP, box 630; J. Ambrose to Gregory, 6 Mar. 1822, SOC, 2375/8.
47 Pastorini, *The general history of the Christian church, from her birth to her final triumphant state in heaven*, p. 249. Italics are original.
48 Eric Hobsbawm, *Bandits* (London: Abacus, 2001), p. 57.
49 J. F. C. Harrison, *The second coming: popular millenarianism 1780–1850* (London and Henley: Routledge & Kegan Paul, 1979), chap. 1, esp. pp. 7–8.
50 James Warner O'Neill, 'Popular culture and peasant rebellion in pre-famine Ireland', Ph. D. thesis, University of Minnesota, 1984, p. 187; Brendán Ó Buachalla, 'From Jacobite to Jacobin', in Thomas Bartlett, David Dickson, Dáire Keogh and Kevin Whelan eds., *1798: a bicentenary perspective* (Dublin: Four Courts Press, 2003), p. 79.
51 Donnelly and Ó Ciosáin argue that because of the distribution of the Bible by evangelical societies lower-class Catholics in Munster may have acquired sufficient knowledge of the biblical texts to accept Pastorini's *General history*. Niall Ó Ciosáin, *Print and popular culture in Ireland, 1750–1850* (Basingstoke and New York: Palgrave, 1997), pp. 193–194; Donnelly, *Captain Rock: the Irish agrarian rebellion of 1821–24*, p. 131. However, an impression to be obtained from testimonies at parliamentary committees and commissions is that in the 1820s the Bible was not fully familiar to the bulk of Catholics. E.g. Evidence of the Archbishop of Dublin, 29 Apr. 1825, BPP, Select committee of House of Lords to inquire into state of Ireland with reference to disturbances, Minutes of evidence, 1825 (521) IX. 249, p. 386. His evidence is corroborated by another witness, who was a Catholic. Evidence of M. Donelan, 8 Dec. 1824, BPP, Royal commission on Irish education, first report, appendix 1825 (400) XII. 1, pp. 487, 489.
52 Evidence of M. B. Dunphy, 12 Jan. 1825, BPP, Royal commission on Irish education, first report, appendix 1825 (400) XII. 1, p. 757.
53 Geoffrey Scott, '"The times are fast approaching": Bishop Charles Walmesley OSB (1722–1797) as prophet', *Journal of Ecclesiastical History*, vol. xxxvi, no. 4, 1985, pp. 597–598.
54 Donnelly, *Captain Rock: the Irish agrarian rebellion of 1821–24*, p. 123.
55 See also *ibid.*, pp. 134–135.
56 Colgan, 'Prophecy against reason', p. 216, note 7; Scott, '"The times are fast approaching"', pp. 602–603.

57 Evidence of F. Blackburne, 14 May 1824, BPP, Select committee to inquire into disturbances in Ireland, minutes of evidence, 1825 (20) VII. 1, p. 23; Evidence of Major Warbuton, 20 May 1825, *ibid.*, p. 144; Donnelly, *Captain Rock: the Irish agrarian rebellion of 1821–24*, pp. 123, 130.
58 Evidence of W. H. W. Newenham, 11, 14 June 1824, Select committee . . . 1825 (200) VII. 501, pp. 198–199.
59 Connolly argues that Pastorini seems to have been important less influencing the content of the Rockite movement than in giving it added energy and cohesion. Connolly, 'Mass politics and sectarian conflict', 1823–30, p. 81.
60 Gearóid Ó Crualaoich, 'The French are on the say', in John A. Murphy ed., *The French are in the bay: the expedition to Bantry Bay, 1796* (Cork: Mercier Press, 1997), p. 120.
61 O'Neill, *Popular culture and peasant rebellion in pre-famine Ireland*, p. 182; Ó Buachalla, 'From Jacobite to Jacobin', p. 80; Éamonn Ó Ciardha, *Ireland and the Jacobite cause, 1685–1766: a fatal attachment* (reprint, Dublin: Four Courts Press, 2004), pp. 161, 233, 274, 325; Vincent Morley, *Irish opinion and the American Revolution, 1760–1783* (Cambridge: Cambridge University Press, 2002), p. 7; David Dickson, 'Jacobitism in eighteenth-century Ireland: a Munster perspective', *Éire-Ireland*, vol. xxxix, nos. 3–4, 2004, p. 66.
62 'Indigator' to Goulburn, 29 Jan. 1822, SOC, 2350/30.
63 Evidence of J. McCarthy, 9 June 1824, Select committee . . . 1825 (20) VII.1, pp. 323–324.
64 Louis M. Cullen, 'The Irish diaspora of the seventeenth and eighteenth centuries', in Nicholas Canny ed., *Europeans on the move: studies on European migration, 1500–1800* (Oxford: Clarendon Press, 1994), p. 129; Dickson, 'Jacobitism in eighteenth-century Ireland', pp. 71–75.
65 Dickson, 'Jacobitism in eighteenth-century Ireland', *passim*, esp. p. 44.
66 See note 61 of Chapter 3 of this book.
67 Dickson, 'Jacobitism in eighteenth-century Ireland', p. 62.
68 F. Drew to Goulburn, 30 Jan. 1822, SOC, 2344/68.
69 Rev. R. Kirchhoffer to Goulburn, 22 Aug. 1822, CSORP, 1822/2970.
70 S. J. Connolly, 'Jacobites, Whiteboys and republicans: varieties of disaffection in eighteenth-century Ireland', *Eighteenth-century Ireland*, vol. xviii, 2003, p. 76; Dickson, 'Jacobitism in eighteenth-century Ireland', p. 52. See also Louis M. Cullen, *The hidden Ireland: reassessemnt of a concept* (Mullingar: Lilliput Press, 1988), pp. 10–11, 16–17, 27–28.
71 Morley, *Irish opinion and the American Revolution*, p. 333; Dickson, *Old world colony*, p. 442.
72 Marianne Elliott, *Partners in revolution: the United Irishmen and France* (New Haven and London: Yale University Press, 1982), chap. 4; Hugh Gough, 'Anatomy of a failure', in Murphy ed., *The French are in the bay*.
73 Ó Crualaoich, 'The French are on the say', pp. 120–122.
74 J. Church to –, 30 Nov. 1821, CSORP, box 631.
75 *Limerick Chronicle*, 29 Dec. 1821.
76 *Limerick Chronicle*, 13 Feb. 1822.
77 *Times*, 13 Sept. 1798; *Limerick Chronicle*, 16 Feb. 1822.
78 Information of J. Houlahan, no. 12, [Mar.] 1822, SOC, 2349/22; M. Barrington to Gregory, 14 Aug. 1822, SOC, 2349/54.
79 *Limerick Chronicle*, 27 Feb. 1822; *Limerick News*, 28 Feb. 1822.
80 J. Connery to E. Johnston, 5 June 1822, SOC, 2345/77. Major Carter had some doubts about the informer, but not about that case. Major Carter to Goulburn, 27 Nov. 1823, SOC, 2516/32. In this case Connery's information led to the arrest and the conviction of a Rockite leader. A. Keily to Gregory, 19 June 1823, CSORP, 1823/6590.

81 C. O'Leary to –, 1 Feb. 1822, SOC, 2344/6; same to –, 3 Mar. 1822, SOC, 2345/7.
82 J. Longfield to Gregory, 10 Dec. 1821, CSORP, box 634.
83 Lord Doneraile to Gregory, 2 Apr. 1822, SOC, 2345/52; *Cork Constitution*, 24 Mar. 1823, 23 Sept. 1824.
84 McCarthy to Gregory, 10 Aug. 1823, SOC, 2514/4; Information of J. Walsh, 13 Jan. 1824, SOC, 2614/13.
85 Catechism, no date, Gough Papers, 8303/105/232.
86 Seán Ó Coindealbháin, 'The United Irishmen in Cork county: I-VI', *Journal of the Cork Historical and Archaeological Society*, vols. liii-lvi, nos. 178, 180–184, 1948–51.
87 Dickson, *Old world colony*, p. 468. The following catechism was reportedly used by United Irishmen in or around 1797 in County Cork: '. . . What is that in your hand to a switch or whip? / It is a branch. Of what [?] / Of the Tree of Liberty. Where did it first grow [?] / In America. Where does it bloom [?] / In France. Where did the seeds fall [?] / In Ireland'. I. Collins to Lord Shannon, 2 Dec. [1797], Public Record Office of Northern Ireland, Shannon Papers, D/2707/A/2/2/150–151. However, the circumstances of this catechism are not clear.
88 David Dickson, 'Smoke without fire? Munster and the 1798 rebellion', in Bartlett, Dickson, Keogh and Whelan eds., *1798: a bicentenary perspective*, p. 162.
89 James G. Patterson, *In the wake of the great rebellion: republicanism, agrarianism and banditry in Ireland after 1798* (Manchester and New York: Manchester University Press, 2008), p. 105.
90 Cf. The existence of Defender organisations in the south in the 1790s is indeed not fully confirmed. Dickson, *Old world colony*, p. 458.
91 Anon., *Report of the trial of Edward Browne & others for administering, and of Laurence Woods for taking an unlawful oath* (Dublin: J. Exshaw, 1822), p. 88; Anon., *Report of the trial of Michael Keenan for administering an unlawful oath* (Dublin: J. Exshaw, 1822), pp. 23–24; J. Harnett to Grant, 5 Dec. 1821, CSORP, box 633; Captain Andrews to Grant, 13 Dec. 1821, CSORP, box 630.
92 Brigade Major Croker to Gregory, 30 Aug. 1820, SOC, 2189/26. An informer told Major Willcocks that 'If it had not been for the death of a person in England [the Queen], you would not be sitting on the chair you now are.' Evidence of Major Willcocks, 21 May 1824, Select committee . . . 1825 (200) VII. 501, p. 59. See also Evidence of Major Warburton, 26 May 1824, *ibid.*, p. 84.
93 W. H. W. Newenham to –, 13 Apr. 1823, SOC, 2512/16; Evidence of the same, 11, 14 June 1824, Select committee . . . 1825 (200) VII. 501, pp. 182–184.
94 Michael Collins, 'The battle of the Big Cross', in Tim Crowley and Traolach Ó Donnabháin eds., *The battle of the Big Cross* (Clonakilty: Clonakilty District 1798 Bi-Centenary Commemoration Committee, 1998); *idem*, 'Inquest and aftermath', *ibid.*; Tom O'Leary, 'Miscellaneous aspects of the 1798 rising in Clonakilty', *ibid.*; Philip M. O'Neill, *The barrow uncrossed: Fr. Peter O'Neill, and the events in east Co. Cork during the 1798 rebellion, which surrounded his arrest and transporation* (Dublin: Ballydaniel Publications, 1998), chaps. 5–6; Dickson, 'Smoke without fire?', pp. 168–169; *idem*, *Old world colony*, pp. 470–471.
95 Ó Coindealbháin, 'The United Irishmen in Cork county: IV', p. 73.
96 James Grove White, *An account of the yeomanry of Ireland, 1796 to 1834: with a list of corps in County Cork, and the records of the Doneraile Yeomanry Cavalry* (Cork: Guy & County Ltd. . . ., 1893), pp. 12–13.
97 *New Cork Evening Post*, 5, 9 Apr. 1798; 'Information collected from various letters respecting the state of Ireland', no date, TNA, HO 100/70/43–48.

98 Tom Bogue, 'Cork in 1798', in Crowley and Ó Donnabháin eds., *The battle of the Big Cross*, pp. 10–11; Dickson, 'Smoke without fire?', pp. 168–169; *idem*, *Old world colony*, pp. 470–471.
99 Basil O'Connell, 'The Nagles of Annakissy', *Irish Genealogist*, vol. ii, no. 11, 1954, p. 343.
100 James G. Patterson, '"Educated Whiteboyism": the Cork tithe war, 1798–9', *History Ireland*, vol. xii, no. 4, 2004, pp. 25–27.
101 Ó Coindealbháin, 'The United Irishmen in Cork county: IV', pp. 73–80.
102 Ivan F. Nelson, *The Irish militia, 1793–1802: Ireland's forgotten army* (Dublin: Four Courts Press, 2007), p. 232.
103 Ó Coindealbháin, 'The United Irishmen in Cork county: II-VI': James O'Donovan, 'The anatomy of the volunteers in Cork, 1775–1782: Part I', *Journal of the Cork Historical and Archaeological Society*, vol. lxxxvii, no. 245, 1982, esp. pp. 38–39; *idem*, 'The anatomy of the Volunteers in Cork, 1775–1782: Part II', *Journal of the Cork Historical and Archaeological Society*, vol. lxxxvii, no. 246, 1982, p. 120, map; Dickson, *Old world colony*, pp. 455–473.
104 d'Alton, *Protestant society and politics in Cork*, pp. 124–125; R. G. Thorne ed., *The history of parliament: the House of Commons 1790–1820, ii, constituencies* (London: Secker & Warburg, published for the History of Parliament Trust, 1986), pp. 634–641. See also Peter J. Jupp and Stephen A. Royle, 'The social geography of Cork city elections, 1801–30', *Irish Historical Sstudies*, vol. xxix, no. 113, 1994, p. 14.
105 Dickson, *Old world colony*, pp. 477–478.
106 John T. Collins, 'Some Munster landed gentry', *Journal of the Cork Historical and Archaeological Society*, vol. lxiv, no. 199, 1959, p. 66; d'Alton, *Protestant society and politics in Cork*, p. 29.
107 White, *An account of the yeomanry of Ireland*, p. 13.
108 R. G. Thorne ed., *The history of parliament: the House of Commons 1790–1820, iv, members G-P* (London: Secker & Warburg, published for the History of Parliament Trust, 1986), p. 305.
109 Speeches of Cotter, *Hansard's*, first series, vol. 34, c. 676, vol. 37, c. 439.
110 *Dublin Evening Post*, 25 June 1818; *Limerick Evening Post*, 2 July 1818; Thorne, *The history of parliament: the House of Commons 1790–1820, ii*, pp. 639–640.
111 d'Alton, *Protestant society and politics in Cork*, pp. 110–111.
112 D. R. Fisher ed., *The history of parliament: the House of Commons 1820–1832, v, members E-K* (Cambridge: Cambridge University Press, published for the History of Parliament Trust, 2009), p. 858.
113 *Dublin Evening Post*, 21 Mar. 1820.
114 d'Alton, *Protestant society and politics in Cork*, pp. 29, 110–111.
115 O'Connell to his wife, 19 Mar. 1820, Maurice R. O'Connell ed., *The correspondence of Daniel O'Connell, vol. II 1815–1823* (Dublin: Irish University Press for the Irish Manuscripts Commission, 1973), letter 823.
116 D. R. Fisher ed., *The history of parliament: the House of Commons 1820–1832, iii, constituencies part 2* (Cambridge: Cambridge University Press, published for the History of Parliament Trust, 2009), pp. 715–716.
117 *Dublin Evening Post*, 23, 30 Mar. 1820.
118 Evidence of the Rev. O'Brien, 10 May 1825, Select committee . . . 1825 (129) VIII. 1, p. 588.
119 *Dublin Evening Post*, 23, 30 Mar. 1820.
120 *Cork Morning Intelligencer*, 7 Aug. 1821; *Dublin Evening Post*, 9 Aug. 1821.
121 BPP, Return of number of troops or corps of effective yeomanry and volunteers in Ireland, 1820, 1821 (306) XIX.177, p. 180.

122 He added he himself was 'far from satisfied that the result will be rebellion or actual civil war'. Goulburn to Peel, 26 Jan. 1822, HO 100/203/120–121.
123 Thomas Bartlett, *The fall and rise of the Irish nation: the Catholic question 1690–1830* (Dublin: Gill & Macmillan, 1992), pp. 307–310.
124 Fergus O'Ferrall, *Catholic Emancipation: Daniel O'Connell and the birth of Irish democracy 1820–1830* (Dublin: Gill & MacMillan, 1985), p. 4.
125 Thomas McGrath, *Politics, interdenominational relations and education in the public ministry of Bishop James Doyle of Kildare and Leighlin, 1786–1834* (Dublin: Four Courts Press, 1999), pp. 10–11; Desmond Keenan, *Ireland 1800–1850* (United States of America: Xlibris, 2001), pp. 109–110.
126 Bartlett, *The fall and rise of the Irish nation*, p. 293.
127 S. J. Connolly, 'Union government, 1812–23', in Vaughan ed., *A new history of Ireland V*, pp. 53–54; Bartlett, *The fall and rise of the Irish nation*, p. 294.
128 *Saunders's Newsletters*, 21 Mar. 1821; *Dublin Evening Post*, 22 Mar. 1822.
129 F. Hely-Hutchinson to Lord Donoughmore, 2, 5 Apr. 1821, Trinity College Dublin, Donoughmore Papers, D/48/184–185.
130 *Limerick Chronicle*, 28 Mar. 1821; *Dublin Evening Post*, 3, 5 Apr. 1821.
131 *Dublin Evening Post*, 3, 5, 7, 10 Apr. 1821.
132 *Ibid.*, 5 Apr. 1822.
133 Reproduced in *Dublin Evening Post*, 5 Apr. 1822.
134 See p. 3 of this book.
135 CSORP, box 634; Gregory to Major Stewart, 23 Oct. 1821, CSORP, box 634; Major Stewart to Grant, 27 Oct. 1821, CSORP, box 634.
136 Donnelly, *Captain Rock: the Irish agrarian rebellion of 1821–24*, p. 356.
137 *Cork Constitution*, 5 Aug. 1822.
138 O'Connell to M. Staunton, 24 Nov. 1830, M. R. O'Connell ed., *Correspondence of Daniel O'Connell, vol. IV 1829–1832* (Dublin: Stationary Office for the Irish Manuscripts Commission, 1977), letter 1728.
139 Fergus O'Ferrall, *Daniel O'Connell* (Dublin: Gill & MacMillan, 1981), pp. 17–21.
140 Major Holmes to R. Peel, 26 June 1818, SOC, 1958/6.
141 CSORP, box 634; Gregory to Major Stewart, 23 Oct. 1821, CSORP, box 634; Major Stewart to Grant, 27 Oct. 1821, CSORP, box 634. O'Connell could be styled by the Catholics even as Moses. Ríonach Uí Ógáin, *Immortal Dan: Daniel O'Connell in Irish folk tradition* (Dublin: Geography Publications, 1995), pp. 104–106; Dickson, *Old world colony*, pp. 490–491.
142 Ó hÓgáin, Dáithí, *The hero in Irish folk history* (Dublin: Gill & Macmillan; New York: St Martin's Press, 1985), pp. 281–284.
143 Uí Ógáin, *Immortal Dan*, pp. 1, 177–179.
144 O'Ferrall, *Catholic emancipation*, p. 65–68, 171.
145 Cited in James A. Reynolds, *The Catholic emancipation crisis in Ireland, 1823–1829* (New Haven: Yale University Press; London: Oxford University Press, 1954), p. 138.
146 J. Norcott to Goulburn, 17 Feb. 1825, CSORP, 1825/11421.

4 Rockites and the government

Strengthening of the authorities: the military and police

Because the Rockites were a more formidable threat than their predecessors, they faced a more determined attitude on the part of the authorities. It must be noted here that this was evident in several ways, and that it also had a permanent effect on policy, for it led to a transformation of the machinery of law and order. In fact, the early 1820s marked the true beginning of the process of dissolving the older system of law and order, the principal pillar of which had been local magistrates: magistrates themselves were even judged to be a cause of the disturbances and became the object of reform.

The first reaction of the London government to the outbreak of the Rockite disturbances was astonishment. Receiving reports from the Irish administration, Viscount Sidmouth, the Home Secretary, judged that 'Some risque must be incurred in England for the purpose of putting down [an] actual, & most formidable danger in Ireland', and he sent five regiments to Ireland.[1] In consequence, by November 1821, the regular army left in Britain was reduced to four cavalry and four infantry regiments.[2] Since the regular armies in both regions before the Rockite disturbances was 22,600 men in Britain and 14,500 in Ireland,[3] the Rockites temporarily reversed the balance.

The Irish administration at Dublin Castle, backed with this massively increased military force, poured troops into Munster, where three regiments of cavalry and eight battalions of infantry were deployed by November 1821.[4] When County Cork became the main theatre of the disturbances in 1822, two regiments were put under the command of Colonel Gough who deployed them in the four baronies in the north of the county.[5] At the time of the first Whiteboy disturbances in 1761, the total military force deployed in Munster was only two regiments,[6] which shows that the physical force at the disposal of the Irish authorities had grown substantially. It should be noted, however, that an increased number of troops was a mere quantitative, as well as a temporary, measure. The real and enduring innovation of the 1820s was the introduction of a new constabulary force, arguably the first national 'police' force not only of Ireland but of the British Isles as a whole.

It is true that the acts of 1787 and 1792 had introduced constabulary forces into Ireland. However, they were limited in scale and competence. The former body had a relatively large complement of 500 men, but the act to establish the body was meant to be in effect only for three years (to be renewed triannually) and the body was introduced only into four out of a total of thirty-two counties.[7] Although it was later expanded in personnel to cover an additional seven counties, the 1787 constabulary seems to have been not effective in peace-keeping activities and the act was not renewed after 1815.[8] What constituted the principal rural constabulary force in the early years of the nineteenth century was that of the 1792 act, which was introduced into nineteen counties. However, because the members of the 1792 constabulary were appointed by county grand juries and because they were part-time jobbers (without uniform), their effectiveness was severely curtailed.[9] Major Carter, commanding the 1814 and 1822 constabulary forces in County Cork, judged them to be not only ineffective because of their partiality to local interests, but corrupt because of being influenced by motives of personal emolument.[10]

In 1814, with the 1787 constabulary act imminent to expire, Robert Peel, the Irish Chief Secretary, established a new force, a body which became known as Peelers. Peelers were to be formed and sent into a disturbed region by proclamation of the lord lieutenant. Although Peelers are known to have marked the beginning of a centralised, armed and fully-employed constabulary force in Ireland, they were but a temporary corps, to be withdrawn and dissolved with the ending of the disturbances.[11] In 1822, at their highest stage of development, only sixteen counties in Ireland saw Peelers active within their boundaries.[12] Hence, another constabulary force was established in 1822, prompted by the Rockite disturbances. Three hundred and twenty-five men were sent into County Cork, while Limerick had 176 men under the 1822 act.[13] All the other counties soon followed and the 1822 constabulary became the first national constabulary force in the history of the British Isles. From then on, constables wearing green trousers and a short jacket, armed with a sabre, a pistol and a short carbine with a bayonet attached became a common scene in rural Ireland.[14] They were expected not only to apprehend suspects but also to prevent crime and violence.[15] The process of building up the 'police' force in Ireland was completed in 1836 with the establishment of the Irish Constabulary (later renamed the Royal Irish Constabulary). In 1839, when Ireland was not suffering from large-scale rural disturbances and when there were virtually no policemen in rural England, more than 8,000 policemen were deployed at more than 1,000 locations in Ireland.[16]

That constructive process was accompanied by a reverse process which dissolved an older agent for maintaining law and order, i.e. the yeomanry led by local magistrates. Before looking at that process, however, it is necessary to see how the physical force of the government, strengthened both by means of the military and the constabulary, was employed. The key here is the legal basis on which strengthened hand of law and order could be used.

In terms of legal power as well, the authorities in the nineteenth century were better equipped against rural disturbances than their eighteenth-century predecessors. The eighteenth-century Irish government's main legal weapon against disturbers was the Whiteboy Act which was enacted in 1765 and amended in 1776.[17] That act decreed that most Whiteboy activities, including use of threatening notices, were capital offences. As the act remained in force after the formation of the United Kingdom, it was under that act that David Nagle and John Hickey were sentenced to death. However, the most formidable obstacle to nineteenth-century rural disturbers was the Insurrection Act. That statute was first enacted in 1796, amended in 1807, re-introduced in 1814 and 1822.[18]

The Insurrection Act gave the power to the Irish Lord Lieutenant to declare a certain district (barony or half barony) to be in a disturbed state. In the proclaimed district a curfew was imposed and power was invested in magistrates to conduct summary searches of houses (without warrant) for curfew breaking or illegal possession of arms. Under the Insurrection Act, trials by jury were superseded and suspects were tried at special sessions courts, while the penalty for breaking the curfew was transportation for life or for seven years. Thus, the act targeted not individual disturbers but an entire disturbed region, restricted the everyday activities of the residents and gave the authorities extensive powers of surveillance.

The Insurrection Act of 1822 was the first act to be passed in the parliament of 1822. Because Dublin Castle had been strongly pressing for it,[19] the London government agreed that 'it was absolutely necessary to propose without delay, & to carry through both Houses with as much dispatch as possible' the Insurrection Act.[20] Within a month of its enactment, the Lord Lieutenant introduced the Insurrection Act by proclamation into the entire counties of Cork, Limerick and Kerry, as well as parts of Carlow, Tipperary and Westmeath. Shortly afterwards, parts of Clare, Kildare and King's Counties were proclaimed.[21] Thus, all the counties of Munster excepting Waterford were, at least partly, put under this act. In March 1822, William Gregory, Under-Secretary at Dublin Castle, wrote to Henry Goulburn, the Irish Chief Secretary, that 'the executive is more strongly armed, & no seeming demonstration of tranquillity should relax any one measure of meeting terror by terror.'[22]

It seems that the powers provided by the Insurrection Act were used rigorously by the local authorities in practice. All houses in Duhallow, Orrery and Kilmore and Fermoy baronies were entered by magistrates and lists of the residents were made for the purpose of strictly enforcing the curfew and conducting house searches.[23] Colonel Gough regularly despatched nightly patrols from the eleven military stations under his command to search numerous houses in the north of County Cork.[24] House searches were deeply disliked. An active magistrate in Cork was warned by 'John Rock Commander in Chief' for his conduct:

> Mr. Batwell you will not obey all the orders I gave you not to be searching the poor people[']s houses and sending them to jail; I hear you threaten to torment us as you did last winter[;] take care if you will live so long to do so . . .[25]

This Batwell was, according to Hickey, on the Rockites' assassination list.[26]

While 110 Cork men were deported to Australia in the two years between February 1822 and February 1824,[27] in the whole of Munster, within a year of its enactment, more than 1,500 men were brought to trial under the Insurrection Act, of whom 239 were convicted.[28] Taking Ireland as a whole, the act was introduced into nine counties, where about 3,000 men were tried and 500 were convicted between February 1822 and January 1824.[29] The Insurrection Act of 1815–16, brought into operation in four counties, convicted only about sixty men in the whole island,[30] after which disturbances were effectively over. In the case of the Swing Riots in England, the total number of those tried at various courts in thirty-four counties was about 2,000, of whom 481 were deported and nineteen were executed.[31] Considering the fact that there were numerous other Rockites who were tried and convicted at assizes or special commissions, such figures show the Irish authorities' very severe response to the Rockites as well as the extraordinarily violent character of the Rockite disturbances.[32]

It was after the introduction of the Insurrection Act that the Cork Rockites abandoned large-scale mobilisation and adopted arson as their main tactic. It is possible to argue that what happened to the Cork Rockites as a short-term phenomenon had longer-term effects: because nineteenth-century rural disturbers had to face an enemy which was much stronger, both in physical force and surveillance, than its eighteenth-century predecessors, they were gradually forced to change their tactics. The following testimony of Major Warburton, a veteran police officer, illustrates the change: 'I think there have been more crimes of an isolated character latterly than there had been before. I think there were greater disturbances previously to 1835; but I think there were not perhaps so many isolated cases of assassination and personal attacks as since.'[33]

Not only did the scale of rural mobilisation shrink, but also it became dangerous to use ritualised forms of protest. Eighteenth-century Whiteboys could appear in the daytime exhibiting some elements of 'rough music', being preceded by the music of 'bagpipes or the sounding of horns'. They also occasionally resorted to simple symbolism such as erecting gallows or performing mimick burials.[34] However, the law of 1787 prohibited under pain of the death penalty such symbolic acts,[35] in addition to which the authorities' hand and vigilance were greatly strengthened in the nineteenth century. No room was left for nineteenth-century disturbers to display themselves openly or to use rituals, which enhanced their character as nightly marauders.[36]

In any event, the process of strengthening the authorities forced changes not only on disturbers' patterns of action but also on the authorities themselves: the presence and weight of resident magistrates commanding yeomanry would begin to fade away in front of more professional bodies of military and police officers. It was at the time of the Rockite disturbances that the deficiency of the older magistrate-led system of law and order became fully evident for the first time since the Union, leading in turn to the reform of the magistracy and ultimately to the future abolition of the yeomanry.

The transformation of the structure of law and order

The introduction of the new constabulary forces would lead, particularly in the eyes of the government, to the diminution of the role, and eventually the abolition, of another agent of law and order: the yeomanry. The yeomanry had been established as a loyalist force in 1796 in the age of revolution. It was a semi-official military corps with a local nature: its officers were formed of local gentry while the rank and file were collected from local inhabitants. Although the brunt of the rebellion of 1798 was borne mainly by the militia, the yeomanry also formed an important component of the government forces immediately after the rebellion.[37] In the early nineteenth century before the constabulary force was fully developed, the yeomanry continued to play an important role in the law and order of the locality.[38] In County Cork in 1804 there existed nearly sixty yeomanry corps with about 4,000 members.[39] In ordinary times yeomanry soldiers were summoned for one day every three months for training and inspection, while in disturbed times they were placed on permanent duty by the Lord Lieutenant to conduct police-like duties. Although drastically reduced with the ending of the Napoleonic Wars, the yeomanry was still a substantial force. In County Cork there existed nine yeomanry corps with 665 officers and men in 1821,[40] which was more than the 1814 and the 1822 constabulary forces in the county combined.

These two types of forces were markedly different. While more than one-third (in County Cork, 155 out of a total of 412) of the 1822 constabulary force were Catholics,[41] the yeomanry in the nineteenth century was an almost exclusively Protestant, sometimes Orange, force.[42] Hence, skirmishes accompanied with bloodshed were frequent particularly in the north of Ireland.[43] That the yeomanry also was inflammatory in Cork can be inferred from a report of a yeomanry officer at Mallow, who observed in 1814 that the district was tranquil 'in consequence of many of the yeomanry corps . . . having been lately disbanded.'[44]

In addition, yeomanry gained a poor reputation for their harsh conduct against those suspected of being rebels in the late 1790s (cases in Cork were seen in Chapter 3). Regular soldiers and militia men were essentially outsiders who would leave the place in time, which may help to explain why the Cork Rockites showed no particular enmity to former members of the North Cork Militia, who with their high profile Orange sentiments had behaved notoriously badly in County Wexford in 1798.[45] In contrast, yeomen were men of locality, which meant the psychological scar would not heal easily. The enmity against the yeomanry was so strong that even a motion to call out the yeomanry could lead to a strong reaction. When the officers of a yeomanry corps in Cork City met in January 1822 to discuss the possibility of putting their corps on permanent duty, a gentleman opposed it on the ground that 'it will only have the effect of embodying party, and rousing those angry feelings which have slept so long.'[46] Captain Rock himself sent a warning against the embodiment of yeomanry, as was shown in the following threatening notice in County Cork:

> READ AND BE WISE.—REMEMBER 98!!!!
>
> To JOSEPH LEYCECTER and all the other heretic raskals this is to give notise and solem [*sic*] warnin [*sic*]
>
> SIR
>
> We have herd [*sic*] that you made yourself very busy about this busines of Rogers and that the notise we sent to him put it into your head to rise [*sic*] a corpse [*sic*] of yomanry. . . . As you attempt to take arms again [*sic*] us so shure you will meet the fate of Hoskins and major Going and your bodys given to the dogs limb by limb. . . . we dont expect the noble Welsly [*sic*] will give arms to Orangemen to tiranize over his loyal Catholick subjects. . . . You all know my power and the number of my subjects. . . . Be advised all of you[,] reflect or prepare for hell!!!
>
> In the absence of sir John Rock K.C.B. gon to inspect his patriots.
>
> signed by order in full councel
>
> Captains JOHN FIREBRAND
>
> PATRICK FURY
>
> TIMOTHY BLOODSUCKER
>
> All sworn to walk knee deep in Orange blood.
>
> Done, at midnight in full asembly of the Royal Irish levellers this 15 day of May 1823 the last year but one for tirants.[47]

The last sentence of this notice refers to Pastorini's millenarian prophecy discussed in Chapter 3.

Considering the fact that the Orange Order was a creation of the upheavals of the 1790s, the yeomanry as a factional body may be regarded as a negative legacy of the age of revolution, which made it rather a troublesome, although perhaps necessary in times of disturbances, force in the eyes of contemporaries. Dublin Castle found itself in a difficult position on the question of yeomanry.[48] It was that difficulty, surfacing in the Rockite disturbances, which became the immediate cause of the recall and replacement of the Irish Lord Lieutenant and the Chief Secretary in late 1821.

With the outbreak of Rockite disturbances, letters requesting that the yeomanry corps be placed on permanent duty poured in to Dublin Castle from various quarters in Munster.[49] Dublin Castle, pressed with the deficiency of regular troops, was forced to comply with them.[50] However, the London government judged the measure insufficient and suggested that all corps in Ireland should be placed on permanent duty.[51] The logic was that by using yeomanry in the north, regulars there could be spared to be sent to the disturbed south. Although the Lord Lieutenant agreed to the suggestion,[52] the Chief Secretary objected on the grounds that placing northern 'Orange' corps on duty would inflame the situation.[53] This suggestion was not ultimately acted upon.[54] Home Secretary Sidmouth, seeing the division and indecision within Dublin Castle and judging that the Irish administration could not cope with the Rockites, recalled both the Lord Lieutenant and the Chief Secretary.[55] Under Marquess of Wellesley and Henry Goulburn, the new Irish administration began to launch measures to counter the Rockites including the Insurrection Act and the 1822 constabulary.

In contrast to the yeomanry, the new constabulary forces were much more centralised. The staff of the 1814 constabulary was appointed by the Lord Lieutenant and they were to serve outside their native counties, which meant no room was left for influence from the local gentry.[56] Almost the same thing can be said about the 1822 constabulary, as will be seen immediately below. The arrival of those outsiders was naturally accompanied by friction. Peelers were highly unpopular at the time of their arrival. When they were introduced in the barony of Orrery and Kilmore in November 1821, the first introduction of the force into County Cork, allegedly about 150 local gentry, magistrates, clergymen and others met and passed a resolution against them.[57] The military commander in Munster district observed of this meeting that farmers were also strongly against it, and 'those gentlemen who had taken the lead in expressing their sentiments against the measure, were hailed by them as deliverers'.[58] The unpopularity of the Peelers was reported also from Mallow.[59] And yet, in less than two years attitudes towards the Peelers would undergo a radical change.

In April 1823, the magistrates of Orrery and Kilmore demanded an increase in Peelers.[60] When Major Carter complied with the demand, the magistrates of Duhallow in turn requested an increase in the Peelers in their barony.[61] At the end of 1822, at a meeting in Condons and Clangibbon barony a resolution was passed for the introduction of the Peelers,[62] and that was later followed by another resolution for an increase in the force.[63]

Attitudes amongst local magistrates and gentry were also warming towards the 1822 constabulary. While the right to dismiss the staff of that constabulary force was solely in the hand of the Lord Lieutenant, the right to appoint the ordinary constables belonged to local magistrates. This sharing of the right of appointment was a concession made by Goulburn to local interests.[64] However, immediately after the introduction of the force Cork magistrates met and resolved that they should share the appointments between themselves and Major Willcocks, who became the Inspector General of Munster district.[65] The Cork magistrates' attitude was not exceptional: in every county, excepting Kerry, magistrates displayed the same attitude.[66]

The above process suggests that while local magistrates still looked to the yeomanry to cope with disturbances, they were accepting the necessity of centralised constabulary forces. It should be noted here that the government's long-term intention was to supersede the yeomanry by the police. With the introduction of the 1822 constabulary, the yeomanry began to be absolved from permanent duty.[67] In time the final abolition of the yeomanry and the establishment of the Irish Constabulary followed in 1836. In short, when magistrates conceded the necessity of the centralised police, they themselves made a step towards the transformation of the structure of law and order in the direction of centralisation.[68] That was not all, however. The government's next target was the magistracy itself.

Magistrates earned a bad reputation, added to their existing reputation, during the Rockite disturbances. In County Limerick, Major Willcocks and Colonel Thornton complained about the inactivity of magistrates who would dare 'not even to take out the police or military'.[69] Dublin Castle had to issue commissions of the peace to all military officers in Limerick.[70] In contrast, Cork magistrates showed a more aggressive stance. Allegedly one hundred magistrates in County Cork met in April 1823 to send an address to the Lord Lieutenant that 'whatever further measures may be adopted, they cannot be too promptly or vigorously carried into effect'.[71] In the same April, the Cork gentry visited Goulburn and complained that 'the Insurrection Act from the mode in which it has been executed has produced no terror, that the terror of the insurgents is therefore predominant'.[72] Responding to this, Gregory wrote to Goulburn, 'I am not surprised at the despair of the resident gentry of the south, they would be formed of materials very different from the rest of mankind if they were not . . . but it really deprives them of all reason, in their opinions no measure will now answer but proclaiming martial law'.[73]

Hence, given such intolerant attitudes, there is a possibility that the power given by the Insurrection Act was overused. A Cork gentleman observed immediately after the enactment of the statute, 'How will the Insurrection Act be executed[?] A night barbarism & discipline are nearly on equal terms.'[74] Peel as Home Secretary was also worried when he advised Goulburn to ascertain the law counsellors' opinion 'for the prevention of abuses which the magistrates unwatched & unassisted might commit.'[75] Despite Peel's caution, the government could not prevent cases of abuse. In February 1823, near Donoughmore in County Cork, Edward Murphy was arrested under the Insurrection Act by a patrol when he was sitting at the fire with the family of his brother at the latter's house. The judge acquitted him, observing that what Murphy was doing was 'most praiseworthy, sitting in the midst of his family quietly at home.'[76] However magistrates found the judge too lenient and forced him to resign by refusing to cooperate with him.[77]

This kind of over-zealousness by magistrates seems to have been reflected in the result of the trials under the Insurrection Act. The conviction rate at the special session courts under that act between 1822 and 1824 was only about 17 percent both in Munster and Ireland as a whole,[78] which was far below the rate at the assizes in the same period.[79] One probable cause for this was that many men were indicted without sufficient evidence. Moreover, there seem to have been many cases when arrests were made without sufficient ground. The commander of the forces expressed his anxiety about the fact that many of those who were arrested under the Insurrection Act were in fact easily discharged.[80]

In any event, Lord Donoughmore, a Cork magnate, observed that 'There are not certainly, in any civilized country, such a set of magistrates as we have been so long cursed with.'[81] His words may sound extreme, but they were not without grounds, considering another problem with Irish magistrates: corruption. Numerous cases of corruption darkened the image of the Irish magistracy. In April 1822, John Hayes was tried under the Insurrection Act in Cork City. One Donoghue, the main witness against Hayes, while swearing, kissed his own thumb instead of the Bible. The judge declined to examine him and acquitted Hayes. Hunson, a magistrate, proceeded to state the circumstances: Donoghue attempted to prosecute Hayes on a charge of robbery, but the magistrates in their locality declined on account of the insufficiency of evidence; Donoghue then went to the city and met another magistrate there, who issued warrants against Hayes; as a result, he had been in gaol for six months. Hunson further stated that 'if the laws of the land were thus administered by their guardians, who could wonder that Captain Rock, or any other imaginary redresser of grievances, had such influence on the minds of an ignorant people?'[82] Donoghue, acting out of personal enmity against Hayes, must have bribed the magistrate in Cork City.

In County Limerick, no less a person than Walter Fitzmaurice, Captain Rock, seems to have benefited from that kind of underhand dealing. He surrendered himself to George Blennerhassett, a magistrate near Rathkeale,[83] probably on some kind of understanding. Major Carter warned against the possibility of Fitzmaurice's escaping justice since 'considerable interest' was being used in his behalf.[84] In court Fitzmaurice pleaded for suspension of the trial because Blennerhassett, 'a material witness' on his side, could not attend.[85] This Blennerhassett was eventually dismissed from the commission by the reform of the magistracy.[86]

Criticism of the Irish magistracy was in fact universal. Peel, who knew Ireland well from his experience of serving as the Irish Chief Secretary from 1812 to 1818, admitted in his correspondence to Wellesley: 'No one can deny that there are in the commission of the peace many persons in want of almost every qualification which fits a man to act as a magistrate'.[87] In another context he even declared that one half of the disturbances were attributable to the idleness, corruption and partisanship of magistrates.[88] Charles Grant, whose political view was rather different from his predecessor Peel's, also admitted that 'The two great wants of this country are, a good clergy & a good magistracy.'[89] Wellesley agreed to their judgement when he wrote to Peel that because it was unquestionable that the state of the magistracy impaired the confidence of the people in the administration of the law, he deemed it to be his duty to submit to his consideration the necessity of 'a complete and effectual reformation of the magistracy.'[90]

Thus, the time had come for the reform of the magistracy, which was carried out in 1822–23. According to the Irish Lord Chancellor, the policy was to omit 'the names of many persons who never ought to have been justices of the peace'.[91] At least 600 of about 3,600 magistrates throughout Ireland were decommissioned, while in County Cork eighty-one out of about 300 were put aside.[92] While this reform of the magistracy was widely admired,[93] the measure was not a completely new idea. Several attempts at reform had been made before the 1820s. Proposals made in 1787 and 1806 were not implemented because of the possibility of a numerical deficiency of magistrates in certain counties.[94] Peel himself gave up another attempt at reform in 1816 because he feared a counter-productive psychological effect on local society.[95] What made possible the reform of 1822–23 was allegedly the death of King George III in 1820.[96] All commissions were supposed to lapse on the death of a king and new ones had to be issued. However, this process did not necessarily entail a reform, i.e. decommissioning a substantial number of magistrates. No reform of magistrates seems to have been implemented in England on the death of George III,[97] and in the case of Ireland it was fairly possible that the attempt of decommissioning on that scale would have been abandoned – like its predecessors. In fact, a bill reforming the Irish magistracy had been ready for the 1820–21 session of parliament but it was postponed and eventually cancelled.[98] It was the intervention of Wellesley who saw its necessity in the light of the Rockite disturbances that eventually brought about the reform of magistracy.[99]

Furthermore, Wellesley knew that reform of the magistracy itself was not sufficient. It was accompanied with another reform in the local administration of justice: the petty sessions. Before its introduction in 1822, a magistrate could preside over a court at his house where he could judge cases whose value was below £10. This court was a closed, and hence often corrupt, one as the magistrate had a right to refuse attendance of the public. As a result, people would not bring cases such as non-payment of wages by their employer before a magistrate in Cork, for they knew that they would not be treated fairly.[100] The new petty sessions aimed at securing the publicity and fairness of a trial by having at least two magistrates presiding over the proceedings.[101] Major Willcocks wrote to Wellesley that 'There is now nearly an end to the system of corruption in the private chamber', and that 'They are satisfied that justice has been done without favour or affection, which to my own knowledge was not formerly the case.'[102] Wellesley was no less outspoken, perhaps trying to impress the achievement of his Irish government on London: 'The useful practice of assembling frequently and regularly in petty session has been introduced into some counties, and the dangerous habit of administering justice by separate magistrates is gradually subsiding.'[103]

Thus, in the first 'age of reform' in Ireland since the Union, the process of strengthening the local machinery of law and order went hand in hand with that of transforming it. It might be argued that this latter process constituted a part of a broader pattern, i.e. 'the trend towards an interventionist state and towards centralised control over local agencies, which was to be one of the most striking features of the development of government in post-union Ireland'.[104] In this way the Rockites occasioned, or at least accelerated, changes in the way rural Ireland was governed. However, centralisation of government machinery was not the whole story. The next task is to analyse other measures of reform, by putting the Rockites, as well as Ireland, in the context of the politics of the United Kingdom.

Tithe reform and the Rockites' place in parliament

The most basic attitude of the London government towards Rockite disturbances can be seen in a parliamentary speech made by Earl of Liverpool, the Prime Minister. As soon as the Westminster parliament opened in 1822, the Rockites became an issue. Liverpool stated, 'When a house was in flames, the first object was, to extinguish them; the next, to consider by what means a repetition of the conflagration was to be prevented.'[105] While his words were to an extent a justification for the introduction of severe repressive measures, they also showed that reforming a rural Ireland haunted with chronic disturbances was within the scope of government.

In fact, the early 1820s saw the introduction of several measures for the reform of rural Ireland.[106] In 1825 Liverpool would ask parliament: 'Has not, during the last few years, more been done for the peace, the prosperity, and the happiness of Ireland, than was done for centuries before?'[107] The early 1820s was the first 'age of reform' in Ireland since the Union, which may have meant that Ireland, together with Britain, shared the attention of 'Liberal Toryism'.[108] However, the term itself was coined by a twentieth-century posterity, and it would be misleading to regard the reform measures introduced either in Britain or in Ireland in the early 1820s simply as 'liberal'.[109] The adjectives to describe Liverpool's basic stance, where Ireland was concerned, were not 'liberal' but 'defensive' and 'parliamentarian', as was illustrated by the tithe reform, which was the first in eighty years. It deserves attention, not only because tithe was a major Rockite grievance but because they show the place of Ireland in the parliamentary politics of the day.

Tithe reform was carried out by means of two parliamentary acts in 1822–23.[110] The reform act of 1822 enabled the incumbent to enter into leases for twenty-one years for his tithe with the proprietors of land. The incumbent would receive a fixed sum of money from the landed proprietors during the term of the lease while the occupiers of the land, paying a fixed amount of tithe to the proprietor, should not suffer from any uncertainty in each year's tithe valuation and payment.[111] The next reform act, that of 1823, covered a wider range of issues and became a very long act. While it abolished both the exemption of grasslands from tithe and payment in kind, it enabled the incumbent and the parishioners to negotiate, via a third party, the sum of tithe to be paid in money for a period of twenty-one years.[112] The last part was important because it defined, in principle, that tithe was not the property of an incumbent alone, by allowing a say to parishioners in the determination of the sum involved.

Nevertheless, the tithe reform of 1823 was limited in its effect. Only 966 parishes of a total of 2,259 in Ireland decided to hold a vestry to discuss its introduction. In addition, of those 966 parishes only 216 had decided by early 1824 on its introduction.[113] Neither the act of 1823, nor (still less so) that of 1822, was radical in their conception, as Goulburn, the chief architect of the two acts, admitted.[114] The partial nature of the reform was also reflected in the divided responses from the Church of Ireland.[115]

The main purpose of the acts was not to lessen the burden of tithe itself but to remove the arbitrariness and uncertainties in its valuation and payment.[116] In fact, the two acts were themselves belated measures. Various proposals for the reform of tithe had been made well before 1822, as in the 1780s a reform was contemplated in the form of commutation.[117] At the time of the Anglo-Irish Union, Prime Minister Pitt was envisioning comprehensive church reforms of both England and Ireland, and the possibility of commutation of tithe into rent in Ireland was considered.[118] Although Pitt resigned in 1801 without realising his schemes, tithe remained an object of much controversy in Ireland and several attempts at its reform were made, though unsuccessfully, in the parliament in the early years of the nineteenth century.[119] Hence, what should be questioned about the tithe reform acts of 1822–23 are not their effects or concept but their timing. To answer this question, it is necessary to turn to their background, the trend of the parliament of the day.

Before the introduction of the reform bill of 1822, about sixty Irish peers and gentry held a meeting and passed a unanimous resolution that tithe should be unconditionally commuted for rent.[120] Although that movement simply reflected an argument prevalent among the landed interest, which regarded tithe as a hindrance to agricultural improvement, it was a cause of worry to Goulburn, a Tory who feared that it might encourage parliament to adopt a radical line on the question of tithe.[121] In fact, in the parliament of 1822 a few MPs did propose a radical reform of tithe (commutation), and a motion was made urging the parliament to 'take into consideration the state of the established church of Ireland, and the manner in which tithes are there collected' early in the next session.[122] In addition, an amendment to this motion was proposed which tried to add the words 'with a view to the tranquillity and happiness of Ireland . . . [and] with a view of substituting for the present precarious and vexatious mode of supporting the established church'. The motion and the amendment were eventually both rejected, but only at a small margin of seven votes.[123] Hence, Goulburn had to try to protect tithes by introducing some sort of reform as a preventive action against the possibility of the introduction of more radical measures.[124]

Goulburn himself may have been encouraged by Liverpool, who had written to Wellesley before the introduction of the reform bill of 1822 to take up the question of tithe in parliament on government initiative.[125] After that reform bill had been passed in parliament, Liverpool further wrote to Peel:

> I think it will be quite impossible not to do something more effectual on this subject, than what was intended to be done by the bill of last session. I should very much regret that so delicate a question should be thrown loose on a committee of the House of Commons, composed as it would be, in a large proportion, of members, who, if not hostile to the establishment itself, would certainly be ready to sacrifice its interests to their own . . . it should be kept in the hands of the government . . .[126]

Thus, Liverpool fully realised the increasing difficulty of defending the Church of Ireland from the criticism of the Irish landed interest. It should be added, however, that not only the landed interest but also the radicals in the parliament attacked the Church of Ireland.

Here an important background was that Ireland of that period was a chief target of the Westminster legislation. While almost a half of the total public general acts passed by the Westminster parliament between 1817 and 1829 were enacted for Great Britain or the United Kingdom as a whole, about a quarter were specifically Irish acts, and this fraction was higher than English and Welsh acts of the same category.[127] That does not necessarily mean that British MPs took active interest in Irish affairs, of course. In some cases only Irish MPs (100 in total) may have attended when Irish affairs were debated in parliament. However, it seems that Ireland in the early 1820s could attract 'British' attentions. For instance, such noted British radicals as Joseph Hume, James Abercromby and Sir Francis Burdett made parliamentary speeches to criticise the Orange Order in Ireland in early 1823, while 404 MPs voted to set up a committee of the whole House of Commons in order to examine the conduct of the sheriff of Dublin in May of that year.[128] The parliament of 1823 in particular became in a way an 'Irish parliament'. By the eighty-fourth day of the session forty-nine days had been appropriated to the discussion of Irish subjects.[129] Although British politicians in general may not have known Ireland, it seems too much to say that they were gloried in their lack of interest in Irish affairs, at least in the early 1820s.[130]

It is in this context that Rockite disturbances arrived as a question on the scene of parliamentary politics. The above-mentioned motion urging the parliament to take tithe into consideration was introduced by Hume, who stated:

> In looking to the state of Ireland for many years past, and in attempting to ascertain the source of the constant succession of inquietude, disturbance, and rebellion in that country, he had observed several powerful causes . . . of which the tithe system was certainly one of the principal.[131]

Hume was not alone to link tithe with rural disturbances: it was rather a common logic among the MPs desirous to introduce radical reform of tithe, against which the government had introduced defensive measures of reform.[132]

However, the Rockites' role in the parliament was not solely providing a convenient ground to criticise government on the question of tithe. When the Insurrection Bill was introduced into parliament in 1822, Burdett took the opportunity to criticise the government by stating:

> Let his majesty's ministers take into their most serious consideration the state of that country. Let them come down to parliament with whatever plans of amelioration might, in their opinion, be best calculated to remedy the evils which had so long existed in that unhappy country. . . . Unless ministers entered into such a consideration, and with such views, he was at a loss to conceive how they would be able to apologize for their gross and criminal negligence.[133]

The division for the first reading of the bill drew 246 votes, a fair comparison to a 260 votes on the proposed amendment of the royal address.[134] Although the bill eventually passed the House of Commons, the government had to face another wave of criticism in the House of Lords. Baron Holland, a major Whig in the Lords, made a long speech where he referred to Liverpool's former speech:

> A noble lord had said, that when a house was on fire, it was the first duty of the inhabitants to extinguish the flames. So, with regard to the measures now proposed for the tranquillizing of Ireland, he should say to ministers, 'It is your duty to restore that country to a state of peace and order: you are now proposing most rigid and severe measures to effect that object; be it so – but it was your duty to have provided means, if not to have prevented the existence, at least to have retarded the progress on its first appearance, of that spirit of discontent which is aiming at the destruction of the whole fabric of public security.'[135]

In other words, the opposition ascribed such difficult problems as the Rockites to the government's inept policies. In 1822 and 1823, at the height of the Rockite disturbances, opposition members moved for the creation of a committee on the state of the nation, which was a favourite tactic to attack the government.[136] When Sir John Newport had moved on the necessity of an inquiry into the state of Ireland in 1817, he 'lamented the evident indifference that appeared to prevail among the members towards that subject, by the very thin attendance then present.'[137] However, when he again moved on the state of Ireland in 1822, his motion occasioned long debates, where several British MPs took part.[138] This time Newport could openly criticise the government:

> . . . the House is called upon to legislate – to rescue them [the Irish people] from the system under which they have so long suffered, and to teach them . . . that legislation is a blessing. They have had, indeed, no reason to believe their government to be a blessing.[139]

Moreover, in 1823 Duke of Devonshire, in making a motion on the state of Ireland, argued that 'the distracted state of Ireland at this moment, the distress and discontent which prevail there, shew that there is something essentially wrong in the nature of its government.'[140]

On other occasions, the government could have simply let these bursts of censure go by. At the time of the Rockite disturbances, however, the government was sensitive to criticism, because of a new development in United Kingdom politics after the post-war period of repression. On the one hand, the end of the Napoleonic Wars meant the arrival of the age of reform, when management of parliament by patronage became difficult with the 'waning of old corruption'.[141] On the other, parliamentary parties which could control the votes of their members were yet to develop.[142] Hence, the government was not on so solid a foundation as it may appear. It was the government of Lord Liverpool, which was in power between 1812 and 1827, which faced that structural problem. In addition, the early 1820s were a particularly difficult period for Liverpool. While he was alienated from the new king George IV on the question of the royal divorce, the opposition in parliament, though small in number, severely attacked his government.[143]

Furthermore, there was always a danger that discussion about matters relevant to Ireland could occasion a debate on the troublesome Catholic question. Ireland and Great Britain formed the United Kingdom in 1801, but the Union was a half measure, which failed to realise Catholic Emancipation, i.e. to remove the remaining legal disabilities imposed upon Catholics, largely because of the firm opposition by George III. After that, the Catholic question would remain a difficult issue in British politics for nearly thirty years, because, with the king's adamant opposition, it had the potential to bring about a constitutional crisis. In fact, this question had occasioned the fall of Pitt's government in 1801, as well as that of 1807.[144] The Prince of Wales, future George IV, was known to be sympathetic to Catholic Emancipation, and his accession to the throne was expected by some, and feared by others, to realise it. However, he switched his allegiance to the anti-Emancipation side after he became the Prince Regent in 1811, and the Emancipation bill of 1813 was rejected in the Commons.[145] After the defeat, the momentum for Catholic Emancipation would remain sluggish for several years, but the episode of the 1813 bill showed that the House of Commons was already pro-Emancipation, to be seen by the very narrow margin of the votes (251 versus 247).[146] When the momentum was revived in the early 1820, the Emancipation Bill of 1821 finally passed the Commons, as is shown in Chapter 3. With the two chambers taking the opposite sides, Liverpool's government naturally did not want to let an Irish question stir up the Catholic question.

Thus, the introduction and the nature of the policies to prevent a repetition of the Rockite conflagration could be strongly influenced by Liverpool's concern with the parliamentary politics of the day. To some extent, the replacement of the high-ranking officials at Dublin Castle in late 1821 was also influenced by the parliamentary politics. When Earl of Talbot was recalled, Sidmouth proposed Duke of Wellington, then the Master-General of the Ordnance, as the new Lord Lieutenant, but Liverpool opposed it and chose Wellesley, a former Grenvillite. While the presence of Wellington in the cabinet was expected to enhance its popularity, the appointment of Wellesley was expected to improve the government's relationship with the Grenvillites. Furthermore, Wellesley was an advocate of Catholic Emancipation, and his appointment necessitated a balancer. This political consideration seems to have been the biggest factor when Goulburn was nominated as the new Chief Secretary.[147]

The attitude of the London government suggests that it did not see the Rockites as a serious threat to the state but merely as an unsettling factor to the government's position in parliament.[148] Although Sidmouth's initial reaction against the Rockites was astonishment, his successor Peel was never shaken. When he was exchanging opinions with Lord Lieutenant Wellesley in April 1822, he wrote that he expected parliament would be interested in:

> the tithe question, the state of the magistracy, and the defective means of enforcing the laws, not only under circumstances of extraordinary disturbance (perhaps I am hardly warranted in calling any species or degree of disturbance in Ireland extraordinary), but in what are considered the most peaceable times, and the best regulated districts.[149]

In Peel's experienced eyes, the Rockites' extraordinary behaviour was, by the standard of the Irish rural disturbances, normal.

Prime Minister Liverpool thought still less of the Rockites than Peel did. Although Liverpool had some knowledge of Ireland from his experience as Home Secretary in 1804–09, he regarded Rockite disturbances as merely a localised agrarian disorder. He stated on the first day of the parliament of 1822: 'It was, indeed, observable, that in all their discontents and excesses, these people never quarrelled with the government, as a government; nor did religion enter largely into the motives or pretexts of their outrages.'[150] Liverpool's view, which he repeated in his private correspondence with Wellesley,[151] was strikingly wide of the mark to those in the other side of the Irish Sea. Immediately after his speech, the Under-Secretary, Gregory, wrote to Goulburn, 'How this insurrection can be called one unmixed with religions, or political feeling, by any person, who has had access to the communication made to the government, I cannot understand.'[152]

However mistaken Liverpool may have been in his view of the Rockites, and however defensive and parliamentarian his motives may have been in introducing reforms to Ireland, it is true that reforms were in fact introduced. Nevertheless, viewing the Irish policy of the 1820s from another angle can present a completely different picture. Liverpool's defensive and parliamentary concern was reflected in not only what was done, but also what was not done. The Catholic question had been left on the shelf since 1801, while no measures to solve the problem of poverty in the Irish countryside had been introduced in the form of reform of land system. A proposal of land reform would have raised as difficult a problem in parliament as the Catholic question. In short, despite Liverpool's words, the measures actually introduced did not tackle fundamental problems and the government upheld the basically conservative attitude towards Ireland which had been followed since the Union.

The question of poverty

It was in fact widely acknowledged that something had to be done to ameliorate the condition of the Irish rural poor. Lord Talbot, Lord Lieutenant at the time of the rural disturbances in the west of the country in 1819–20, wrote to Sidmouth:

> . . . while I advocated strong measures for repressing disturbance, it is my duty no less broadly to state, that the peasantry of Ireland have great cause of complaint, & that but little hopes can be cherished of the permanent establishment of peace & real security, unless the gentry of the country are disposed to alleviate the pressure that weighs down the far greater part of its excessive population.[153]

Talbot was not alone in advocating amelioration. Majors Warburton and Willcocks, when they were sent to investigate the state of County Limerick at the outbreak of the Rockite disturbances, added to their report the following observation:

> . . . we sensibly feel that our poorer fellow subjects and countrymen had many hardships to contend with, and in many cases grievances to complain of. We sincerely wish their condition amended, their habits improved and their comforts encreased.[154]

Dublin Castle conducted an investigation of rural Ireland on a county by county basis in the years of 1813, 1819 and 1820.[155] It might be added that the London government was never indifferent to the condition of the rural poor in Ireland. Between 1800 and 1833, more than 90 parliamentary select committees and royal commissions were set up to investigate various matters related to Ireland,[156] nearly ten of which dealt with the question of the rural poverty or that of the rural disturbances.[157]

Nevertheless, it is suggestive that on the occasion of setting up a select committee in parliament in 1824, Goulburn wrote to Wellesley:

> I see nothing however to make me repent having moved for such a committee and if no other advantage should be derived from it than that of shewing the number of evils affecting Ireland which are beyond the control of any government it will produce a useful result.[158]

Goulburn, who introduced tithe reforms, thought that the evils affecting Ireland were in principle beyond the reach of government. Wellesley seems to have held the same view. He confessed to Peel that:

> I cannot perceive any symptom of improvement in the general spirit of disobedience to the law . . . The origin of this destructive temper is intimately connected with the actual and long existing state of society. . . . Evils of such inveterate malignity, whose causes are so deeply seated, whose effects are so widely diffused, cannot be remedied by any one act of legislature or executive power.[159]

Behind this thinking may have been not only the government's concern about the reaction of parliament against a proposal for land reform, but also political economy, which may be regarded as 'dedicated to the justification of an existing social structure and especially of its social and economic inequalities.'[160] However, the true problem was not that political economy despaired of saving Ireland, but that the political economists' prescription to relieve poverty in rural Ireland was practically impossible to implement.[161] According to political economists, the real problem of rural Ireland was the disparity between the growth in capital and that in population. The resulting insufficiency of capital meant lower wages. Hence, it was difficult to improve one's standard of living while at the same time it was relatively easy to live, thanks to the nutritiously excellent crops of the potato. Under those circumstances there was no incentive to live an industrious life or to limit the number of one's children. Hence, population increase could not be halted and that meant that the disparity between population and capital was worsening.[162]

Because this diagnosis was drawn from a comparison with the model of the English land system,[163] the prescription was to make Ireland another England, which meant that by consolidating numerous potato plots a large farm could be created, where a farmer should employ a few wage labourers and run commercial farming. Under this system, the capital-population rate would be significantly improved.[164]

Although Peel admitted this prescription to be the only rational reasoning to cope with the problem in Ireland,[165] it was a completely unrealistic measure. The conversion of the numerous potato-growing rural poor into a smaller number of wage-earning agricultural labourers would have been ruinous to them in a country where other forms of employment were limited. Migration to a foreign country or to newly-reclaimed land might have offered an outlet for the redundant population who would have been created by this prescription, but the former measure was too costly to be a realistic measure, while the latter began only in the 1830s.[166] In addition, Ireland had no poor relief before 1838.

Most important of all, it was exactly such a conversion that rural disturbers in Ireland tried to oppose, where every peasant clung 'with the tenacity of a drowning man to his cabin and patch of potato-ground.'[167] In addition, the prescription had to face not only the problem of Whiteboyism, but also that of humanity. Judge Blackburn, who tried numerous Rockites in County Limerick, summarised the dilemma:

> The change of possession . . . is . . . attended with the most grievous . . . distress. . . [There will be a] greater number of families . . . all at once deprived of their houses, and of the means of subsistence. . . . I therefore view a great many of the outrages, which wear the appearance of system or confederacy, as the natural and necessary result of a change, in the mode of dealing with land, and of a correction of the errors of a mischievous system. . . . If a landlord after the fall of lease finds his estate covered with numerous paupers, he must dispossess them and he must be placed in [a] state in which if he asserts his legal rights he must appear to violate the first principles of humanity and endanger the public tranquillity.[168]

It should be noted, however, that the ministers were not in a helpless situation, at least not in their own minds, as to the problem of poverty of Ireland. There was one thing which was expected to solve the problem, and that was the long-term effect of 'proper' education. Here it might be recalled that Malthus argued in his second edition of *An essay on the principle of population* in 1803 that moral restraint inculcated at school was 'the only effectual mode of improving the condition of the poor'.[169]

Education

Marquess of Londonderry (Castlereagh), who had been once the Irish Chief Secretary, stated in parliament in February 1822 that 'The influence of time, the extension of civilization, and the encouragement of education, would render triumphant that conciliatory feeling'.[170] In the next year, Goulburn spoke in a similar fashion:

> Ireland was afflicted by two kinds of evils – one of them was of a temporary nature, and immediate relief might be applied to it; but the other had grown up through a long period of time, and could only be cured by the adoption of measures, the progress of which must necessarily, from the nature of the disease, be slow in their operation. The encouragement of education, with a view to a perfect eradication of the disturbances which too often prevailed in Ireland, was a matter of very great moment . . . by persevering in the introduction of a regular system of education, not merely that of learning the people to read and write, but teaching them the due observance of their moral duties – of those duties which they owed to God and man – and proving to them, that obedience to the law was a religious as well as a moral obligation, very great benefit would result from it.[171]

Thus, it was expected that universal education, particularly primary education, would bring about material benefits by civilising the Irish poor. The necessity of education in Ireland was shared by a variety of people. Peel as Irish Chief Secretary observed in parliament in 1816 that 'Time alone, the prevalence of a kind and paternal system of government, and the extension of education, were the remedies which must be chiefly relied upon.'[172] Expectations of the effect of education were widely held. Hume spoke in parliament in 1822: 'If we wished to make Ireland happy, we must give them education, revise the existing tithe system, and discourage, as much as possible, the tendency to become absentees'.[173] Newport made a motion on the education of the poor in Ireland both in 1823 and 1824, stating: 'However gentlemen might differ on other points, he believed they all agreed on this – that general education was the most certain mode by which the situation of Ireland could be ameliorated'.[174]

Well before the outbreak of Rockite disturbances, the government had begun to take a pro-active approach to the question of Irish primary education. Primary education had become a major public concern in Ireland in the late eighteenth century, but no measure to improve the condition of primary education was implemented. The Union government could not ignore the problem, and education was a priority for Grenville's government of 1806–07, which set up a commission on Irish education.[175] By 1812 the commissioners had compiled fourteen reports,[176] followed by a further eight reports submitted by 1821.[177] A parliamentary committee of 1825 on the state of Ireland referred to the question of education as a 'subject of urgent and pressing importance'.[178] The most famous initiative was the establishment of the Kildare Place Society in 1812, which aimed at a new and comprehensive system of primary education to cover both Protestant and Catholic children. The Society began to receive public grants from the government in 1814 and the number of children studying at schools supervised by the Society jumped from a mere 600 in 1816 to about 100,000 in 1824, according to the calculations of the Society.[179]

However, the ambitious project of the Kildare Place Society was eventually unsuccessful. The fourteenth report of the Board of Education in 1812, well-known for its advocacy of the 'mixed' education, concealed a serious divide between the anti-Catholic attitude of the Church of Ireland and the more liberal view of other commissioners.[180] This divide was reflected in the management of the schools supervised by the Kildare Place Society, and after 1820 Catholic politicians, notably Daniel O'Connell, seceded from the Society and, together with Catholic clergymen began an anti-Kildare Place Society agitation.[181] This kind of religious divide was in fact to remain the biggest stumbling block in matters relevant to education in Ireland in the nineteenth century. In short, contrary to its expectation most Catholic children remained beyond the reach of the government in the early nineteenth century.

Although the number of children who received primary education in various ways at that period in Ireland increased from about 200,000 in 1811 to about 500,000 in 1824,[182] only about 7 percent of Catholic children receiving an education in 1824 were going to schools supervised by the Kildare Place Society. In County Cork in particular, the rate was about 3 percent.[183] In addition, speaking about the Rockites, they must have been beyond the age of formal education when schools under the control of the Kildare Place Society were fully established in rural Ireland.

The kind of school which most of the future Rockites had attended was the so-called hedge schools.[184] These were often criticised for the contents of their education. The Commissioners of the Board of Education concluded in 1812 that 'instead of being improved by religious and moral instruction, their minds are corrupted by books calculated to incite to lawless and profligate adventure, to cherish superstition, or to lead to dissension or disloyalty'.[185] Thomas Spring Rice, a Whig MP, calling the education at hedge schools 'vicious and bad', asked in parliament, 'What would the House think, for instance, of the circulation among the boys, as a sort of textbook, of the history of [a] freebooter who figured 50 years ago in Ireland, as captain Rock was now represented to figure?'[186] The book he was referring to was probably *Irish Highwaymen, Tories and Rapparees*. As seen in Chapter 1, this book must have contributed to the spread of the image of a 'captain' among the Irish population in general. It would be simplistic, of course, to conclude that children who had read this book at school would became Rockites. The most fundamental influence of the education at hedge schools was in the sphere of language and culture.

While many forms of literature were used at hedge schools, most of the textbooks were imported from England, as there was a general dearth of Irish printed books between the seventeenth and nineteenth century. In consequence, hedge schools functioned, in effect, also as English-language schools.[187] According to the 1841 census, 47 percent of the population above five years of age could read in English. This is an extremely high figure considering the fact that English was a new language to be learned at these schools.[188]

Although Irish was not a dead language in early nineteenth-century Ireland by any means,[189] a Gaelic revival had little meaning at hedge schools, which served as preparatory schools for students intending for the priesthood, for service in foreign armies, for trading on the continent or for employment at home.[190] In other words, their greatest *raison d'être* was, from a parental viewpoint, the perspective that the education provided there would give chances to children, particularly boys, to escape from their parents' low status in society. Thus, while the hedge-school education, in some cases supervised by Catholic priests, was emphatically Catholic, it was a channel for Catholics to find better ways of living in eighteenth- and early nineteenth-century Protestant-dominated Ireland.[191]

The hedge-school education and the consequent widespread literacy in English may explain why the language of the Rockites, seen in their notices, proclamations, catechisms and oaths, was solely English. This is in contrast to the Whiteboys of the 1760s, who had been surrounded by Irish vernacular manuscripts.[192] At the same time, there were considerable internal differences within the county. The west and the south of County Cork were still Irish-speaking in the early nineteenth century, while the region around the Mallow committee was seeing the fastest advance of English in rural Cork.[193] The members of the Mallow committee had a good command over the English language which enabled them to discuss their insurrectionary plans in English.

The disparities in the prevalence of English within County Cork would largely remain until the Great Famine,[194] notwithstanding the continuing concern of successive governments of the United Kingdom with primary education in Ireland, which should be conducted in the English language. By that time, a new system of primary education had been established by the national school system of 1831, which constituted another attempt to put education of Irish children under governmental surveillance. The question of the influence of national schools on rural disturbances is, of course, beyond the scope of this book, but it deserves a note, so as to see one aspect of the aftermath of Rockite disturbances. The concluding chapter will, after summarising the argument of this book, briefly describe the aftermath from another perspective.

Notes

1 Lord Sidmouth to Lord Talbot, 23 Oct. 1821, TNA, HO 100/201/154; same to same, 8 Nov. 1821, HO 100/202/55–56.
2 J. E. Cookson, *Lord Liverpool's administration: the crucial years 1815–22* (Edinburgh: Archon Books, 1975), p. 342.
3 Stanley H. Palmer, *Police and protest in England and Ireland 1780–1850* (Cambridge: Cambridge University Press, 1988), pp. 174, 224.
4 C. Grant to Lord Sidmouth, 25 Nov. 1821, HO 100/202/201–204.
5 Major General Lambert to Lt. Col. Sorell, 27 Sept. 1822, NAI, SOC, 2346/69.
6 James S. Donnelly Jr, 'The Whiteboy movement, 1761–5', *Irish Historical Studies*, vol. xxi, no. 81, 1978, pp. 44–45.
7 Palmer, *Police and protest in England and Ireland*, pp. 111–114, 136.

8 *Ibid.*, p. 139.
9 *Ibid.*, pp. 137–138.
10 Major Carter to —, no date, NAI, CSORP, 1822/2885. See also R. Hare to —, 10 Oct. 1815, SOC, 1715/31; W. Sanders to Grant, 15 Nov. 1818, SOC, 1958/10; Rev. Chester to Grant, 26 Oct. 1821, CSORP, box 631.
11 Galen Broeker, *Rural disorder and police reform in Ireland, 1812–36* (London: Routledge & Kegan Paul; Toronto: University of Toronto Press, 1970), chap. 4; Palmer, *Police and protest in England and Ireland*, pp. 199–203.
12 Palmer, *Police and protest in England and Ireland*, pp. 224–225.
13 *Cork Constitution*, 6 Nov. 1822; *Limerick Chronicle*, 13, 20 Nov. 1822. In addition, these two counties had about 100 Peelers respectively. List of the districts under Peace Preservation Force, SOC, 2375/22; *Limerick Chronicle*, 13, 20 Nov. 1822; Sergeant Torrens to H. Goulburn, 29 Oct. 1822, SOC, 2354/36.
14 Palmer, *Police and protest in England and Ireland*, p. 252.
15 However, they were also used by local magistrates to assist collecting and distraining civil claims. *Ibid.*, pp. 262–263.
16 Palmer, *Police and protest in England and Ireland*, pp. 267, 558.
17 5 Geo. III (Irish), chap. 8; 15 & 16 Geo. III (Irish), chap. 21.
18 36 Geo. III (Irish), chap. 20; 47 Geo. III (2), chap. 13; 54 Geo. III, chap. 180; 3 Geo. IV, chap. 1.
19 Lord Wellesley to R. Peel, 31 Jan. 1822, HO 100/203/192–199.
20 Peel to Lord Wellesley, 5 Feb. 1822, HO 79/7/4.
21 Virginia Crossman, 'Emergency legislation and agrarian disorder in Ireland, 1821–41', *Irish Historical Studies*, vol. xxvii, no. 108, 1991, p. 316.
22 W. Gregory to Goulburn, 22 Mar. 1822, Surrey History Centre, Goulburn Papers, 304/69.
23 *Cork Constitution*, 27 Sept. 1822.
24 Col. Gough to Lt. Col. Sorell, 15 Sept. 1822, SOC, 2346/51; same to same, 1 Oct. 1822, SOC, 2347/3; Col. Gough to Lt. Col. Finch, 22 Nov. 1822, SOC, 2347/38.
25 A. Batwell to Major Carter, [28] June 1822, SOC, 2345/86.
26 *Cork Constitution*, 25 Apr. 1823.
27 BPP, Return of persons tried in counties in Ireland under Insurrection Act, 1823, 1823 (311) XVI. 687; BPP, Return of persons committed under Insurrection Act in Ireland, 1823–24, 1824 (174) XXII. 189.
28 Return of persons tried . . . under Insurrection Act, 1823, 1823 (311) XVI. 687.
29 Crossman, 'Emergency legislation and agrarian disorder in Ireland', p. 316.
30 Virginia Crossman, *Politics, law and order in nineteenth-century Ireland* (Dublin: Gill & Macmillan, 1996), p. 23.
31 E. J. Hobsbawm and George Rudé, *Captain Swing* (London: Pimlico, 1993), pp. 262–263.
32 After the Rockites, the Insurrection Act was superseded by the similarly repressive Coercion Act of 1833 (3 & 4 Will. IV, chap. 4).
33 Evidence of Major Warburton, 25 Apr. 1839, BPP, Select committee to inquire into the state of Ireland since 1835 in respect to crime and outrage, report and evidence, 1839 (486) XI.1, XII.1, question 680. See also Michael Beames, *Peasants and power: the Whiteboy movements and their control in pre-Famine Ireland* (Sussex: The Harvester Press; New York: St Martin's Press, 1983), pp. 51–52.
34 Maurice J. Bric, 'The Whiteboy movement in Tipperary, 1760–80', in William Nolan in association with Thomas G. McGrath ed., *Tipperary: history and society: interdisciplinary essays on the history of an Irish county* (Dublin: Geography Publications, 1985), pp. 153–154; *idem*, 'Priests, parsons and politics: the Rightboy protest in county Cork, 1785–1788', in C. H. E. Philpin ed., *Nationalism*

and popular protest in Ireland (Cambridge: Cambridge University Press, 1987), p. 177.

35 27 Geo. III (Irish), chap. 15.

36 This may explain why little has produced since E. P. Thompson expressed his expectations about the future study of charivari in Ireland in 1972. E.P. Thompson, '"Rough Music": Le Charivari anglais', *Annales. Économies, Sociétés, Civilisations*, vol. 27, no. 2, 1972, p. 308. Cf. James Warner O'Neill, *Popular culture and peasant rebellion in pre-famine Ireland*, Ph. D. thesis, University of Minnesota, 1984, p. 208.

37 Thomas Bartlett, 'Defence, counter-insurgency and rebellion: Ireland, 1793–1803', in Thomas Bartlett and Keith Jeffery eds., *A military history of Ireland* (Cambridge: Cambridge University Press, 1996), p. 249.

38 Allan Blackstock, *An ascendancy army: the Irish yeomanry, 1796–1834* (Dublin: Four Courts Press, 1998), pp. 243–252.

39 James Grove White, *An account of the yeomanry of Ireland, 1796 to 1834: with a list of corps in County Cork, and the records of the Doneraile Yeomanry Cavalry* (Cork: Guy & Co. Ltd. . . ., 1893), pp. 14–15.

40 BPP, Return of number of troops or corps of the effective yeomanry and volunteers in Ireland, 1820, 1821 (306) VIX. 177, p. 4.

41 BPP, Abstract return of number of magistrates, constables and sub-constables in provinces of Connaught, Leinster and Munster, 1824 (257) XXII. 405; Palmer, *Police and protest in England and Ireland*, p. 258.

42 Blackstock, *An ascendancy army*, pp. 128–136; *idem*, *Loyalism in Ireland 1789–1829* (Woodbridge: The Boydell Press, 2007), pp. 5–6. For the case of Cork, Major Maxwell to Major General Lambert, 7 Nov. 1821, SOC, 2293/20.

43 Numerous cases can be seen in HO. For a notorious one, HO 100/153/364-370.

44 Brigade Major Croker to Peel, 1 Nov. 1814, SOC, 1560/73.

45 L. M. Cullen, 'The 1798 rebellion in Wexford: United Irishman organisation, membership, leadeship', in Kevin Whelan in association with William Nolan eds., *Wexford: history and society: interdisciplinary essays on the history of an Irish county* (Dublin: Geography Publications, 1987), p. 267; Kevin Whelan, 'Introduction to section VI', in Thomas Bartlett, David Dickson, Dáire Keogh and Kevin Whelan eds., *1798: a bicentenary perspective* (Dublin: Four Courts Press, 2003), p. 469.

46 J. M. Travers to Lord Donoughmore, [18] Jan. 1822, Trinity College Dublin, Donoughmore Papers, D/32/72.

47 *Cork Constitution*, 21 May 1823. For other cases, *Limerick Chronicle*, 20, 27 Oct. 1821; Grant to W. W. Quin, 27 Oct. 1821, SOC, 2296/25; *Cork Morning Intelligencer*, 3 Nov. 1821; J. Godfrey to Grant, 26 Nov. 1821, CSORP, box 633; *Waterford Chronicle*, 4 Dec. 1821; Godfrey to Goulburn, 2 Feb. 1822, SOC, 2348/33; G. Blennerhassett to Gregory, 1 Mar. 1822, SOC, box 170.

48 Blackstock, *An ascendancy army*, pp. 265–266.

49 For County Cork, W. Hill to Grant, 10 Nov. 1821, CSORP, box 633; Resolutions of magistrates at Fermoy, 17 Nov. 1821, CSORP, box 631; the same, 27 Dec. 1821, SOC, box 170; Hare to Grant, 30 Nov. 1821, box 633; J. Conveney to —, 17 Dec. 1821, CSORP, box 631; W. H. H. Hodder to Gregory, 17 Dec. 1821, CSORP, box 633; Lord Carbery to —, 27 Dec. 1821, CSORP, box 631; Provost of Bandon to Goulburn, 27 Dec. 1821, CSORP, box 630; A. Sealy to Goulburn, 30 Dec. 1821, CSORP, box 636.

50 Major Stewart to Gregory, 9 Oct. 1821, CSORP, box 636; Lt. Col. Sorell to Gregory, 18 Oct. 1821, SOC, 2295/11; Grant to Quin, 27 Oct. 1821, SOC, 2296/25; Grant to Lord Sidmouth, 24 Dec. 1821, HO 100/202/385–386.

51 Lord Sidmouth to Lord Talbot, 17 Nov. 1821, HO 100/202/95–96.
52 Grant to Lord Sidmouth, 8 Nov. 1821, HO 100/200/47–48; Lord Talbot to Lord Sidmouth, 13 Nov. 1821, HO 100/202/73–74.
53 Grant to Lord Sidmouth, 18 Nov. 1821, HO 100/202/113–116.
54 Lord Sidmouth to Grant, 21 Nov. 1821, HO 100/202/93–94.
55 Lord Sidmouth to Lord Liverpool, 21 Nov. 1821, Devon Record Office, Sidmouth Papers, 152M/1821/OI/56; same to same, 22 Nov. 1821, *ibid.*, 152M/1821/OI/57.
56 Palmer, *Police and protest in England and Ireland*, pp. 225–227.
57 Magistrates to the Lord Lieutenant, 22 Nov. 1821, CSORP, box 632; J. Anderson to Grant, 23 Nov. 1821, CSORP, box 630.
58 Major General Aylmer to Lt. Col. Sorell, 23 Nov. 1821, SOC, 2293/30. See also Hare to Grant, 18 Nov. 1821, CSORP, box 633.
59 Major General Aylmer to —, 13 Nov. 1821, SOC, 2293/25.
60 Magistrates to Major Carter, [23] Apr. 1823, SOC, 2512/34.
61 Major Carter to Gregory, 6 May 1823, SOC, 2513/8.
62 T. Pinott to Goulburn, 1 Dec. 1822, SOC, 2347/44. Cf. T. Disney to Goulburn, 24 Dec. 1822, SOC, 2347/57.
63 Major Carter to Goulburn, 20 Dec. 1823, SOC, 2516/49.
64 Palmer, *Police and protest in England and Ireland*, p. 243.
65 *Cork Constitution*, 27 Nov. 1822.
66 Goulburn to Peel, 28 Nov. 1822, BL, Peel Papers, Add. Mss, 40328/258–259.
67 Lt. Col. Sorell to Gregory, 25 June 1822, National Library of Ireland, Kilmainham Papers, 1043; *Cork Constitution*, 3 July 1822; *Limerick Chronicle*, 3 July 1822.
68 Crossman, *Politics, law and order in nineteenth-century Ireland*, p. 4.
69 Major Willcocks to Gregory, 30 Nov. 1821, CSORP, box 637; Col. Thornton to Lt. Col. Sorell, 13 Feb. 1822, SOC, 2350/61; Evidence of Major Willcocks, 18 May 1824, BPP, Select committee to inquire into disturbances in Ireland, minutes of evidence, 1825 (20) VII. 1, p. 108.
70 Lord Talbot to Lord Sidmouth, 7 Nov. 1821, HO 100/202/44–45; Lt. Col. Sorell to Grant, 8 Nov. 1821, SOC, 2296/34. That measure was approved by Home Secretary Sidmouth as 'reasonable and judicious'. Lord Sidmouth to Lord Talbot, 11 Nov. 1821, HO 100/202/65–66. The same proposal at the time of the Luddite disturbances in England had been turned down. Frank Ongley Darvall, *Popular disturbances and public order in regency England: being an account of the Luddite and other disorders in England during the years 1811–1817 and of the attitude and activity of the authorities* (reprint, London: William Clowes and Sons, 1969), p. 239.
71 BPP, Addresses from grand jury of County and City of Cork on disturbances in Ireland, 1823 (302) XVI.613, p. 3.
72 Goulburn to Lord Wellesley, 19 Apr. 1823, BL, Wellesley Papers, Add. Mss, 37301/18–19.
73 Gregory to Goulburn, 23 Apr. 1823, Goulburn Papers, 304/71.
74 Unsigned memo of 23 Feb. 1822 written in the handwriting of Arthur Hutchins, Cork City and County Archives, Hutchins Papers, U254(2), p. 1.
75 Peel to Goulburn, 21 Jan. 1822, Goulburn Papers, 304/36.
76 *Cork Constitution*, 14 Mar. 1823.
77 Crossman, *Politics, law and order in nineteenth-century Ireland*, pp. 30–34.
78 Return of persons tried . . . under Insurrection Act, 1823, 1823 (311) XVI. 687; Return of persons committed under Insurrection Act in Ireland, 1823–24, 1824 (174) XXII. 189.
79 Crossman, 'Emergency legislation and agrarian disorder in Ireland', p. 316.

80 Lord Combermere to Lord Wellesley, 18 Mar. 1823, HO 100/208/145–154.
81 Lord Donoughmore to Lord Kingston, 5 Sept. 1822, Donoughmore Papers, D/28/05.
82 *Cork Morning Intelligencer*, 20 Apr. 1822.
83 Blennerhassett to Gregory, 11 July 1822, SOC, box 170.
84 W. Allen to Major Carter, 2 Aug. 1822, SOC, 2346/22; Major Carter to Gregory, 3 Aug. 1822, SOC, 2346/22; *Dublin Evening Post*, 27 Aug. 1822.
85 *Cork Constitution*, 26 Aug. 1822. Although Fitzmaurice was eventually sentenced for death, his execution was suspended, while his comrade in the same case was actually hanged. John Archdeacon Begley, *The diocese of Limerick from 1691 to the present time* (Dublin: Browne and Nolan, 1938), pp. 344–346. The eventual fate of Fitzmaurice is not known, but it seems scarcely possible that the execution of a man of his notoriety could go uncovered.
86 Evidence of F. Blackburn, 15 May 1824, Select committee . . . 1825 (20) VII.1, p. 47.
87 Peel to Lord Wellesley, 12 Apr. 1822, HO 79/8/1–21.
88 Brian Jenkins, *Era of emancipation: British government of Ireland, 1812–1830* (Kingston and Montreal: McGill-Queen's University Press, 1988), p. 122.
89 Grant to [? Lord Sidmouth], 28 Sept. 1820, HO 100/199/230–235.
90 Lord Wellesley to Peel, 27 Sept. 1822, HO 100/206/176–179.
91 Lord Manners to Lord Wellesley, 21 Oct. 1822, Wellesley Papers, Add. Mss, 37299/342–343.
92 Palmer, *Police and protest in England and Ireland*, pp. 245–246, 681, note 35.
93 Evidence of Major Willcocks, 21 May 1824, BPP, Select committee of House of Lords on nature and extent of disturbances in Ireland, minutes of evidence, 1825 (200) VII. 501, pp. 50, 52; Evidence of J. Church, 18 June 1824, Select committee . . . 1825 (20) VII. 1, p. 450.
94 Palmer, *Police and protest in England and Ireland*, p. 137; Crossman, *Politics, law and order in nineteenth-century Ireland*, p. 34.
95 Palmer, *Police and protest in England and Ireland*, p. 210.
96 Speech of Grant, 7 June 1822, *Hansard's parliamentary debates*, second series, vol. vii, c. 871–873.
97 Palmer, *Police and protest in England and Ireland*, p. 245; Sir Thomas Skyrme, *History of the justices of the peace: vol. 2 England 1689–1989* (Chichester: B. Rose, 1991), pp. 165–168.
98 Palmer, *Police and protest in England and Ireland*, p. 242.
99 F. Hely-Hutchinson to Lord Donoughmore, 23 Oct. 1822, Donoughmore Papers, D/49/47.
100 Evidence of W. Wrixon Becher, 1 June 1824, Select committee . . . 1825 (200) VII. 501, p. 137.
101 The petty sessions were at first a recommendation by the lord lieutenant. It became the norm in 1827. R. B. McDowell, *The Irish administration 1801–1914* (London: Routledge & Kegan Paul, 1964), p. 113; Jenkins, *Era of emancipation*, pp. 199–200.
102 Major Willcocks to Lord Wellesley, 29 Dec. 1824, HO 100/211/142–145.
103 Lord Wellesley to Peel, 29 Jan. 1823, HO 100/208/21–36.
104 S. J. Connolly, 'Union government, 1812–23', in W. E. Vaughan ed., *A new history of Ireland V: Ireland under the Union, I 1801–70* (Oxford: Clarendon Press, 1989), p. 64.
105 Speech of Lord Liverpool, 10 Feb. 1822, *Hansard's*, second series, vol. vi, c. 186.
106 Jenkins, *Era of emancipation*, chap. 7.
107 Speech of Lord Liverpool, 3 Mar. 1825, *Hansard's*, second series, vol. xii, c. 874. See also Jenkins, *Era of emancipation*, p. 209.

108 For Liberal Toryism, W. R. Brock, *Lord Liverpool and Liberal Toryism 1820 to 1827* (second edition, London: Frank Cass & Co., 1967), esp. chaps. 5–7; Cookson, *Lord Liverpool's administration*, esp. chaps. 6–7; Norman Gash, 'Lord Liverpool and the foundation of conservative policy', in Lord Butler ed., *The conservatives: a history from their origins to 1965* (London: George Allen & Unwin, 1977), pp. 48–49; *idem, Lord Liverpool: the life and political career of Robert Banks Jenkinson, second Earl of Liverpool 1770–1828* (Cambridge, Mass.: Harvard University Press, 1984), esp. chaps. 9–10; Boyd Hilton, 'The political arts of Lord Liverpool', *Transactions of the Royal Historical Society*, 5th series, vol. xxxviii, 1988, esp. pp. 159–170; Philip Harling, *The waning of 'old corruption': the politics of economical reform in Britain, 1779–1846* (Oxford: Clarendon Press, 1996), pp. 153–154; Stephen M. Lee, *George Canning and Liberal Toryism, 1801–1827* (London: Royal Historical Society, 2008), esp. chaps. 6–7.

109 Michael Bentley, 'Liberal Toryism in the twentieth century', *Transactions of the Royal Historical Society*, 6th series, vol. iv, 1994, pp. 184–185.

110 3 Geo IV, chap. 125; 4 Geo IV, chap. 99.

111 Speech of Goulburn, 13 June 1822, *Hansard's*, second series, vol. vii, c. 1029–1035.

112 Speech of Goulburn, 16 May 1823, *Hansard's*, second series, vol. ix, c. 368–371; R. B. McDowell, *Public opinion and government policy in Ireland, 1801–1846* (London: Faber & Faber, 1952), p. 73; Jenkins, *Era of emancipation*, pp. 201–203.

113 Speech of J. Hume, 19 June 1822, *Hansard's,* second series, vol. vii, c. 1160–1161; Goulburn to Peel, no date, Goulburn Papers, 304/35; Goulburn to Lord Wellesley, 3 Feb. 1824, Wellesley Papers, Add. Mss, 37302/68–69. However, the reform act of 1823 became, 'within its own limitations', 'reasonably successful' in a decade. Donald Harman Akenson, *The Church of Ireland: ecclesiastical reform and revolution, 1800–1885* (New Haven and London: Yale University Press, 1971), p. 109; Jenkins, *Era of emancipation*, pp. 203–204.

114 Goulburn to Peel, 7 Sept. 1822, HO 100/206/120–121; Goulburn to Peel, no date, Goulburn Papers, 304/35.

115 While the Archbishop of Armagh was opposed to the reform of 1823, the Archbishop of Cashel welcomed the measure which he judged would save tithe. Archbishop of Armagh to Lord Liverpool, 23 Apr. 1823, BL, Liverpool Papers, Add. Mss, 38294/8–13; Archbishop of Cashel to [Lord Liverpool], 23 Feb. 1823, *ibid.*, Add. Mss, 38292/91–94.

116 Goulburn to Peel, no date, Goulburn Papers, 304/35; Speech of Goulburn, 16 May 1823, *Hansard's*, second series, vol. ix, c. 368–371.

117 James Kelly, 'The genesis of "Protestant Ascendancy": the Rightboy disturbances of the 1780s and their impact upon Protestant opinion', in Gerard O'Brien ed., *Parliament, politics and people: essays in eighteenth-century Irish history* (Dublin: Irish Academic Press, 1989), pp. 106–107.

118 'No. 8, eighth paper', Sept. 1800, HO 100/99/120–127; McDowell, *Public opinion and government policy in Ireland*, pp. 20–21; Joanna Innes, 'Parliament and church reform: off and on the agenda', in Gordon Pentland and Michael T. Davis eds., *Liberty, property and popular politics: England and Scotland, 1688–1815: essays in honour of H. T. Dickinson* (Edinburgh: Edinburgh University Press, 2016), p. 45. I am grateful to Professor Innes for letting me read her work before publication.

119 Akenson, *The Church of Ireland*, pp. 87, 98–103.

120 Goulburn to Lord Wellesley, 1 June 1822, Goulburn Papers, 304/43; Lord Limerick to Goulburn, 5 June 1822, Wellesley Papers, Add. Mss, 37299/183–184.

121 Goulburn to Peel, 7 Sept. 1822, HO 100/206/120–121; Goulburn to Peel, no date, Goulburn Papers, 304/35.
122 Speeches of Sir H. Parnell and Sir John Newport, 13 June 1822, *Hansard's*, second series, vol. vii, c. 1037–1040; 'Mr. Hume's motion respecting tithes; and the church establishment in Ireland', 19 June 1822, *ibid.*, c. 1147–1178.
123 Speech of Newport, 19 June 1822, *ibid.*, c. 1185; Division, 19 June 1822, *ibid.*, 1197.
124 Goulburn to Peel, 16 Oct. 1822, Peel Papers, Add. Mss, 40328/147–148; same to same, 18 Nov. 1822, *ibid.*, Add. Mss, 40328/234–235.
125 Lord Liverpool to Lord Wellesley, 22 Mar. 1822, Wellesley Papers, Add. Mss, 37298/336–339.
126 Lord Liverpool to Peel, 9 Oct. 1822, Peel Papers, Add. Mss, 40304/80–83. Cf. Lord Liverpool to Lord Wellesley, 9 Dec. 1822, Wellesley Papers, Add. Mss, 37300/88–91.
127 Joanna Innes, 'Legislating for three kingdoms: how the Westminster parliament legislated for England, Scotland and Ireland, 1707–1830', in Julian Hoppit ed., *Parliaments, nations and identities in Britain and Ireland, 1660–1850* (Manchester and New York: Manchester University Press, 2003), p. 19, figure 2.2, pp. 22, 33–34.
128 Speech of Hume, 11 Feb. 1823, *Hansard's*, second series, vol. viii, c. 93–94; Speech of Abercromby, 5 Mar. 1823, *ibid.*, c. 443–444; Speech of Burdett, 22 Apr. 1823, *ibid.*, c. 1149–1167, 1151; 'Conduct of the sheriff of Dublin', 22 Apr. 1823, *ibid.*, c. 1167.
129 Speech of Peel, 26 June 1823, *Hansard's*, second series, vol. ix, c. 1306. Cf. Niall Ó Ciosáin, '"114 commissions and 60 committees": phantom figures from a surveillance state', *Proceedings of the Royal Irish Academy. Section C: Archaeology, Celtic Studies, History, Linguistics, Literature*, vol. 109C, 2009, p. 379.
130 K. Theodore Hoppen, *Governing Hibernia: British politicians and Ireland 1800–1921* (Oxford: Oxford University Press, 2016), p. 34.
131 'Mr. Hume's motion respecting tithes; and the church establishment in Ireland', 19 June 1822, *Hansard's*, second series, vol. vii, c. 1148.
132 For instance, speech of S. Cooper, 15 May 1822, *Hansard's*, second series, vol. vii, c. 597; Speech of Newport, 15 May 1822, *ibid*, c. 598; Speech of Parnell, 13 June 1822, *ibid.*, c. 1037; Speech of D. Browne, 13 June 1822, *ibid.*, c. 1041; Speech of G. Dawson, 13 June 1822, *ibid.*, c. 1042; Speech of [S.] O'Grady, 13 June 1822, *ibid.*, c. 1043.
133 Speech of Burdett, 7 Feb. 1822, *Hansard's*, second series, vol. vi, c. 131.
134 'Address on the king's speech at the opening of the session', 5 Feb. 1822, *Hansard's*, second series, vol. vi, c. 93; 'State of Ireland – Irish Insurrection Bill – Irish Habeas Corpus Suspension Bill', 7 Feb. 1822, *ibid.*, c. 150.
135 Speech of Lord Holland, 10 Feb. 1822, *Hansard's*, second series, vol. vi, c. 131.
136 James J. Sack, *The Grenvillites 1801–29: party politics and factionalism in the age of Pitt and Liverpool* (Urbana and London: University of Illinois Press, 1979), p. 51. Cf. Cookson, *Lord Liverpool's administration*, p. 172.
137 Speech of Newport, 19 June 1817, *Hansard*'s, first series, vol. xxxvi, c. 1076.
138 'Sir John Newport's Motion on the State of Ireland', 22 April 1822, *Hansard's*, second series, vol. vi, c. 1469–1556.
139 Speech of Newport, 22 Apr. 1822, *Hansard's*, second series, vol. vi, c. 1469–1478.
140 Speech of Lord Devonshire, 19 June 1823, *Hansard's*, second series, vol. ix, c. 1033–1034.
141 Harling, *The waning of 'old corruption'*, pp. 179–182.
142 Hilton, 'The political arts of Lord Liverpool', pp. 154–155.
143 Hilton, 'The political arts of Lord Liverpool', p. 159.

144 G. I. T. Machin, *The Catholic question in English politics 1820 to 1830* (Oxford: Clarendon Press, 1964), pp. 1–15; Thomas Bartlett, *The fall and rise of the Irish nation: the Catholic question 1690–1830* (Dublin: Gill & Macmillan, 1992), pp. 287–291; Patrick M. Geoghegan, *The Irish Act of Union: a study in high politics 1798–1801* (Dublin: Gill & Macmillan, 1999), chap 7. Cf. Boyd Hilton, *A mad, bad, & dangerous people? England 1783–1846* (Oxford: Clarendon Press, 2006), pp. 97–98.
145 Bartlett, *The fall and rise of the Irish nation*, pp. 301–302, 304–305.
146 *Times*, 25, 27 May 1813. See also *ibid.*, 3 May 1819.
147 Lord Liverpool to Lord Talbot, 29 Nov. 1821, Liverpool Papers, Add. Mss, 38290/104–107; Arthur Aspinall ed., *The diary of Henry Hobhouse (1820–1827)* (London: Home & Van Thal, 1947), pp. 80–81; Jenkins, *Era of emancipation*, p. 165; *idem, Henry Goulburn 1784–1856: a political biography* (Liverpool: Liverpool University Press, 1996), p. 131.
148 Dublin Castle under Wellesley did not see the Rockites as a threat to the government, either. Wellesley wrote to Peel on the engagements in January 1822, 'For a military view, these hostile assemblies of the populace cannot be estimated, as in any degree formidable to regular troops.' Lord Wellesley to Peel, 29 Jan. 1822, HO 100/203/152–157.
149 Peel to Lord Wellesley, 12 Apr. 1822, HO 79/8/1–21.
150 Speech of Lord Liverpool, 5 Feb. 1822, *Hansard's*, second series, vol. vi, c. 17–18.
151 Lord Liverpool to Lord Wellesley, 22 Mar. 1822, Wellesley Papers, Add. Mss, 37298/336–339.
152 Gregory to Goulburn, 23 Feb. 1822, Goulburn Papers, 304/69.
153 Lord Talbot to Lord Sidmouth, 8 Apr. 1820, HO 100/198/327–330.
154 Majors Willcocks and Warburton to Grant, 23 Oct. 1821, HO 100/202/25.
155 See pp. 20–22 of this book.
156 Ó Ciosáin, '"114 commissions and 60 committees"', p. 370.
157 See Bibliography of this book.
158 Goulburn to Lord Wellesley, 26 May 1824, Wellesley Papers, Add. Mss, 37302/273–276.
159 Lord Wellesley to Peel, 27 Apr. 1823, HO 100/208/171–176.
160 Cited in A. M. C. Waterman, *Revolution, economics and religion: Christian political economy, 1798–1833* (Cambridge: Cambridge University Press, 1991), pp. 75–76.
161 R. D. Collison Black, *Economic thought and the Irish question 1817–1870* (Cambridge: Cambridge University Press, 1960), pp. 19–20, 23.
162 *Ibid.*, pp. 19, 86–87. Cf. David A. Valone, 'Economic identity and the Irish peasantry on the eve of the Great Hunger', in David A. Valone and Jill Marie Bradbury eds., *Anglo-Irish identities, 1571–1845* (Lewisburg: Bucknell University Press, 2008), pp. 240–242.
163 David Ricardo admitted that his theory could not fully explain Ireland. Barry Gordon, *Political economy in parliament 1819–1823* (London: Macmillan, 1976), p. 233, note 33; Jenkins, *Era of emancipation*, p. 208.
164 Black, *Economic thought and the Irish question*, pp. 18, 87. Cf. After the Great Famine, this argument was criticised. Thomas A. Boylan and Timothy P. Foley, *Political economy and colonial Ireland: the propagation and ideological function of economic discourse in the nineteenth century* (London and New York: Routledge, 1992), pp. 117–118.
165 Robert Carl Shipkey, *Robert Peel's Irish policy: 1812–1846* (New York and London: Garland Publishing, 1987), p. 516.
166 Black, *Economic thought and the Irish question*, pp. 178, 182–189, 203–209.

167 George Cornwall Lewis, *Local disturbances in Ireland* (reprint, Cork: Tower Books, 1977), p. 63.
168 Blackburn to Goulburn, 1 Apr. 1824, SOC, 2613/27. On this letter a note was written to the effect that this report should be copied for transmission to England.
169 Waterman, *Revolution, economics and religion*, pp. 138, 142, 144.
170 Speech of Lord Londonderry, 7 Feb. 1822, *Hansard's*, second series, vol. vi, c. 111.
171 Speech of Goulburn, 24 June 1823, *Hansard's*, second series, vol. ix, c. 1191.
172 Jenkins, *Era of emancipation*, p. 122. At the same time, however, Peel knew that education did not possess magical powers. *Ibid.*, p. 116.
173 Speech of Hume, 11 Apr. 1822, *Hansard's*, second series, vol. vi, c. 833.
174 Speech of Newport, 25 June 1823, *Hansard's*, second series, vol. ix, c. 1241–1242; Speech of the same, 25 May 1824, *Hansard's*, second series, vol. x, c. 1399–1406.
175 Antonia McManus, *The Irish hedge school and its books, 1695–1831* (Dublin: Four Courts Press, 2002), p. 44.
176 *Ibid.*, p. 45.
177 BPP, Commissioners of education in Ireland, annual report, 1820–21, 1821 (510) XI.129.
178 BPP, Select committee to inquire into state of Ireland with reference to disturbances, reports, 1825 (129) VIII. 1, p. 4.
179 BPP, Royal commission on Irish education, first report, appendix, 1825 (400) XII. 1, p. 40. The number of children regularly attending school must have been below 100,000. The second report, calculating from parish returns sent by local clergymen, states the figure as being between 57,000 and 58,000. BPP, Royal commission on Irish education, second report, appendix, 1826–27 (12) XII. 1, pp. 72–73; Evidence of J. D. Jackson, 3 Jan. 1826, *ibid.*, p. 196.
180 Harold Hislop, 'The 1806–12 Board of Education and non-denominational education in Ireland', *Oideads*, vol. xl, 1993, pp. 52–54.
181 Donald H. Akenson, *The Irish education experiment: the national system of education in the nineteenth century* (London: Routledge & Kegan Paul; Toronto: University of Toronto Press, 1970), pp. 89–94; Irene Whelan, *The Bible war in Ireland: the 'Second Reformation' and the polarisation of Protestant-Catholic relations, 1800–1840* (Madison, Wis.: University of Wisconsin Press, 2005), p. 137. The opposition of the Catholic Church to the Society was at its strongest in Munster. Evidence of Jackson, 1 Dec. 1824, Royal Commission on Irish education, first report, appendix, 1825 (400) XII. 1, p. 425.
182 *Ibid.*, pp. 101–102.
183 Royal commission on Irish education, second report, appendix, 1826–27 (12) XII. 1, pp. 32–34, 70–73.
184 In 1824 it was estimated that each parish had about six hedge schools, which meant that about 400,000 Catholic children were educated in hedge schools in the whole island. Akenson, *The Irish education experiment*, p. 57; McManus, *The Irish hedge school and its books*, pp. 21, 31.
185 Cited in McManus, *The Irish hedge school and its books*, p. 46.
186 Speech of Spring Rice, 22 Apr. 1822, *Hansard's*, second series, vol. vi, c. 1498.
187 Akenson, *The Irish education experiment*, p. 51; McManus, *The Irish hedge school and its books*, pp. 182, 185–186.
188 Niall Ó Ciosáin, *Print and popular culture in Ireland, 1750–1850* (London: MacMillan Press; New York: St. Martin's Press, 1997), pp. 32–33; Cormac Ó Gráda, 'School attendance and literacy before the Famine: a simple

baronial analysis', *UCD Centre for Economic Research, Working Paper Series*, WP10/22, 2010, pp. 3–4.

189 David Dickson, *Old world colony: Cork and south Munster 1630–1830* (Cork: Cork University Press, 2005), pp. 495–496.

190 McManus, *The Irish hedge school and its books*, pp. 13, 182.

191 *Ibid.*, pp. 23–24, 127.

192 Vincent Morley, *Irish opinion and the American Revolution, 1760–1783* (Cambridge: Cambridge University Press, 2002), pp. 48–50. However, to what extent such manuscripts reflected the real mental world of the Whiteboys is another question. See S. J. Connolly, 'Jacobites, Whiteboys and republicans: varieties of disaffection in eighteenth-century Ireland', *Eighteenth-Century Ireland*, vol. xviii, 2003, esp. p. 72.

193 Garret FitzGerald, 'Irish-speaking in the pre-Famine period: a study based on the 1911 census data for people born before 1851 and still alive in 1911', *Proceedings of the Royal Irish Academy: Section C: Archaeology, Celtic Studies, History, Linguistics, Literature*, vol. 103C, no. 5, 2003, pp. 202–203.

194 *Ibid.*, maps 1–3.

Conclusion
The Rockites in context

By their very nature, insurrectionary movements made few if any records. Secrecy was at a premium. Business was conducted by word of mouth. If they resorted to paper, it was chiefly to circulate threatening but anonymous letters or, at times, internal rules or oaths of their organisation. Hence, historians have to rely heavily on the accounts of the authorities, and the information they obtained from informers or men who turned king's evidence. All of this is useful but often ill-informed and biased. The case of the Rockites is no exception, but the relatively rich documentation enables historians to avoid seeing the Rockites simply as agrarian and millenarian-cum-sectarian disturbers. The Rockite disturbances were, like every popular upheaval, a complex phenomenon. This conclusion attempts to summarise the argument of the book briefly and place the Rockite disturbances in longer-term contexts.

The most important single factor in the outbreak of the Rockite disturbances was the economic hardship of the early 1820s caused by the fall in agricultural prices and the widespread failure of Munster banks. The Rockites responded to hardship with the well-established method of protest in rural Ireland, Whiteboyism, i.e. clandestine night-time activities led by the captains of oath-bound secret societies. At the same time, the Rockites' use of violence, arson in particular, was much more serious and widespread than that of their eighteenth-century predecessors.

However, the Rockites were not simply agrarian disturbers. Ireland in the early 1820s saw a wide circulation of the millenarian and sectarian prophecy of Pastorini. Influenced by his prophecy, the Rockites dreamed of a social revolution to be effected by the help of the intervention of a supernatural force. Prophecies may have constituted an important element of Irish popular culture, but Pastorini seems to have gripped popular minds to an unprecedented degree.

The Rockites were something new in other respects too. They had a transregional underground network connecting various places in Munster, which was a graft of the committee-based organisational structure of the Dublin Ribbonmen onto local Whiteboy organisations. This was a novel phenomenon in the history of Irish rural disturbances. Furthermore, using the Ribbon network, the Rockites formed an independent movement which developed distinct political notions not necessarily connected with Pastorini's prophecy. What was decisive in the development of their political notions was firstly the divide in local politics since the revolutionary decade of the 1790s and secondly the new popular politics of the O'Connellite agitation for Catholic Emancipation begun in 1821. The Rockites' degree of politicisation was dimensionally different from that of the eighteenth-century Whiteboys.

While the Rockite disturbances were thus a creation of local as well as national circumstances, the Rockites themselves became an agent of change. In the Westminster parliament of the early 1820s, the Rockites became a useful tool for the Opposition to criticise the government's Irish policy. In consequence, the government was forced not only to introduce severe repressive measures against the Rockites but also to implement controversial tithe reforms, which symbolised the beginning of an age of reform in Ireland. It must be added that the violence of the Rockites forced the government to introduce law-and-order reforms as well, such as the establishment of the first national 'police' force and the decommissioning of a significant number of magistrates, which means that a structural change in the local machinery of law and order towards a more centralised control was taking place. In other words, the central administration in Dublin, backed by the London government, was coping not only with the disturbers but also with partisan local structure of justices of the peace and grand jury. In summary, while the Rockites, magistrates and parliamentarians, in reference to the title of this book, were at enmity with each other, they were also interacting among themselves.

In order to place the Rockites in contexts, it is appropriate to begin with the question of the central-local relationship since the eighteenth century. At the time of the first Whiteboy disturbances of the early 1760s, in the heightened atmosphere of the Seven Years' War, the Munster gentry easily formed an inflammatory impression about the Whiteboys, who were mostly Catholic and hence, in the eyes of the authorities, potentially pro-French or Jacobites. Rumours were circulated across the south of Ireland that French money and French-trained military officers were involved in the disturbances, and that a day had been fixed to rise and massacre the Protestants.[1] With its geographical position and the Catholic networks with France, County Cork in particular already had a longstanding anti-Jacobite and anti-Catholic tradition. Over the decades French recruiting agents, officers of the Irish Brigade serving in France, were arrested and executed up to the middle of the eighteenth century, with the latest one occurring as late as 1764. Viscount Boyle, destined to inherit his father's powerful political interest in the county as the second Earl of Shannon, and his brother-in-law Earl of Carrick were well known in the early 1760s for their anti-Catholic stance, and Carrick stuck to the story of the 'rise and massacre' for several years after the supposed date for a rising had passed.[2] In fact, the Whiteboy disturbances neither originated in County Cork, nor did the disturbances spread widely in the county (they were limited to the northeast).[3] However, the Cork authorities imprisoned 237 suspected Whiteboys, exceptionally numerous by the standard of the day, in early 1762.[4]

In contrast, the central administration at Dublin Castle adopted a level-headed approach to the situation and tried to calm the panic by refuting, in both parliament and the press, a political interpretation of the Whiteboy disturbances. It seems that the Irish Chief Secretary's private secretary, Edmund Burke, who was related to Cork Catholics and critical of the Munster gentry's anti-Catholic attitude, played a part in this.[5] When the administration sent a special commission to Munster, it found that the Whiteboys were essentially agrarian disturbers and that many of the prisoners had been arrested by the local authorities without sufficient justification. Accordingly, the judges released most of the prisoners, with only three men receiving capital sentences in Cork.[6]

The story of the 1760s makes a contrast to the Rightboy disturbances, which broke out in County Cork and spread through south Munster in the latter half of the 1780s. The Rightboy disturbances were more impressive than the first Whiteboy disturbances in terms of the scale of mobilisation and geographical extent. The primary issue raised by the Rightboys was tithe, on which there was a wide variety of opinion among members of the Church of Ireland. The laity of the Church of Ireland had as much cause as Catholics and Presbyterians to resent both what was in effect a tax and its often oppressive methods of collection. Dublin Castle itself admitted that tithe reform was desirable.[7] As a result of these several factors, and in contrast to the 1760s, the response at the Cork spring assizes of 1786 was moderate. All but one of the twenty-six alleged Rightboys indicted for felony were admitted to bail by the grand jury and eventually liberated.[8] Another factor responsible for the absence of a frenzied response comparable to that in 1761–62 was the fact that the threat of Jacobitism, which earlier had been used to stoke fears over the Whiteboys, had lost meaning with the death of Young Pretender in 1766. In addition, Ireland and Britain were not at war with France in the late 1780s, and a fear of invasion, so potent in the early 1760s, was not present.

However, moderation in punishment of Rightboys did not signify a comparable political moderation. During the War of American Independence, concessions to Catholics had been made in statutes of 1778 and 1782. These measures were in effect engineered by the Irish administration under the direction of the British government, not by the Irish parliament acting freely. Combined with suggestions of tithe reform, they led the conservative section of the Protestants to read events as a serious challenge to church and state, i.e. the Protestant constitution. In Cork in particular, a close analysis reveals a complex and ultimately unreassuring local background.

The Rightboys and tithe reform became central in the local politics of County Cork. The 'aristocratic combination' led by the second Earl of Shannon was losing its former grip on the politics of the county and faced the challenge of the rival Longfield interest. Some lesser individuals, so-called 'Independents', opportunistically took up the issue of tithe, claiming that tithe was a hindrance to agricultural improvement and a symbol of oppression by the 'aristocratic combination'. Prominent though they were at the outset, the weakness of the 'gentlemen Whiteboys' is seen in the fact that their role did not last beyond the initial stage of the disturbances.[9]

From late 1786 a conservative Protestant counter-offensive began, set out in pamphlets, in which Richard Woodward, bishop of Cloyne, County Cork, played a prominent role. His diocese was the worst hit by the Rightboy campaign against tithe. Woodward argued that the Rightboys were determined to 'extinguish the Protestant religion in Munster and Connaught' and urged Protestants to oppose tithe reform and defend the established church. His pamphlet, establishing the phrase Protestant Ascendancy, had both a local and national impact. One consequence was that Dublin Castle was forced to give up any idea of tithe reform.[10] Another was the establishment, though a timid one, of a new 'police' force by an act of 1787. Although the original idea of establishing this new 'police' in eleven counties had to be abandoned by the widespread opposition over constitutional concerns, pecuniary distress and the paucity of Protestants to man the police force, Cork was one of only four counties to have the new police.[11] In fact, the police was claimed by opponents of Lord Shannon, including one of the former 'gentlemen Whiteboys', to have been adopted simply to serve as a source of patronage for the Shannon interest.[12]

The turmoils of the 1790s posed a serious challenge to both the local and central authorities. On the one hand, rural disturbances, though not frequent or widespread, were coloured by the radicalism of the day in the first half of the decade.[13] In addition, disturbers became more violent than in the former period. In the late 1790s they could resort to extreme measures of violence, even murder, when they dealt with the traditional issue of tithe.[14] On the other hand, the decade saw another war with France which brought a new fear, that of Jacobinism, which meant in the Irish context fear of invasion by French revolutionaries. In 1796 a large French fleet under the leading French general of the day, Louis Lazare Hoche, failed to make landing only because of winter storms. Had it made a landing on the coast of Bantry, it would have found a Munster devoid of defence. Though Munster experienced no overt rebellion eventually, the politicisation by the United Irishmen became vigorous enough in early 1797.[15] The combination of the fear caused by the Bantry fleet, and an awareness of the existence of plans for further attempts at invasion, served to panic the leaders of local Protestant society. The response was harsh measures of repression, as is discussed in Chapters 3 and 4. On this occasion the central administration and the magistrates and gentry of Cork found common ground in tolerating repression.

However, they faced the challenge of Sir Ralph Abercromby, the Commander in Chief of the army, who had broad view of the army's role. He was intent on building up the army as a force to resist invasion and was opposed to its dispersion throughout the countryside. In other words, he was opposed to those gentry who desired to use the army as a tool for supporting the questionable activity of local magistrates, e.g. flogging or house burning, targeted on those figures suspected in partisan fashion by local loyalists.[16] General Moore, one of Abercromby's most capable senior officers, was like Abercromby highly critical of the local gentry's activities.[17] When he was put in charge of a disarming campaign in County Cork, Moore was under no illusions about the local gentry:

> The common people have been so ill-treated by them, and so often deceived, that neither attachment nor confidence any longer exists. They have yielded in this instance to force, are humbled, but irritated to a great degree, and unless the gentlemen change their conduct and manner towards them, or government steps in with regulations for the protection of the lower order from the upper order, the pike will appear again very soon.[18]

Pikes appeared again in the 1820s and the central government stepped in. Dublin Castle at the outbreak of the Rockite disturbances saw itself as having no alternative but to seek wide degree of support in what was becoming in law and order terms a challenging situation. At the same time, however, the central administration, as well as Colonel Gough, the military commander in Cork, held a low opinion of the local gentry and magistrates, and saw them as one of the causes of the disturbances.[19] Marquess of Wellesley, the Irish Lord Lieutenant, and Robert Peel, the Home Secretary, agreed that many of the magistrates were not sufficiently qualified to discharge the duties,[20] and removed a substantial part of their number. As is seen in Chapter 4, this measure was accompanied with the introduction of a Dublin-controlled police force.

However, the local power structure of County Cork showed its durability. The experience of the Rockite disturbances and the O'Connellite mass agitation may have even hardened the anti-Catholic mentality of the Protestant authorities of Cork. In the Mallow committee region in particular, they tried to demonstrate where the real power lay in the county by recalling the danger of the Rockites. In January 1829, an attempt had been made to assassinate an unpopular landlord and magistrate in Doneraile. While the magistrate had been a target of the Rockites several times earlier,[21] in retaliation the local authorities brought capital charges against some Catholics by using spies and informers to invent evidence of a conspiracy to assassinate two other magistrates.[22] The allegation of the false conspiracy led to more than twenty men to be tried at the special commission in Cork in October 1829.

The Doneraile magistrates had formally put the depositions on record in April 1829. In that month the Roman Catholic Relief Bill passed the parliament and obtained the royal assent, and the magistrates' action seems to have an aspect of vindictive reaction to Catholic Emancipation. In addition, Dublin Castle at that time, headed by the anti-Catholic Duke of Northumberland, sided with the Cork authorities. The Crown prosecutor at the special commission was to be John Doherty, the Solicitor General. Doherty had presided at the Clonmel assizes in the summer of 1829 over a case in which policemen were tried for having killed six people allegedly without sufficient cause and Doherty acquitted all of the accused.[23] After the Clonmel assizes O'Connell expressed strong disapproval of the new administration:

> There is more of unjust and unnatural virulence towards the Catholics in the present administration than existed even before the passing of the Emancipation Bill. . . . The Relief Bill has just enabled them to act with distrust – immediate and personal rancour on the one hand, and with open and unblushing favouritism on the other.[24]

The special commission for the 'Doneraile conspiracy' which finally met in Cork City in October became 'an outrageous spectacle of fashion' for the gentry,[25] and the Solicitor General's speech was 'much liked by the country gentlemen'.[26] However, O'Connell routed the prosecution and saved the lives of the innocent.[27] O'Connell, knowing the world of the Munster gentry, may have anticipated that a scandal like the case would occur. In March, knowing that the grant of Catholic Emancipation was imminent, O'Connell had perceptively written:

> The people will be taken out of *our* hands by Emancipation as we took them from Capt. Rock by *our* agitation. They may fall back into Rock's hands unless the government have [*sic*] the common sense to take them into their own.[28]

What O'Connell feared was that the granting of Catholic Emancipation would create a loss of direction in the minds of the people which he had so successfully roused. In other words, he feared a power vacuum after Catholic Emancipation in which 'Captain' might establish his authority once more to cope with local issues. As is shown in Chapter 3, to the Catholic lower orders in general the early nineteenth century was an age of O'Connell and 'Captain'. O'Connell himself added a third factor, i.e., 'government', by which he meant both the British government and the Irish administration.

Irish history after Catholic Emancipation was no less complex than the 1820s. The 1830s saw rural disturbances again, e.g. the Blackfeet and Whitefeet movement, while the Irish administration backed by the Whig British government in the latter half of the decade showed a fair attitude to the Catholics by reforms introduced by the Under-Secretary Thomas Drummond. The early 1840s was the period of O'Connell's another mass agitation of the Repeal Movement which almost set up an alternative machinery of government in Ireland. However, O'Connell died during the Great Famine, and the experience of the Famine seems to have eliminated the possibility of the government's establishing itself as the legitimate authority in rural Ireland.

The Famine also hit the landlords badly, and the government tried to replace old and insolvent landlords with new and commercial ones by the introduction of the Encumbered Estates Courts. The new land system seems to have been working, but the crisis of 1879–82, which led to the Land War, showed how precarious the system was. While the Land War necessitated massive intervention of the government in the form of successive land acts, serious rural disturbances recurred during the Land War in which Captain Moonlight was to remake his reappearance in something of his old style. Among the three factors of O'Connell, 'Captain' and the government, only Captain was left.

Notes

1 David Dickson, 'Novel spectacle? The birth of the Whiteboys, 1761–2', in D. W. Hayton and Andrew R. Holmes eds., *Ourselves alone? Religion, society and politics in eighteenth- and nineteenth-century Ireland: essays presented to S. J. Connolly* (Dublin: Four Courts Press, 2016), pp. 69, 73.
2 L. M. Cullen, 'The Blackwater Catholics and county Cork society and politics in the eighteenth century', in Patrick O'Flanagan and Cornelius G. Buttimer eds., *Cork: history and society: interdisciplinary essays on the history of an Irish county* (Dublin: Geography Publications, 1993), pp. 566, 569; Dickson, 'Novel spectacle?', pp. 69, 73.
3 James S. Donnelly Jr, 'The Whiteboy movement 1761–5', *Irish Historical Studies*, vol. xxi, no. 81, 1978, p. 23.
4 Cullen, 'The Blackwater Catholics and county Cork society and politics in the eighteenth century', p. 568.
5 Dickson, 'Novel spectacle?', pp. 69–70.
6 Cullen, 'The Blackwater Catholics and county Cork society and politics in the eighteenth century', pp. 568–569; Dickson, 'Novel spectacle?', p. 79.
7 James S. Donnelly Jr, 'The Rightboy movement 1785–8', *Studia Hibernica*, nos. 17/18, 1977–78, pp. 190–191; James Kelly, 'The genesis of "Protestant Ascendancy": the Rightboy disturbances of the 1780s and their impact upon Protestant opinion', in Gerard O'Brien ed., *Parliament, politics and people: essays in eighteenth-century Irish history* (Dublin: Irish Academic Press, 1989), pp. 102–107.
8 Donnelly, 'The Rightboy movement 1785–8', pp. 195–196.
9 Maurice J. Bric, 'Priests, parsons and politics: the Rightboy protest in county Cork, 1785–1788', in C. H. E. Philpin ed., *Nationalism and popular protest in Ireland* (Cambridge: Cambridge University Press, 1987), pp. 163–168; David Dickson, *Old world colony: Cork and south Munster 1630–1830* (Cork: Cork University Press, 2005), p. 453.
10 Kelly, 'The genesis of "Protestant Ascendancy"', pp. 119–120.
11 Stanley H. Palmer, *Police and protest in England and Ireland 1780–1850* (Cambridge: Cambridge University Press, 1988), pp. 111–116, 136.
12 Bric, 'Priests, parsons and politics', p. 187.
13 Dickson, *Old world colony*, pp. 458–459.
14 James G. Patterson, '"Educated Whiteboyism": the Cork tithe war, 1798–9', *History Ireland*, vol. xii, no. 4, 2004, pp. 25–26.
15 Dickson, *Old world colony*, pp. 462–465.
16 L. M. Cullen, 'The politics of crisis and rebellion, 1792–1798', in Jim Smyth ed., *Revolution, counter-revolution and Union: Ireland in the 1790s* (Cambridge: Cambridge University Press, 2000), pp. 29–31.

17 David Dickson, 'Smoke without fire? Munster and the 1798 rebellion', in Thomas Bartlett, David Dickson, Dáire Keogh and Kevin Whelan eds., *1798: a bicentenary perspective* (Dublin: Four Courts Press, 2003), pp. 168–170; Dickson, *Old world colony*, pp. 470–471.
18 Sir John Moore, ed. by Major General Sir J. F. Maurice, K. C. B., *The diary of Sir John Moore, with portrait and maps*, 2 vols (London: Edward Arnold, 1904), vol. 1, p. 290.
19 Col. Gough to Lt. Col. Sorell, 31 Oct. 1822, TNA, HO 100/206/323–326; H. Goulburn to Lord Wellesley, 22 Apr. 1823, BL, Wellesley Papers, 37301/27–28.
20 R. Peel to Lord Wellesley, 12 Apr. 1822, HO 79/8/1–21; Lord Wellesley to Peel, 27 Sept. 1822, HO 100/206/176–179.
21 Major Maxwell to Col. Gough, 17 Mar. 1823, NAI, SOC, 2511/55; *Cork Constitution*, 19 Mar. 1823; Major Carter to Goulburn, 10 Oct. 1824, SOC, 2617/10; same to same, 9 Nov. 1823, SOC, 2516/6.
22 At least one of the two had been on the assassination list of the Rockites. Col. Gough to Lt. Col. Finch, 12 May 1823, SOC, 2513/24.
23 D. O'Connell to P. Mahony, 11 Aug. 1829, Maurice R. O'Connell ed., *The correspondence of Daniel O'Connell, vol. IV 1829–1832* (Dublin: Stationary Office for the Irish Manuscripts Commission, 1977), letter 1601, note 6.
24 O'Connell to the Knight of Kerry, 24 Sept. 1829, O'Connell ed., *The correspondence of Daniel O'Connell, vol. IV 1829–1832*, letter 1608.
25 Ian d'Alton, *Protestant society and politics in Cork 1812–1844* (Cork: Cork University Press, 1980), pp. 201, 231.
26 From C. Lyne to O'Connell, 26 Oct. 1829, O'Connell ed., *The correspondence of Daniel O'Connell, vol. IV 1829–1832*, letter 1616.
27 Patrick M. Geoghegan, *King Dan: the rise of Daniel O'Connell, 1775–1829* (Dublin: Gill & Macmillan, 2008), prologue.
28 O'Connell to Mahony, 28 [and 29] Mar. 1829, O'Connell ed., *The correspondence of Daniel O'Connell, vol. IV 1829–1832*, letter 1544. Italics are original.

Bibliography

1 Primary sources

1a Manuscripts

National Archives of Ireland, Dublin

State of the Country Papers, series I, boxes 100–145; series II, boxes 154–178

Chief Secretary's Office Registered Papers, boxes 605–1129, 1158

Chief Secretary's Office Official Papers, series II, 1790–1831, boxes 506–588AAL

Frazer Mss, no. 43

General Private Correspondence, letterbooks 430–431

Home Office Letterbook, letterbook 466

Prisoners' Petitions

Private Official Correspondence, letterbooks 421–422

Rebellion Papers, boxes 1–67

Tithe Applotment Books

National Library of Ireland, Dublin

Bourke Papers, Mss 8476–77

Cotter Papers, Mss 711

Doneraile Papers, Mss 32855, 32950, 32972, 34006, 34016, 34017, 34022, 34027, 34028, 34059, 34130, 34135

Fitz-Simon Papers, Accession List 5697

Kilmainham Papers, Mss 1042–1044

Letter from the Marquis of Wellesley, Lord Lieutenant of Ireland to Sir Robert Peel, relating to the state of the south of Ireland during the course of the 'Whiteboy rebellion', 1822 February 11, Mss 27645

Monteagle Papers, Mss 11140, 13351, 13356, 13365, 13367

O'Connell Papers, Mss 13621–13651, 33565/19–53

Plunket Papers, Mss 796

Trinity College Dublin

Donoughmore Papers, D/3–50, F/13

Sirr Papers, Mss 869/1–4

University College, Dublin

Irish Folklore Commission

O'Connell Papers, P12

Kildare and Leighlin Diocesan Archives, Carlow

Bishop Doyle Papers, 1821–23

Cork Archives Institute, Cork

Ferris Papers, U60, boxes 1–2
Ryan Purcell Papers, U 139, boxes 40–42
The National Archives, London
Colonial Office Papers, CO 904/7, 906/9
Home Office Papers, HO 79, Private and Secret Entry Books, Ireland 79/7–8
Home Office Papers, HO 100/99–212
Home Office Papers, HO 101/5, King's letter-books, entry book, 1820–28
Home Office Papers, HO 122, Ireland: General Letter Books, 122/13
Home Office Papers, HO 123/9, /19
War Office Papers, WO 35/23, /25–26
Public Record Office of Northern Ireland, Belfast
Castlereagh Papers, D/3030
Redesdale Papers, T/3030
Shannon Papers, D/2707
Talbot/Gregory Papers, D/4100
British Library, London
A long memorandum on Wellesley's administration as Lord Lieutenant of Ireland, Add. Mss 38103/12/129–154
Liverpool Papers, Add Mss. 38195–38576
Peel Papers, Add. Mss 40299–40374
Wellesley Papers, Add. Mss 37298–37310
Surrey History Centre, Woking
Goulburn Papers, 304/A1, political correspondence and papers
Devon Record Office, Exeter
Sidmouth Papers, 152M
Staffordshire Record Office, Stafford
Talbot Papers, D/649/9/2–3
National Army Museum, London
Gough Papers, correspondence and papers, 8303/105
Emory University, Atlanta
Gregory Papers, 624

1b Newspapers and periodicals

Belfast Newsletter
Chute's Western Herald
Cork Advertiser
Cork Constitution
Cork Evening Post
Cork Mercantile Chronicle
Cork Morning Intelligencer
Dublin Correspondent
Dublin Evening Mail
Dublin Evening Post
Dublin Journal
Dublin Morning Post
Finn's Leinster Journal
Freeholder
Freeman's Journal
The Irish Protestant, and faithful examiner

Limerick Chronicle
Limerick Evening Post
Limerick News
Morning Chronicle
Munster Farmer's Magazine
New Cork Evening Post
Patriot
Saunders's Newsletters
Warder
Waterford Chronicle
Waterford Mirror
Williamites' Magazine: or Protestants' advocate for civil and religious liberty (Dublin: W. Espy, 1823)

1c British Parliamentary Papers
Hansard's parliamentary debates
Return of number of troops or corps of effective yeomanry and volunteers in Ireland, 1820, 1821 (306) XIX. 177
Abstract of population of Ireland, 1821, 1822 (36) XIV. 737
Minutes of evidence before committee of whole House of Commons on statement of Attorney-General of Ireland on proceedings on trials and conduct of sheriff of city of Dublin, 1823 (308) VI. 545
Return of persons tried in counties in Ireland under Insurrection Act, 1823, 1823 (311) XVI. 687
Report from the select committee appointed to inquire into the condition of the labouring poor, 1823 (561) VI. 331
Return of persons committed under Insurrection Act in Ireland, 1823–24, 1824 (174) XXII. 189
Abstract of answers and returns pursuant to act for taking account of population of Ireland; enumeration abstract, appendix, 1824 (577, 1823) XXII. 411
List of parishes in Ireland, with names of incumbents, 1824 (246) (436) XXI. 227, 333
Select committee to inquire into disturbances in Ireland, minutes of evidence, 1825 (20) VII. 1, report, 1824 (372) VIII.1
Select committee to inquire into state of Ireland with reference to disturbances, minutes of evidence, reports, 1825 (129) VIII. 1
Select committee of House of Lords on nature and extent of disturbances in Ireland, minutes of evidence, 1825 (200) VII. 501
Select committee of House of Lords to inquire into state of Ireland with reference to disturbances, minutes of evidence, 1825 (181) IX. 1, report, 1826 (40) V. 659
Select committee of House of Lords to inquire into state of Ireland with reference to disturbances, minutes of evidence, appendix, 1825 (521) IX. 249
Royal commission on Irish education, first report, appendix 1825 (400) XII. 1, second report, appendix (parochial abstracts) 1826–27 (12) XII. 1, third report, appendix (Dublin) 1826–27 (13) XIII. 1
Select committee on the butter trade of Ireland, minutes of evidence, 1826, 1826 (406) V. 135
Select committee on state of poor in Ireland, and means of improving their condition, summary report, minutes of evidence, appendix, 1830, 1830 (589) VII. 173, 1830 (654) VII. 451, 1830 (665) VII. 323

Report on roads made at public expense in southern district of Ireland, by Richard Griffith, 1831 (119) XII. 61

Papers on experimental improvements on crown lands in county of Cork, and employment of labourers on other estates in Ireland 1831–32 (355) (418) XLV. 207, 237

Select committee on disturbed state of Ireland, report, minutes of evidence, appendix, index, 1831–32 (677)

Abstract of population returns for Ireland, 1831, 1833 (634) XXXIX. 59

Abstract of answers and returns under the population acts, 55 Geo. III, chap. 120, 3 Geo. IV, chap. 5, 2 Geo. IV, chap. 30, 1 Will. IV, chap 19, enumeration 1831 (1833)

Royal commission on state of religious and other public instruction in Ireland, first report, appendix; second report, 1835 (45–47) XXXIII. 1, 829, XXXIV. 1

Royal commission on the condition of poorer classes in Ireland, reports, appendix, supplements, 1835 (369) XXXII, 1836 (35–42) XXX. 35, 221, XXXI. 1, XXXII. 1, XXXIII. 1, XXXIV. 1, 427, 643, 657

Select committee to inquire into the state of Ireland since 1835 in respect to crime and outrage, report and evidence, 1839 (406) XI.1, XII.1

Committees of census of Ireland, 1841, report, appendix, 1843 (504) XXIV. 1.

Royal commission of inquiry into state of law and practice in respect to occupation of land in Ireland, report, minutes of evidence, part 1, 1845 (605) (606) XIX. 1, 57, minutes of evidence, part 2, and part 3, 1845 (616) (657) XX. 1, XXI. 1, appendix to minutes of evidence, part 4; index to minutes of evidence, part 5, 1845 (672) (673) XXII. 1, 225

Return of number of members of established church in each diocese in Ireland, 1834 and 1861; amount of revenues of established church in each diocese, 1861 1863 (204) XLVI. 119

The forty-ninth report of the Deputy Keeper of the public records and Keeper of the state papers in Ireland, 1917–18 [Cd. 8681]

1d Pamphlets and other published sources

Anon., *A full and impartial report of the truly farcical public meeting, got up on Wednesday, 20th January 1819, by Mr. Hedges of Macromp, Lords Carbery, Kingston, &c. &c. &c.* (Cork: Michael Mathes, 1819)

Anon., *Captain Rock in London: or, the chieftain's gazette* (London: James Robins and Co., Joseph Robins, Junr. and Co., [1825–26])

Anon., *Historical notices of the several rebellions, disturbances, and illegal association in Ireland, from the earliest period to the year 1822; and a view of the actual state of the country, and of events generating, or connected with, its past disturbances, and present discontented and demoralized situations; with suggestions for the restoration and maintenance of tranquillity, and for promoting the national prosperity and happiness* (Dublin: Richard Milliken, 1822)

Anon., *Report on the present state of the disturbed district of the south of Ireland, with an enquiry into the causes of the distresses of the peasantry and farmers* (Dublin: J. Charles, 1822)

Anon., *Report of the trial of Edward Browne & others for administering, and of Laurence Woods for taking an unlawful oath* (Dublin: J. Exshaw, 1822)

Anon., *Report of the trial of Michael Keenan for administering an unlawful oath* (Dublin: J. Exshaw, 1822)

Anon., *Report of the trial had at the Court-house, Green-Street, on the 23rd, 24th, 25th, and 29th days of June, 1840, of Richard Jones, who was charged with being a member of an illegal society, the members whereof did communicate with and were known to each other by secret signs and pass words: taken in short-hand, by Andrew Bourne, . . .* (Dublin: Hodges and Smith, 1840)

Aspinall, Arthur, ed., *The diary of Henry Hobhouse (1820–1827)* (London: Home & Van Thal, 1947)

Author of 'A tour in Connaught' (Caeser Otway), *Sketches in Ireland: descriptive of interesting portions of the counties of Donegal, Cork, and Kerry*, second edition (Dublin: W. Curry, Jr. and Co., 1839)

Committee of the county of Limerick agricultural association, *Third report, for the year ending 1st March 1825, to which is subjoined, an appendix, containing the accounts of the year-extracts of correspondence, etc., etc.* (Limerick: R. P. Canter, 1825)

Connery, James, *The reformer, or, an infallible remedy to prevent pauperism and periodical returns of famine . . .* (Dublin: John Cumming, 1837)

Cosgrove, J., *A genuine history of the lives and actions of the most notorious Irish highwaymen, Tories and rapparees, from Redmond O'Brien, the famous gentleman-robber, to Cahier na Gappul, the great horse-catcher, who was executed at Maryborough in August, 1735* (Belfast: N. I., 1776)

Crofts, Charley, *Memoirs of Charley Crofts, containing numerous highly entertaining anecdotes: written by himself* (Cork: Edwards and Savage, 1829)

Croker, T. Crofton, *Researches in the south of Ireland, illustrative of the scenery, architectural remains, and the manners and superstitions of the peasantry: with an appendix, containing a private narrative of the rebellion of 1798* (London: John Murray, 1824)

Dowden, Wilfred S., ed., *Letters of Thomas Moore*, 2 vols (Oxford: Clarendon Press, 1964)

The editor of 'The Windham papers', ed., *The Wellesley papers*, 2 vols (London: H. Jenkins, 1914)

Elizabeth, Charlotte, *The Rockite: an Irish story*, fourth and enlarged edition (London: James Nisbet & Co., 1846), originally published in 1829

England, the Rev. Thomas R., *The life of the reverend Arthur O'Leary, including historical anecdotes, memoirs, and many hitherto unpublished documents, illustrative of the condition of the Irish Catholics, during the eighteenth century* (London: Longman, Hurst, Rees, Orme and Brown, 1822)

First report of the general board of health in the city of Dublin, most respectfully submitted to the most noble Richard Marquess Wellesley, Lord Lieutenant General and General Governor of Ireland (Dublin: Graisberry, 1822)

Fitzgerald, the Rev. P., and J. J. McGregor, *The history, topography, and antiquities, of the county and city of Limerick; with a preliminary view of the history and antiquities of Ireland*, 2 vols (Dublin: George Mckern, 1826–27)

A graduate of Trinity College, *The prophecies of Pastorini, analyzed and refuted, and the powerful tendency of inflammatory predictions to excite insurrection, satisfactorily demonstrated, from incontrovertible historical records, with a cursory view of the dangerous state of Ireland, from an exclusively Popish conspiracy: humbly submitted to the consideration of the Protestants of the British empire* (Dublin: George Bull, 1823)

Gregory, Lady, ed., *Mr. Gregory's letter-box 1813–1835*, second edition (Gerrards Cross, Bucks. Colin Smyth, 1981), originally published in 1898

Hall, Mrs. S. C., *The Whiteboy: a story of Ireland in 1822* (London: Chapman and Hall, 1845)

Idem, *Killarney and the south of Ireland* (London: Virtue, 1865)

Idem, ed. by S. Scott, *Hall's Ireland: Mr. & Mrs. Hall's tour of 1840*, 2 vols (London and Sydney: Sphere Books, 1984), originally published in 1841–43

Hall, the Rev. James, *Tour through Ireland; particularly the interior & least known parts: containing an accurate view of the parties, politics, and improvements, in the different provinces; with reflections and observations on the Union of Britain and Ireland; the practicability and advantages of a telegraphic communication between the two countries, and other matters of importance*, 2 vols (London: R. P. Moore, etc., 1813)

An Irishman (Thomas Spring Rice), *The present state of Ireland, and on the best means of improving the condition of its inhabitants* (London: R. and A. Taylor, 1822)

Kohl, J. G., *Ireland, Scotland, and England* (London: Chapman and Hall, 1844)

Lenihan, Maurice, *Limerick; its history and antiquities, ecclesiastical, civil, and military, from the earliest ages, with copious historical, archaeological, topographical, and genealogical notes and illustrations; maps, plates, and appendices, and an alphabetical index, etc. compiled from the ancient annals, the most authentic ms. and printed records, recent researches, etc., etc.* (Dublin: Hodges, Smith, 1866)

Lewis, George Cornwall, *Local disturbances in Ireland* (Cork: Tower Books, 1977), reprint, first published in 1836

Lewis, Samuel, *A topographical dictionary of Ireland* (Baltimore: Genealogical Publishing, 1995), reprint, originally published in 1837

Marx, Karl, and Frederick Engels, *Ireland and the Irish question* (Moscow: Progress Publishers, 1971)

Mason, William Shaw, ed., *A statistical account or parochial survey of Ireland, drawn up from the communications of the clergy*, 3 vols (Dublin: Graisberry and Campbell, for J. Cumming, 1814–19)

Moore, Sir John, ed. by Major General Sir J. F. Maurice, K. C. B., *The diary of Sir John Moore, with portrait and maps*, 2 vols (London: Edward Arnold, 1904)

Moore, Thomas, *Memoirs of Captain Rock, the celebrated Irish chieftain: with some account of his ancestors* (London: Longman, Hurst, Rees, Orme, Brown, and Green, 1824)

Musgrave, Sir Richard, ed. by Steven W. Myers and Delores E. McKnight, *Memoirs of the different rebellions of Ireland . . .* (Fort Wayne: Round Tower Books, 1995), originally published in 1802

Newenham, Thomas, *A view of the natural, political, and commercial circumstances of Ireland* (London: T. Cadell and W. Davies, 1809)

O'Connell, Maurice R., ed., *The correspondence of Daniel O'Connell, vol. I 1792–1814* (Dublin: Irish University Press for the Irish Manuscripts Commission, 1972)

Idem, ed., *The correspondence of Daniel O'Connell, vol. II 1815–1823* (Dublin: Irish University Press for the Irish Manuscripts Commission, 1973)

Idem, ed., *The correspondence of Daniel O'Connell, vol. III 1824–1828* (Dublin: Irish University Press for the Irish Manuscripts Commission, 1974)

Idem, ed., *The correspondence of Daniel O'Connell, vol. IV 1829–1832* (Dublin: Stationary Office for the Irish Manuscripts Commission, 1977)

O'Sullivan, Mortimer, *Captain Rock detected: or, the origin and character of the recent disturbances and the causes, both moral and political of the present*

alarming condition of the south and west of Ireland, fully and fairly considered and exposed by a Munster farmer (London: T. Cadell, 1824)
Parker, Charles Stuart, *Sir Robert Peel from his private papers, with a chapter on his life and character by his grandson, the hon. George Peel*, 3 vols, second edition (London: John Murray, 1899)
Pastorini, Sig, *The general history of the Christian church, from her birth to her final triumphant state in heaven: chiefly deduced from the apocalypse of St John the apostle and evangelist, second edition, with a few additional remarks and elucidations, by the author* (London: J. P. Coghlan, 1898), first published in 1771
Plowden, Francis, *The history of Ireland from its Union with Great Britain, in January 1801, to October 1810*, 3 vols (Dublin: John Boyce, 1811)
Plunket, David, *The life, letters and speeches of Lord Plunket*, 2 vols (London: Smith Elster and Co., 1867)
Reid, Thomas, *Travels in Ireland, in the year 1822: exhibiting brief sketches of the moral, physical, and political state of the country; with reflections on the best means of improving its condition* (London: Printed for Longman, Hurst, Rees, Orme, and Brown, 1823)
Reid, Thomas, *Sketches of Ireland* (London: printed for Longman, Rees, Orme, Brown, and Green, 1827)
Russell, Lord John, ed., *Memoirs, journal, and correspondence of Thomas Moore*, 8 vols (New York: D. Appleton & Co., 1853–56)
Savage, M. W., ed., *Sketches, legal and political, by the late right honourable Richard Lalor Sheil*, 2 vols (London: Colburn, 1855)
Tocqueville, Alexis de, transl. by George Lawrence and K. P. Mayer, ed. by J. P. Mayer, *Journeys to England and Ireland* (London: Faber and Faber, 1958)
Townsend, the Rev. Horatio, *A general and statistical survey of the county of Cork*, 2 vols, second edition (Cork: Edwards & Savage, 1815)
White, James Grove, *An account of the yeomanry of Ireland, 1796 to 1834: with a list of corps in County Cork, and the records of the Doneraile Yeomanry Cavalry* (Cork: Guy & Co. Ltd. . . ., 1893)
Idem, *Historical and topographical notes, etc., on Buttevant, Castletownroche, Doneraile, Mallow, and places in their vicinity, collected by Colonel James Grove White*, 4 vols (Alabama: Amite and Knocknagee Historical Fund, 1969), reprint, originally published in 1905–18
Wyse, Thomas, *Historical sketch of the late Catholic Association of Ireland*, 2 vols (London: H. Colburn, 1829)

2 Secondary literature

2a Guides

Crawford, E. Margret, *Counting the people: a survey of the Irish censuses, 1813–1911* (Dublin: Four Courts Press, 2003)
General alphabetical index to the townlands and towns, parishes, and baronies of Ireland: based on the census of Ireland for the Year 1851 (Baltimore: Genealogical Publishing Co., 1984), reprint, originally published in 1861
Hayes, Richard J., *Manuscript sources for the history of Irish civilisation*, 11 vols (Boston, Mass.: G. K. Hall, 1965), first supplement, 3 vols (1979)
McVeagh, John, *Irish travel writing: a bibliography* (Dublin: Wolfhound Press, 1996)

O'Higgins, Paul, *A bibliography of Irish trials and other legal proceedings* (Abindon: Professional Books Ltd., 1986)

Public Records in Ireland, *Deputy Keeper's Reports*, vols. 1–59

Quinlan, Tom, 'The registered papers of the Chief Secretary's Office', *Irish Archives: Journal of the Irish Society for Archives*, 1994

Vaughan, W. E., and A. J. Fitzpatrick, eds., *Irish historical statistics: population, 1821–1971* (Dublin: Irish Academic Press, 1971)

2b Irish history

Adams, J. R. R., 'Swine-tax and eat-him-all-magee: the hedge schools and popular education in Ireland', in Donnelly and Miller, eds., *Irish popular culture* (Dublin: Irish Academic Press, 1998)

Akenson, Donald H., *The Irish education experiment: the national system of education in the nineteenth century* (London: Routledge & Kegan Paul, and Toronto: University of Toronto Press, 1970)

Idem, *The Church of Ireland: ecclesiastical reform and revolution, 1800–1885* (New Haven and London: Yale University Press, 1971)

Andrews, J. H., 'The struggle for Ireland's public commons', in O'Flanagan, Ferguson and Whelan, eds., *Rural Ireland 1600–1900* (Cork: Cork University Press, 1987)

Idem, 'Plantation Ireland: a review of settlement history', in Barry, ed., *A history of settlement in Ireland* (London: Routledge, 2000).

Barry, Terry, ed., *A history of settlement in Ireland* (London: Routledge, 2000).

Bartlett, Thomas, 'Select documents XXXVIII: Defenders and Defenderism in 1795', *Irish Historical Studies*, vol. xxiv, no. 95, 1984–85

Idem, 'Indiscipline and disaffection in the armed forced in Ireland in the 1790s', in Corish, ed., *Radicals, rebels and establishments* (Belfast: Appletree Books, 1985)

Idem, 'An end to moral economy: the Irish militia disturbances of 1793', in Philpin, ed., *Nationalism and popular protest in Ireland* (Cambridge: Cambridge University Press, 1987)

Idem, 'Militarization and politicization in Ireland (1780–1820)', in Bergeron and Cullen, eds., *Culture et pratique politiques en France et en Irlande XVIe-XVIIIe siècle* (Paris: Centre de Recherches Historiques, 1991)

Idem, *The fall and rise of the Irish nation: the Catholic question 1690–1830* (Dublin: Gill & Macmillan, 1992)

Idem, 'Defence, counter-insurgency and rebellion: Ireland, 1793–1803', in Thomas Bartlett and Keith Jeffery, eds., *A military history of Ireland* (Cambridge: Cambridge University Press, 1996)

Bartlett, Thomas, David Dickson, Dáire Keogh and Kevin Whelan, eds., *1798: a bicentenary perspective* (Dublin: Four Courts Press, 2003)

Beames, M., 'Cottiers and conacre in pre-Famine Ireland', *Journal of Peasant Studies*, vol. ii, no. 3, 1975

Idem, 'Peasant movements: Ireland, 1785–1795', *Journal of Peasant Studies*, vol. ii, no. 4, 1975

Idem, *Peasants and power: the Whiteboy movements and their control in pre-Famine Ireland* (Sussex: The Harvester Press, and New York: St Martin's Press, 1983)

Idem, 'Rural conflict in pre-Famine Ireland: peasant assassinations in Tipperary, 1837–1847', in Philpin, ed., *Nationalism and popular protest in Ireland* (Cambridge: Cambridge University Press, 1987)

Idem, 'The Ribbon societies: lower-class nationalism in pre-Famine Ireland', in Philpin, ed., *Nationalism and popular protest in Ireland* (Cambridge: Cambridge University Press, 1987)

Begley, John Archdeacon, *The diocese of Limerick from 1691 to the present time* (Dublin: Browne and Nolan, 1938)

Belchem, John, 'English working-class radicalism and the Irish, 1815–50', in Roger Swift and Sheridan Gilley, eds., *The Irish in the Victorian city* (London, Sydney, Dover: Croom Helm, 1985)

Idem, '"Freedom and friendship to Ireland": Ribbonism in early nineteenth-century Liverpool', *International Review of Social History*, vol. 39, no. 1, 1994

Bennett, R. J., 'The rising of 1822', *Ireland's Own*, January 6, 1940

Bergeron, Louis, and Louis Cullen, eds., *Culture et pratique politiques en France et en Irlande XVIe-XVIIIe siècle: actes du colloque de Marseille 28 septembre-2 Octobre 1988* (Paris: Centre de Recherches Historiques, 1991)

Berry, Henry, 'Duhallow cavalry, county Cork, 1822–25', *Journal of the Cork Historical and Archaeological society*, vol. v, 1899

Idem, 'Story of the attack on Lavally Cottage, Ballymagooly, near Mallow, in 1823', *Journal of the Cork Historical and Archaeological Society*, vol. xv, no. 81, 1909

Bew, Paul, *Ireland: the politics of enmity 1789–2006* (Oxford: Oxford University Press, 2007)

Black, R. D. Collison, *Economic thought and the Irish question 1817–1870* (Cambridge: Cambridge University Press, 1960)

Blackstock, Allan F., '"A dangerous species of ally": Orangeism and the Irish yeomanry', *Irish Historical Studies*, vol. xxx, no. 119, 1997

Idem, *An ascendancy army: the Irish yeomanry, 1796–1834* (Dublin: Four Courts Press, 1998)

Idem, *Loyalism in Ireland 1789–1829* (Woodbridge: The Boydell Press, 2007)

Idem, 'Tommy Downshire's Boys: popular protest, social change and political manipulation in mid-Ulster, 1829–1847', *Past and Present*, no. 196, 2007

Blackstock, Allan, and Eoin Magennis, eds., *Politics and political culture in Britain and Ireland 1750–1850: essays in tribute to Peter Jupp* (Belfast: Ulster Historical Foundation, 2007)

Bogue, Tom, 'Cork in 1798', in Crowley and Ó Donnabháin, eds., *The battle of the Big Cross* (Clonakilty: Clonakilty District 1798 Bi-Centenary Commemoration Committee, 1998)

Bolster, Evelyn, *A history of Mallow* (Cork: Cork Historical Guides Committee, 1971)

Bourke, P. M. A., 'The agricultural statistics of the 1841 census of Ireland: a critical review', *Economic History Review*, 2nd series, vol. xviii, 1965

Idem, 'Notes on some agricultural units of measurement in use in pre-Famine Ireland', *Irish Historical Studies*, vol. xiv, no. 55, 1965

Bowen, Desmond, *The Protestant crusade in Ireland, 1800–70: a study of Protestant-Catholic relations between the Act of Union and disestablishment* (Dublin: Gill and Macmillan, & Montreal: McGill Queen's University Press, 1978)

Boyce, D. G., *Nationalism in Ireland*, 3rd edition (New York: Routledge, 1995)

Boylan, Thomas A., and Timothy P. Foley, *Political economy and colonial Ireland: the propagation and ideological function of economic discourse in the nineteenth century* (London and New York: Routledge, 1992)

Brennan, Brian, *Máire Bhuí Ní Laoire: a poet of her people* (Cork: The Collins Press, 2000)

Bric, Maurice J., 'Popular protest movements in Kerry, 1770–1800', *Journal of the Kerry Archaeological and Historical Society*, no. 18, 1985

Idem, 'The Whiteboy movement in Tipperary, 1760–80', in William Nolan in association with Thomas G. McGrath, eds., *Tipperary: history and society: interdisciplinary essays on the history of an Irish county* (Dublin: Geography Publications, 1985)

Idem, 'The tithe system in eighteenth-century Ireland', *Proceedings of the Royal Irish Academy*, section C, vol. lxxxvi, 1986

Idem, 'Priests, parsons and politics: the Rightboy protest in county Cork, 1785–1788', in Philpin, ed., *Nationalism and popular protest in Ireland* (Cambridge: Cambridge University Press, 1987)

Broeker, Galen, *Rural disorder and police reform in Ireland, 1812–36* (London: Routledge & Kegan Paul, and Toronto: University of Toronto Press, 1970)

Brown, Michael, Patrick M. Geoghegan and James Kelly, eds., *The Irish Act of Union, 1800: bicentennial essays* (Dublin: Irish Academic Press, 2003)

Brown, Stewart J., 'The new reformation movement in the Church of Ireland, 1801–29', in Stewart J. Brown and David W. Miller, eds., *Piety and power in Ireland 1760–1960: essays in honour of Emmet Larkin* (Queen's University of Belfast: Institute of Irish Studies, and Notre Dame: University of Notre Dame Press, 2000)

Brown, Thomas N., 'Nationalism and the Irish peasant, 1800–1848', *Review of Politics*, vol. xv, no. 4, 1953

Buckley, James, 'The yeomanry corps of county Cork, 1823–1834', *Journal of the Cork Historical and Archaeological society*, vol. xix, 1913

Buttimer, Cornelius G., 'A Cork Gaelic text on a Napoleonic campaign', *Journal of the Cork Historical and Archaeological society*, vol. xcv, no. 254, 1990

Idem, 'Gaelic literature and contemporary work', in O'Flanagan and Buttimer, eds., *Cork: history and society* (Dublin: Geography Publications, 1993)

C., J., 'Notes on the Cotter family of Rockforest, Co. Cork', *Journal of the Cork Historical and Archaeological Society*, vol. xiv, 1908

Campbell, M., 'Thomas Moore's wild song: the 1821 Irish Melodies', *Bullán*, vol. iv, no. 2, 2000

Casey, Albert Eugene, *O'Kief, Coshe Mang, Slieve Logher and upper Blackwater in Ireland, vol. vi, historical and genealogical items relating to north Cork and east Kerry* (Birmingham, Ala.: Knockagree Historical Fund, 1963)

Casey, Daniel J., and Robert E. Rhodes, eds., *Views of the Irish peasantry 1800–1916* (Hamden, Conn.: Aechon Books, 1977)

Christianson, Gale E., 'Secret societies and agrarian violence in Ireland, 1780–1840', *Agricultural History*, vol. xlvi, no. 3, 1972

Clark, Samuel, 'The importance of agrarian classes: agrarian class structure and collective action in nineteenth-century Ireland', *British Journal of Sociology*, vol. xxix, no. 1, 1978

Idem, *Social origins of the Irish land war* (Princeton: Princeton University Press, 1979)

Idem, and James S. Donnelly Jr., eds., *Irish peasants: violence and political unrest 1780–1914* (Dublin: Gill & Macmillan, 1983)

Colgan, Maurice, 'Prophecy against reason: Ireland and the apocalypse', *British Journal for Eighteenth-Century Studies*, vol. viii, 1985

Collins, John T., 'Some Munster landed gentry', *Journal of the Cork Historical and Archaeological Society*, vol. lxiv, no. 199, 1959

Collins, Michael, 'Inquest and aftermath', in Crowley and Ó Donnabháin, eds., *The battle of the Big Cross* (Clonakilty: Clonakilty District 1798 Bi-Centenary Commemoration Committee, 1998)

Idem, 'The battle of the Big Cross', in Crowley and Ó Donnabháin, eds., *The battle of the Big Cross* (Clonakilty: Clonakilty District 1798 Bi-Centenary Commemoration Committee, 1998)

Comerford, R. V., Mary Cullen, Jacqueline R. Hill and Colm Lennon, eds., *Religion, conflict and coexistence in Ireland: essays presented to Monsignor Patrick J. Corish* (Dublin: Gill & Macmillan, 1990)

Connolly, S. J., 'The "blessed turf": cholera and popular panic in Ireland, June 1832', *Irish Historical Studies*, vol. xxiii, no. 91, 1983

Idem, 'Law, order and popular protest in early eighteenth-century Ireland: the case of the Houghers' in Corish, ed., *Radicals, rebels and establishments* (Belfast: Appletree Books, 1985)

Idem, *Religion and society in nineteenth-century Ireland* (Dundalk: Dundalgan Press [for Economic and Social History Society of Ireland], 1985)

Idem, 'The Houghers: agrarian protest in early eighteenth-century Connacht', in Philpin, ed., *Nationalism and popular protest in Ireland* (Cambridge: Cambridge University Press, 1987)

Idem, 'Violence and order in the eighteenth century', in O'Flanagan, Ferguson and Whelan, eds., *Rural Ireland 1600–1900* (Cork: Cork University Press, 1987)

Idem, 'Mass politics and sectarian conflict, 1823–30', in Vaughan, ed., *A new history of Ireland V* (Oxford: Clarendon Press, 1989)

Idem, 'Union government, 1812–23', in Vaughan, ed., *A new history of Ireland V* (Oxford: Clarendon Press, 1989)

Idem, *Religion, law and power: the making of Protestant Ireland 1660–1760* (Oxford: Clarendon Press, 1992)

Idem, 'Eighteenth-century Ireland: colony or ancien régime?', in D. G. Boyce and Alan O'Day, eds., *The making of modern Irish history: revisionism and the revisionistic controversy* (London: Routledge, 1996)

Idem, '"Ag Déanamh commanding": elite responses to popular culture, 1660–1850', in Donnelly and Miller, eds., *Irish popular culture* (Dublin: Irish Academic Press, 1998)

Idem, 'Jacobites, Whiteboys and republicans: varieties of disaffection in eighteenth-century Ireland', *Eighteenth-Century Ireland*, vol. xviii, 2003

Conzemius, V., 'The place of Daniel O'Connell in the liberal Catholic movement of the nineteenth century', in Donal McCartney, ed., *The world of Daniel O'Connell* (Dublin and Cork: Mercier Press, 1980)

Corish, Patrick J., ed., *Radicals, rebels and establishments. Historical Studies XV: papers read before the Irish Conference of Historians, Maynooth, 16–19 June 1983* (Belfast: Appletree Books, 1985)

Cotter, G. de P., 'The Cotter family of Rock-forest, Co. Cork, being portion of a history of the family by Rev. Charles P. Cotter', *Journal of the Cork Historical and Archaeological Society*, vol. xliii, 1938

Cronin, Denis A., *Who killed the Franks family? Agrarian violence in pre- Famine Cork* (Dublin: Four Courts Press, 2009)

Cronin, Maura, 'Memory, story and balladry: 1798 and its place in popular memory in pre-Famine Ireland', in Geary, ed., *Rebellion and remembrance in modern Ireland* (Dublin: Four Courts Press, 2000)

Idem, *Agrarian protest in Ireland 1750–1960* (Dundalk: Dundalgan Press for the Economic and Social History Society of Ireland, 2012)

Crossman, Virginia, 'Emergency legislation and agrarian disorder in Ireland, 1821–41', *Irish Historical Studies*, vol. xxvii, no. 108, 1991

Idem, *Politics, law and order in nineteenth-century Ireland* (Dublin: Gill & Macmillan, 1996)

Crotty, Raymond D., *Irish agricultural production: its volume and structure* (Cork: Cork University Press, 1966)

Crowley, Tim, and Traolach Ó Donnabháin, eds., *The battle of the Big Cross* (Clonakilty: Clonakilty District 1798 Bi-Centenary Commemoration Committee, 1998)

Cullen, L. M., and F. Furet, eds., *Ireland and France 17th-20th centuries: towards a comparative study of rural history: proceedings of the first Franco-Irish symposium on social and economic history · Dublin* ([n.p.]: Éditions de l'Ecole des Hautes Études en Sciences Sociales, 1980)

Cullen, L. M., *The emergence of modern Ireland 1600–1900* (New York: Holmes & Meier Publishers, 1981)

Idem, *An economic history of Ireland since 1660*, second edition (London: Batsford, 1987)

Idem, 'The 1798 rebellion in Wexford: United Irishman organisation, membership, leadeship', in Kevin Whelan in association with William Nolan, eds., *Wexford: history and society: interdisciplinary essays on the history of an Irish county* (Dublin: Geography Publications, 1987)

Idem, *The hidden Ireland: reassessemnt of a concept* (Mullingar: Lilliput Press, 1988)

Idem, 'The political structures of the Defenders', in Gough and Dickson, eds., *Ireland and the French revolution* (Dublin: Irish Academic Press, 1990)

Idem, 'The Blackwater Catholics and county Cork society and politics in the eighteenth century', in O'Flanagan and Buttimer, eds., *Cork: history and society* (Dublin: Geography Publications, 1993)

Idem, 'The internal politics of the United Irishmen', in Dickson, Keogh and Whelan, eds., *The United Irishmen* (Dublin: Lilliput Press, 1993)

Idem, 'Politics and rebellion: Wicklow in the 1790s', in Ken Hannigan and William Nolan, eds., *Wicklow: history and society* (Dublin: Geography Publications, 1994)

Idem, 'The Irish diaspora of the seventeenth and eighteenth centuries', in Nicholas Canny, ed., *Europeans on the move: studies on European migration, 1500–1800* (Oxford: Clarendon Press, 1994)

Idem, 'Humphrey O'Sullivan's Callan: before and after', in Noreen McDonnell, ed., *Callan Co-operative Agricultural and Dairy Society Ltd. 1899–1999* (Callan: Callan Co-operative Agricultural and Dairy Society Ltd., 1999)

Idem, 'The politics of crisis and rebellion, 1792–1798', in Jim Smyth, ed., *Revolution, counter-revolution and union: Ireland in the 1790s* (Cambridge: Cambridge University Press, 2000)

Idem, 'The "suppression" of the Volunteers and United Irishmen: sources and interpretation 1792–4', in Bernard Browne, ed., *The Wexford man: essays in honour of Nicky Furlong* (Dublin: Geography Publications, 2007)

Curtin, Gerald, 'Opposition to the payment of tithes in West Limerick 1821–1838', *Old Limerick Journal*, no. 26, 2006

Curtin, Nancy J., 'The transformation of the Society of United Irishmen into a mass-based revolutionary organisation, 1794–6', *Irish Historical Studies*, vol. xxiv, no. 96, 1985

Idem, 'Symbols and rituals of United Irish mobilisation', in Gough and Dickson, eds., *Ireland and the French revolution* (Dublin: Irish Academic Press, 1990)

Idem, *The United Irishmen: popular politics in Ulster and Dublin 1791–1798* (Oxford: Clarendon Press, 1994)

d'Alton, Ian, *Protestant society and politics in Cork 1812–1844* (Cork: Cork University Press, 1980)

Idem, 'Keeping faith: an evocation of the Cork Protestant character, 1820–1920', in O'Flanagan and Buttimer, eds., *Cork: history and society* (Dublin: Geography Publications, 1993)

Davis, R. W., 'The Tories, the Whigs, and Catholic emancipation, 1827–1829', *English Historical Review*, vol. xcvii, no. 382, 1982

Dickson, David, 'An economic history of the Cork region in the eighteenth century', unpublished Ph. D. thesis, Trinity College Dublin, 1977

Idem, 'Butter comes to the market: the origins of commercial dairying in county Cork', in O'Flanagan and Buttimer, eds., *Cork: history and society* (Dublin: Geography Publications, 1993)

Idem, 'Paine and Ireland', in Dickson, Keogh and Whelan, eds., *The United Irishmen* (Dublin: Lilliput Press, 1993)

Idem, Dáire Keogh and Kevin Whelan, eds., *The United Irishmen: republicanism, radicalism and rebellion* (Dublin: Lilliput Press, 1993)

Idem, 'The south Munster region in the 1790s', in Murphy, ed., *The French are in the bay* (Cork: Mercier Press, 1997)

Idem, *New Foundations: Ireland, 1660–1800* second revised and enlarged edition (Dublin: Irish Academic Press, 2000)

Idem, 'Smoke without fire? Munster and the 1798 rebellion', in Bartlett, Dickson, Keogh and Whelan, eds., *1798: a bicentenary perspective* (Dublin: Four Courts Press, 2003)

Idem, 'Jacobitism in eighteenth-century Ireland: a Munster perspective', *Éire-Ireland*, vol. xxxix, nos. 3–4, 2004

Idem, *Old world colony: Cork and south Munster 1630–1830* (Cork: Cork University Press, 2005)

Idem, 'Novel Spectacle? The birth of the Whiteboys, 1761–2', in D. W. Hayton and Andrew R. Holmes, eds., *Ourselves alone? Religion, society and politics in eighteenth- and nineteenth-century Ireland: essays presented to S. J. Connolly* (Dublin: Four Courts Press, 2016)

Donnelly, J. S., Jr, 'The journals of Sir John Benn-Walsh relating to the management of his Irish estates, 1823–64', *Journal of the Cork Historical and Archaeological Society*, vol. lxxix, 1974

Idem, *The land and the people of nineteenth-century Cork: the rural economy and the land question* (London: Routledge & Kegan Paul, 1975)

Idem, 'The Rightboy movement 1785–8', *Studia Hibernica*, nos. 17/18, 1977–78

Idem, 'The Whiteboy movement, 1761–5', *Irish Historical Studies*, vol. xxi, no. 81, 1978

Idem, 'Propagating the cause of the United Irishmen', *Studies*, vol. lxix, no. 273, 1980

Idem, 'Hearts of Oak, Hearts of Steel', *Studia Hibernica*, no. 21, 1981

Idem, 'Irish agrarian rebellion: the Whiteboys of 1769–76', *Proceedings of the Royal Irish Academy*, section C, vol. lxxxiii, no. 12, 1983

Idem, 'Pastorini and Captain Rock: millenarianism and sectarianism in the Rockite movement of 1821–4', in Clark and Donnelly, eds., *Irish Peasants* (Dublin: Gill & Macmillan, 1983)

Idem, 'The social composition of agrarian rebellions in early nineteenth-century Ireland: the case of the Carders and Caravats, 1813–16', in Corish, ed., *Radicals, rebels and establishments* (Belfast: Appletree Books, 1985)

Idem, 'The Terry Alt movement 1829–31', *History Ireland*, vol. ii, no. 4, 1994

Idem, and Kerby A. Miller, eds., *Irish popular culture 1650–1850* (Dublin: Irish Academic Press, 1998)

Idem, 'Sectarianism in 1798 and in Catholic nationalist memory', in Geary, ed., *Rebellion and remembrance in modern Ireland* (Dublin: Four Courts Press, 2000)

Idem, 'Captain Rock: ideology and organization in the Irish agrarian rebellion of 1821–24', *Éire-Ireland*, vol. lxii, nos. 3–4, 2007

Idem, 'Captain Rock: the origins of the Irish agrarian rebellion of 1821–24', *New Hibernia Review*, vol. xi, no. 4, 2007

Idem, *Captain Rock: the Irish agrarian rebellion of 1821–24* (Cork: The Collins Press, 2009)

Dooley, Terence, *The murders at Wildgoose Lodge: agrarian crime and punishment in pre-Famine Ireland* (Dublin: Four Courts Press, 2007)

Dore, M., 'The murder of Thomas Hoskins', *Annual Observer* (Newcastle West Historical Society), vol. v, 1983

Dunne, Tom, 'Popular ballads, revolutionary rhetoric and politicisation', in Gough and Dickson, eds., *Ireland and the French revolution* (Dublin: Irish Academic Press, 1990)

Idem, '"In the service of the French republic"? Wolfe Tone in Bantry bay', in Murphy, ed., *The French are in the bay* (Cork: Mercier Press, 1997)

Elliott, Marianne, 'The origins and transformation of early Irish republicanism', *International Review of Social History*, vol. xxiii, no. 3, 1978

Idem, *Partners in revolution: the United Irishmen and France* (New Haven and London: Yale University Press, 1982)

Idem, *Wolfe Tone: prophet of Irish independence* (New Haven and London: Yale University Press, 1989)

Idem, 'The Defenders in Ulster', in Dickson, Keogh and Whelan, eds., *The United Irishmen* (Dublin: Lilliput Press, 1993)

Evans, E. Estyn, 'Peasant beliefs in nineteenth-century Ireland', in Casey and Rhodes, eds., *Views of the Irish peasantry 1800–1916* (Hamden, Conn.: Aechon Books, 1977)

FitzGerald, Garret, 'Estimates for baronies of minimum level of Irish-speaking amongst successive decennial cohorts: 1771–1781 to 1861–1871', *Proceedings of the Royal Irish Academy. Section C: Archaeology, Celtic Studies, History, Linguistics, Literature*, vol. 84C, 1984

Idem, 'Irish-speaking in the pre-Famine period: a study based on the 1911 census data for people born before 1851 and still alive in 1911', *Proceedings of the Royal Irish Academy: Section C: Archaeology, Celtic Studies, History, Linguistics, Literature*, vol. 103C, no. 5, 2003

Idem, with contributions by John Fitzgerald, Gillian O'Brien and Cormac Ó Gráda, *Irish Primary Education in the early nineteenth century: an analysis of the First and Second Reports of the Commissioners of Irish Education Inquiry, 1825–6* (Dublin: Royal Irish Academy, 2013)

Fitzpatrick, David, 'Class, family and rural unrest in nineteenth-century Ireland', in P. J. Drudy, ed., *Ireland: land, politics and people: Irish studies II* (Cambridge: Cambridge University Press, 1982)

Idem, 'Unrest in rural Ireland', *Irish Economic and Social History*, vol. xii, 1985

Idem, 'Was Ireland special? Recent writing on the Irish economy and society in the nineteenth century', *Historical Journal*, vol. xxxiii, no. 1, 1990

Fitzpatrick, W. J., *The life, times, and correspondence of the right Rev. Dr. Doyle, Bishop of Kildare and Leighlin*, 2 vols, new edition (Dublin: James Duffy & Co., M. H. Gill & Son, 1880)

Foster, R. F., *Modern Ireland 1600–1972* (London: Penguin Books, 1989)

Friel, Mary, *Dancing as a social pastime in the south-east of Ireland, 1800–1897* (Dublin: Four Courts Press, 2004)

Garnham, Neal, *The courts, crime and the criminal law in Ireland 1692–1760* (Cornwall: Hartnolls, 1996)

Garvin, Tom, 'Defenders, Ribbonmen and others: underground political networks in pre-Famine Ireland', in Philpin, ed., *Nationalism and popular protest in Ireland* (Cambridge: Cambridge University Press, 1987)

Gaughan, J. Anthony, *Doneraile*, second and revised edition (Dublin: Kamac Publications, 1970)

Geary, Laurence M., 'Prince Hohenlohe, Signor Pastorini and miraculous healing in early nineteenth-century Ireland', in E. Malcolm and G. Jones, eds., *Medicine, disease and the state in Ireland, 1650–1940* (Cork: Cork University Press, 1998)

Geary, Laurence M., ed., *Rebellion and remembrance in modern Ireland* (Dublin: Four Courts Press, 2000)

Geoghegan, Patrick M., *The Irish Act of Union: a study in high politics 1798–1801* (Dublin: Gill & Macmillan, 1999)

Idem, *King Dan: the rise of Daniel O'Connell, 1775–1829* (Dublin: Gill & Macmillan, 2008)

Gibbons, Luke, 'Between Captain Rock and a hard place: art and agrarian insurgency', in Tadhg Foley and Seán Ryder, eds., *Ideology and Ireland in the nineteenth century* (Dublin: Four Courts Press, 1998)

Gibbons, Stephen Randolph, *Captain Rock, night errant: the threatening letters of pre-Famine Ireland, 1801–1845* (Dublin: Four Courts Press, 2004)

Gibson, Charles B., *The history of the county and city of Cork*, 2 vols (London: T. C. Newby, 1861)

Gillespie, Raymond, and W. G. Neely, eds., *The laity and the Church of Ireland, 1000–2000: all sorts and conditions* (Dublin: Four Courts Press, 2002)

Goldstrom, J. M., and L. A. Clarkson, eds., *Irish population, economy and society: essays in honour of the late K. H. Connell* (Oxford: Clarendon Press, 1981)

Gough, Hugh, and David Dickson, eds., *Ireland and the French revolution* (Dublin: Irish Academic Press, 1990)

Idem, 'Anatomy of a failure', in Murphy, ed., *The French are in the bay* (Cork: Mercier Press, 1997)

Hammond, Joseph W., 'Town major Henry Charles Sirr', *Dublin Historical Record*, vol. iv, 1941–42

Hayes-McCoy, G. A., 'The government forces which opposed the insurgents of 1798', *Irish Sword*, vol. iv, no. 14, 1959

Hempton, David, and Myrtle Hill, *Evangelical Protestantism in Ulster society 1740–1890* (London: Routledge, 1992)

Hickey, Patrick, *Famine in west Cork: the Mizen Peninsula land and people, 1800–1852: a local study of pre-Famine and Famine Ireland* (Cork: Mercier Press, 2002)

Hickman, Mary J., *Religion, class and identity: the state, the Catholic church and the education of the Irish in Britain* (Avebury, Alder.: Ashgate Publishing, 2005)

Hislop, Harold, 'The 1806–12 Board of Education and non-denominational education in Ireland', *Oideads*, vol. xl, 1993

Hoppen, K. Theodore, *Ireland since 1800: conflict and conformity*, second edition (Harlow and New York: Longman, 1989)

Idem, 'Riding a tiger: Daniel O'Connell, reform, and popular politics in Ireland, 1800–1847', in T. C. W. Blanning and Peter Wende, eds., *Reform in Great Britain and Germany 1750–1850* (Oxford: Oxford University Press, 1999)

Idem, 'An incorporating Union? British politicians and Ireland 1800–1830', *English Historical Review*, vol. cxxiii, no. 501, 2008

Idem, *Governing Hibernia: British politicians and Ireland 1800–1921* (Oxford: Oxford University Press, 2016)

Hoppit, Julian, ed., *Parliaments, nations and identities in Britain and Ireland, 1660–1850* (Manchester and New York: Manchester University Press, 2003)

Huggins, Michael, *Social conflict in pre-Famine Ireland: the case of County Roscommon* (Dublin: Four Courts Press, 2007)

Inglis, Brian, *The freedom of the press in Ireland 1784–1841* (London: Faber and Faber, 1954)

Innes, Joanna, 'Legislating for three kingdoms: how the Westminster parliament legislated for England, Scotland and Ireland, 1707–1830', in Hoppit, ed., *Parliaments, nations and identities in Britain and Ireland, 1660–1850* (Manchester and New York: Manchester University Press, 2003)

Idem, 'Parliament and church reform: off and on the agenda', in Gordon Pentland and Michael T. Davis, eds., *Liberty, property and popular politics: England and Scotland, 1688–1815: essays in honour of H. T. Dickinson* (Edinburgh: Edinburgh University Press, 2016)

Idem, '"National education" in the British Isles 1765–1815: British and Irish variations on a European theme', typescript

Jackson, Alvin, *Ireland, 1798–1998: politics and war* (London: Blackwell, 1999)

Jenkins, Brian, *Sir William Gregory of Coole: the biography of an Anglo-Irishman* (Gerrards Cross, Bucks.: Colin Smythe, 1986)

Idem, *Era of emancipation: British government of Ireland, 1812–1830* (Kingston and Montreal: McGill-Queen's University Press, 1988)

Idem, *Henry Goulburn 1784–1856: a political biography* (Liverpool: Liverpool University Press, 1996)

Jephson, Maurice Denham, *An Anglo-Irish miscellany: some records of the Jephsons of Mallow* (Dublin: Allen Figgis, 1964)

Johnston, Edith Mary, 'Violence transported: aspects of Irish peasant society', in Oliver MacDonagh and W. F. Mandle, eds., *Ireland and Irish-Australia: studies in cultural and political history* (London: Croom Helm, 1986)

Jupp, P. J., 'Irish parlimentary elections and the influence of the Catholic vote, 1801–20', *Historical Journal*, vol. x, no. 2, 1967

Idem, 'Urban politics in Ireland 1801–1831', in David Harkness and Mary O'Dowd, eds., *The town in Ireland. Historical Studies XIII: papers read before the Irish Conference of Historians, Belfast 30 May-2 June, 1979* (Belfast: Appletree Press, 1981)

Idem, and Stephen A. Royle, 'The social geography of Cork city elections, 1801–30', *Irish Historical Studies*, vol. xxix, no. 113, 1994

Idem, and Eoin Magennis, eds., *Crowds in Ireland, c. 1720–1920* (London: Macmillan, 2000)

Idem, 'Government, parliament and politics in Ireland, 1801–41', in Julian Hoppit, ed., *Parliaments, nations and identities in Britain and Ireland, 1650–1850* (Manchester and New York: Manchester University Press, 2003)

Katsuta, Shunsuke, 'The Rockite movement in county Cork in the early 1820s', *Irish Historical Studies*, vol. xxxiii, no. 131, 2003

Idem, 'Conciliation, anti-Orange politics and the sectarian scare: Dublin politics of the early 1820s', *Dublin Historical Record*, vol. lxiv, no. 2, 2011

Idem, 'The proposal for a militia interchange between Great Britain and Ireland', *Irish Sword*, vol. xxix, no. 116, 2013

Keenan, Desmond J., *The Catholic church in nineteenth-century Ireland: a sociological study* (Dublin: Gill & Macmillan, 1983)

Idem, *Pre-Famine Ireland: social structure* (United States of America: Xlibris, 2000)

Idem, *Ireland 1800–1850* (United States of America: Xlibris, 2001)

Kelly, James, 'The genesis of "Protestant Ascendancy": the Rightboy disturbances of the 1780s and their impact upon Protestant opinion', in Gerard O'Brien, ed., *Parliament, politics and people: essays in eighteenth-century Irish history* (Dublin: Irish Academic Press, 1989)

Idem, ed., 'The Whiteboys in 1762: a contemporary account', *Journal of the Cork Historical and Archaeological Society*, vol. xciv, 1989

Idem, '"We were all to have been massacred": Irish Protestants and the experience of rebellion', in Bartlett, Dickson, Keogh and Whelan, eds., *1798: a bicentenary perspective* (Dublin: Four Courts Press, 2003)

Kelly, Jennifer, *'The downfall of Hagan': Sligo Ribbonism in 1842* (Dublin: Four Courts Press, 2008)

Kennedy, Liam, and Peter Solar, *Irish agriculture: a price history from the mid-eighteenth to the eve of the first world war* (Dublin: Royal Irish Academy, 2007)

Keogh, Dáire, and Kevin Whelan, eds., *Acts of Union: the causes, contexts, and consequences of the Act of Union* (Dublin: Four Courts Press, 2001)

Kerr, Donal A., 'Priests, pikes and patriots: the Irish Catholic church and political violence from the Whiteboys to the Fenians', in Brown and Miller, eds., *Piety and power in Ireland* (Queen's University of Belfast: Institute of Irish Studies, and Notre Dame: University of Notre Dame Press, 2000)

Kiely, Brendan, *The Connerys: the making of a Waterford legend* (Dublin: Geography Publications, 1994)

Knott, J. W., 'Land, kinship and identity: the cultural roots of agrarian agitation in eighteenth- and nineteenth-century Ireland', *Journal of Peasant Studies*, vol. xii, no. 1, 1984

Larkin, Emmet, 'Before the devotional revolution', in James H. Murphy, ed., *Evangelicals and Catholics in nineteenth-century Ireland* (Dublin: Four Courts Press, 2005)

Idem, *The pastoral role of the Roman Catholic church in pre-Famine Ireland 1750–1850* (Dublin: Four Courts Press, and Washington D. C.: The Catholic University of America Press, 2006)

Lee, Joseph, 'The Ribbonmen', in Williams, ed., *Secret societies in Ireland* (Dublin: Gill & Macmillan, and New York: Barnes & Noble Books, 1973)

Idem, 'Patterns of rural unrest in nineteenth-century Ireland: a preliminary survey', in Cullen and Furet, eds., *Ireland and France 17th-20th centuries* ([n.p.]: Éditions de l'Ecole des Hautes Études en Sciences Sociales, 1980)

Idem, 'On the accuracy of the pre-Famine Irish censuses', in Goldstrom and Clarkson, eds., *Irish Population, economy and society* (Oxford: Clarendon Press, 1981)

Leerssen, Joep, *Remembrance and imagination: patterns in the historical and literary representation of Ireland in the nineteenth century* (Cork: Cork University Press, 1996)

Leighton, C. D. A., *Catholicism in a Protestant kingdom: a study of the Irish ancien régime* (Dublin: Gill & Macmillan, 1994)

Livesey, James, 'From the ancient constitution to democracy', in Bartlett, Dickson, Keogh and Whelan, eds., *1798: a bicentenary perspective* (Dublin: Four Courts Press, 2003)

MacCurtain, Margaret, 'Pre-Famine peasantry in Ireland: definition and theme', *Irish University Review*, vol. 4, no. 2, 1974

MacDonagh, Oliver, W. F. Mandle and Pauric Travers, eds., *Irish culture and nationalism*, 1750–1950 (London: Macmillan in association with Humanities Research Centre, Australian National University, 1983)

Idem, *The hereditary bondsman: Daniel O'Connell, 1775–1829* (New York: St Martin's Press, 1987)

Idem, 'Ideas and institutions, 1830–45', in Vaughan, ed., *A new history of Ireland V* (Oxford: Clarendon Press, 1989)

Idem, 'The economy and society, 1830–45', in Vaughan, ed., *A new history of Ireland V* (Oxford: Clarendon Press, 1989)

McDonough, Terence, ed., *Was Ireland a colony? Economics, politics and culture in nineteenth-century Ireland* (Dublin: Irish Academic Press, 2005)

McDowell, R. B., *Public opinion and government policy in Ireland, 1801–1846* (London: Faber & Faber, 1952)

Idem, *The Irish administration 1801–1914* (London: Routledge & Kegan Paul, 1964)

McGrath, Thomas, *Politics, interdenominational relations and education in the public ministry of Bishop James Doyle of Kildare and Leighlin, 1786–1834* (Dublin: Four Courts Press, 1999)

Mackenzie, R. Shelton, *Bits of Blarney* (New York: Redfield, 1854)

MacKillop, James, 'Finn MacCool: hero and anti-hero in Irish folk tradition', in Casey and Rhodes, eds., *Views of the Irish peasantry 1800–1916* (Hamden, Conn.: Aechon Books, 1977)

McManus, Antonia, *The Irish hedge school and its books, 1695–1831* (Dublin: Four Courts Press, 2002)

MacLochlainn, Alf, 'Gael and peasant: a case of mistaken identity?', in Casey and Rhodes, eds., *Views of the Irish Peasantry 1800–1916* (Hamden, Conn.: Aechon Books, 1977)

Magennis, Eoin F., 'A "Presbyterian insurrection"? Reconsidering the Hearts of Oak disturbances of July 1763', *Irish Historical Studies*, vol. xxxi, no. 122, 1998

Maguire, W. A., 'Lord Donegall and the Hearts of Steel', *Irish Historical Studies*, vol. xxi, no. 84, 1979

Malcolm, Elizabeth, 'Popular recreation in nineteenth-century Ireland', in MacDonagh, Mandle and Travers eds., *Irish Culture and Nationalism, 1750–1950* (London: Macmillan in association with Humanities Research Centre, Australian National University, 1983)

Matsuo, Taro, 'Transformation of rural societies in nineteenth-century Ireland', *Keizai-Shirin*, vol. lxiv, no. 3, 1996

Miller, David W., 'The Armagh troubles, 1784–95', in Clark and Donnelly, eds., *Irish peasants* (Dublin: Gill & Macmillan, 1983)

Miller, David W., ed., *Peep O'Day Boys and Defenders: selected documents on the disturbances in County Armagh, 1784–1796* (Belfast: Public Record Office of Northern Ireland, 1990)

Idem, 'Politicisation in revolutionary Ireland: the case of the Armagh troubles', *Irish Economic and Social History*, vol. xxiii, 1996

Mokyr, Joel, *Why Ireland starved: a quantitative and analytical history of the Irish economy 1800–1850*, revised edition (Abingdon and New York: Routledge, 2006)

Moody, T. W., and W. E. Vaughan, eds., *A new history of Ireland IV: eighteenth-century Ireland 1691–1800* (Oxford: Clarendon Press, 1986)

Morley, Vincent, *Irish opinion and the American Revolution, 1760–1783* (Cambridge: Cambridge University Press, 2002)

Moyles, M. G., and Pádraig de Brún, 'Charles O'Brien's agricultural survey of Kerry, 1800', *Journal of the Kerry Archaeological and Historical Society*, nos. 1–2, 1968–69

Murphy, John A., ed., *The French are in the bay: the expedition to Bantry Bay, 1796* (Cork: Mercier Press, 1997)

Murray, A. C., 'Agrarian violence and nationalism in nineteenth-century Ireland: the myth of Ribbonism', *Irish Economic and Social History*, vol. xiii, 1986

Nelson, Ivan F., ' "The first chapter of 1798"? Restoring a military perspective to the Irish militia riots of 1793', *Irish Historical Studies*, vol. xxxiii, no. 132, 2003

Idem, *The Irish militia, 1793–1803: Ireland's forgotten army* (Dublin: Four Courts Press, 2007)

Ó Buachalla, Brendán, 'From Jacobite to Jacobin', in Bartlett, Dickson, Keogh and Whelan, eds., *1798: a bicentenary perspective* (Dublin: Four Courts Press, 2003)

Ó Ciardha, Éamonn, *Ireland and the Jacobite cause, 1685–1766: a fatal attachment* (Dublin: Four Courts Press, 2004), reprint

Ó Ciosáin, Niall, *Print and popular culture in Ireland, 1750–1850* (Basingstoke and New York: Palgrave, 1997)

Idem, 'The Irish rogues', in Donnelly and Miller, eds., *Irish popular Culture* (Dublin: Irish Academic Press, 1998)

Idem, ' "114 commissions and 60 committees": phantom figures from a surveillance state', *Proceedings of the Royal Irish Academy: Section C: Archaeology, Celtic Studies, History, Linguistics, Literature*, vol. 109C, 2009

Ó Coindealbháin, Seán, *The story of Iveleary: the history, antiquities and legends of Uibh-Laoghaire* (Dundalk: Dundalgan Press, 1921)

Idem, 'The United Irishmen in Cork county', *Journal of the Cork Historical and Archaeological Society*, vol. liii, no. 178, 1948

Idem, 'The United Irishmen in Cork county: II', *Journal of the Cork Historical and Archaeological Society*, vol. liv, no. 180, 1949

Idem, 'The United Irishmen in Cork county: III', *Journal of the Cork Historical and Archaeological Society*, vol. lv, no. 181, 1950

Idem, 'The United Irishmen in Cork county: IV', *Journal of the Cork Historical and Archaeological Society*, vol. lv, no. 182, 1950

Idem, 'The United Irishmen in Cork county: V', *Journal of the Cork Historical and Archaeological Society*, vol. lvi, no. 183, 1951

Idem, 'The United Irishmen in Cork county: VI', *Journal of the Cork Historical and Archaeological Society*, vol. lvi, no. 184, 1951

Idem, 'The United Irishmen in Cork county: VII', *Journal of the Cork Historical and Archaeological Society*, vol. lvii, no. 186, 1952

Idem, 'The United Irishmen in Cork county: VIII', *Journal of the Cork Historical and Archaeological Society*, vol. lviii, no. 188, 1953

O'Connell, Basil, 'The Nagles of Annakissy', *Irish Genealogist*, vol. ii, no. 11, 1954

O'Connor, John, *The workhouses of Ireland: the fate of Ireland's poor* (Dublin: Anvil Books, and Minneapolis: Irish Books and Media, 1997)

O'Connor, Patrick J., *Exploring Limerick's past: an historical geography of urban development in county and city* (Newcastle West: Oireacht na Mumhan Books, 1987)

Idem, *People make places: the story of the Irish Palatines* (Newcastle West: Oireacht na Mumhan Books, 1989)

Idem, *All Ireland is in and about Rathkeale* (Newcastle West: Oireacht na Mumhan Books, 1996)

Ó Crualaoich, Gearóid, 'The French are on the say', in Murphy, ed., *The French are in the bay* (Cork: Mercier Press, 1997)

O'Dea, Michael, and Kevin Whelan, eds., *Nations and nationalisms: France, Britain, Ireland and the eighteenth-century context* (Oxford: Voltaire Foundation, 1995)

O'Donoghue, Patrick, 'Causes of the opposition to tithes, 1830–38', *Studia Hibernica*, no. 5, 1965

Idem, 'Opposition to tithe payments in 1830–31', *Studia Hibernica*, no. 6, 1966

Idem, 'Opposition to tithe payment in 1832–3', *Studia Hibernica*, no. 12, 1972

O'Donovan, James, 'The anatomy of the Volunteers in Cork, 1775–82: Part I', *Journal of the Cork Historical and Archaeological Society*, vol. lxxxvii, no. 245, 1982

Idem, 'The anatomy of the Volunteers in Cork, 1775–82: Part II', *Journal of the Cork Historical and Archaeological Society*, vol. lxxxvii, no. 246, 1982

O'Dowd, Anne, *Spalpeens and tattie hokers: history and folklore of the Irish migratory agricultural worker in Ireland and Britain* (Dublin: Irish Academic Press, 1991)

Ó Farrell, Patrick, 'Millenialism, messianism and utopianism in Irish history', *Anglo-Irish Studies*, vol. ii, 1976

O'Ferrall, Fergus, *Daniel O'Connell* (Dublin: Gill & MacMillan, 1981)

Idem, *Catholic Emancipation: Daniel O'Connell and the birth of Irish democracy 1820–1830* (Dublin: Gill & MacMillan, 1985)

O'Flanagan, Patrick, Paul Ferguson and Kevin Whelan, eds., *Rural Ireland 1600–1900: modernisation and change* (Cork: Cork University Press, 1987)

Idem, 'Three hundred years of urban life: villages and towns in County Cork *c.* 1600 to 1901', in *idem* and Buttimer, eds., *Cork: history and society* (Dublin: Geography Publications, 1993)

Idem, and Cornelius G. Buttimer, eds., *Cork: history and society: interdisciplinary essays on the history of an Irish county* (Dublin: Geography Publications, 1993)

Ó Grada, Cormac, *The great Irish famine* (Dublin: Gill & Macmillan, 1989)

Idem, 'Poverty, population, and agriculture, 1801–45', in Vaughan, ed., *A new history of Ireland V* (Oxford: Clarendon Press, 1989)

Idem, *Ireland before and after the Famine: explorations in economic history, 1800–1925*, second edition (Manchester and New York: Manchester University Press, 1993)

Idem, *Ireland: a new economic history 1780–1939* (Oxford: Clarendon Press, 1994)

Idem, 'School attendance and literacy before the Famine: a simple baronial analysis', *UCD Centre for Economic Research, Working Paper Series*, WP10/22, 2010

Ó hÓgáin, Dáithí, *The hero in Irish folk history* (Dublin: Gill & Macmillan, and New York: St Martin's Press, 1985)

O'Leary, Tom, 'Miscellaneous aspects of the 1798 rising in Clonakilty', in Crowley and Ó Donnabháin, eds., *The battle of the Big Cross* (Clonakilty: Clonakilty District 1798 Bi-Centenary Commemoration Committee, 1998)

Ó Lúing, Seán, 'Richard Griffith and the roads of Kerry', *Journal of the Kerry Archaeological and Historical Society*, no. 8, 1975

O'Mahony, Jeremiah, *West Cork and its story* (Tralee: Kerryman Ltd, 1961)

O'Neill, James W., 'A look at Captain Rock: agrarian rebellion in Ireland, 1815–1845', *Éire-Ireland*, vol. xvii, no. 3, 1982

Idem, 'Popular culture and peasant rebellion in pre-famine Ireland', Ph. D. thesis, University of Minnesota, 1984

O'Neill, Philip M., *The barrow uncrossed: Fr. Peter O'Neill, and the events in east Co. Cork during the 1798 rebellion, which surrounded his arrest and transporation* (Dublin: Ballydaniel Publications, 1998)

O'Neill, Timothy P., 'The famine of 1822', unpublished M. A. thesis, National University of Ireland, 1966

O Súilleabháin, Seán, *Irish wake amusements* (Cork: Mercier Press, 1967)

O'Sullivan, Patrick, 'A literary difficulty in explaining Ireland: Tom Moore and Captain Rock, 1824', in Roger Swift and Sheridan Gilley, eds., *The Irish in Britain 1815–1939* (Savage: Barnes & Noble Books, 1989)

O'Sullivan, Tadgh, '"The violence of a servile war": three narratives of Irish rural insurgency post-1798', in Geary, ed., *Rebellion and remembrance in modern Ireland* (Dublin: Four Courts Press, 2000)

Ó Tuathaigh, Gearóid, 'Gaelic Ireland, popular politics and Daniel O'Connell', *Journal of the Galway Archaeological and Historical Society*, vol. xxxiv, 1974–75

Palmer, Stanley H., *Police and protest in England and Ireland 1780–1850* (Cambridge: Cambridge University Press, 1988)

Patterson, James G., '"Educated Whiteboyism": the Cork tithe war, 1798–9', *History Ireland*, vol. xii, no. 4, 2004

Idem, 'Republicanism, agrarianism and banditry in the west of Ireland, 1798–1803', *Irish Historical Studies*, vol. xxxv, no. 137, 2006

Idem, *In the wake of the great rebellion: republicanism, agrarianism and banditry in Ireland after 1798* (Manchester and New York: Manchester University Press, 2008)

Petty-Fitzmaurice, H. W. E., 6th Marquis of Lansdowne, *Glanerought and the Petty-Fitzmaurices* (London: Oxford University Press, 1937)

Philpin, C. H. E., ed., *Nationalism and popular protest in Ireland* (Cambridge: Cambridge University Press, 1987)

Powell, Martyn J., 'Popular disturbances in late eighteenth-century Ireland: the origins of the Peep of Day Boys', *Irish Historical Studies*, vol. xxxiv, no. 135, 2005

Reynolds, James A., *The Catholic emancipation crisis in Ireland, 1823–1829* (New Haven: Yale University Press, and London: Oxford University Press, 1954)

Roberts, Paul E. W., 'Caravats and Shanavests: Whiteboyism and faction fighting in east Munster, 1802–11', in Clark and Donnelly, eds., *Irish Peasants* (Dublin: Gill & Macmillan, 1983)

Romani, Robert, 'British views on Irish national character 1800–1846', *History of European Ideas*, vol. xxiii, no. 5, 1997

Senior, Hereward, *Orangeism in Ireland and Britain 1795–1836* (London: Routledge & Kegan Paul, and Toronto: The Ryerson Press, 1966)

Shipkey, Robert Carl, *Robert Peel's Irish policy: 1812–1846* (New York and London: Garland Publishing, 1987)

Simms, Brendan, 'Continental analogies with 1798', in Bartlett, Dickson, Keogh and Whelan eds., *1798: a bicentenary perspective* (Dublin: Four Courts Press, 2003)

Smith, A. W., 'Irish rebels and English radicals 1798–1820', *Past and Present*, no. 7, 1955

Smyth, Jim, 'Popular politicisation, Defenderism and the Catholic question', in Gough and Dickson, eds., *Ireland and the French revolution* (Dublin: Irish Academic Press, 1990)

Idem, *The men of no property: Irish radicals and popular politics in the late eighteenth century* (London: Macmillan, and New York: St. Martin's Press, 1998), reprint

Smyth, William J., 'Social, economic and landscape transformations in county Cork from the mid-eighteenth to the mid-nineteenth century', in O'Flanagan and Buttimer, eds., *Cork: history and society* (Dublin: Geography Publications, 1993)

Takagami, Shin-ichi, 'The Fenian rising in Dublin, March 1867', *Irish Historical Studies*, vol. xxix, no. 115, 1995

Uí Ógáin, Ríonach, *Immortal Dan: Daniel O'Connell in Irish folk tradition* (Dublin: Geography Publications, 1995)

Valone, David A., 'Economic identity and the Irish peasantry on the eve of the Great Hunger', in David A. Valone and Jill Marie Bradbury, eds., *Anglo-Irish identities, 1571–1845* (Lewisburg: Bucknell University Press, 2008)

Vance, Norman, 'Celts, Carthaginians and constitutions: Anglo-Irish literary relations, 1780–1820', *Irish Historical Studies*, vol. xxii, no. 87, 1981

Vaughan, W. E., ed., *A new history of Ireland V: Ireland under the Union, I 1801–70* (Oxford: Clarendon Press, 1989)

Wall, Maureen, 'The Whiteboys', in Williams, ed., *Secret societies in Ireland* (Dublin: Gill & Macmillan, and New York: Barnes & Noble Books, 1973)

Whelan, Irene, *The Bible war in Ireland: the 'Second Reformation' and the polarisation of Protestant-Catholic relations, 1800–1840* (Madison, Wis.: University of Wisconsin Press, 2005)

Whelan, Kevin, *The tree of liberty: radicalism, Catholicism, and the construction of Irish identity* (Cork: Cork University Press, 1996)

Idem, 'Bantry bay: the wider context', in Murphy, ed., *The French are in the bay* (Cork: Mercier Press, 1997)

Idem, 'The modern landscape', in F. H. A. Aalan, Kevin Whelan and Matthew Stout, eds., *Atlas of the Irish rural landscape* (Cork: Cork University Press, 1997)

Idem, 'An underground gentry? Catholic middlemen in eighteenth-century Ireland', in Donnelly and Miller, eds., *Irish popular culture* (Dublin: Irish Academic Press, 1998)

Idem, 'Settlement and society in eighteenth-century Ireland', in Barry, ed., *A history of settlement in Ireland* (London: Routledge, 2000)

Idem, 'Introduction to section IV', in Bartlett, Dickson, Keogh and Whelan, eds., *1798: a bicentenary perspective*

Whooley, Finbarr, 'The Rockite movement in north Cork 1820–25', unpublished M. A. thesis, University College, Cork, 1986

Williams, T. Desmond, ed., *Secret societies in Ireland* (Dublin: Gill and Macmillan, and New York: Barnes & Noble Books, 1973)

Yates, Nigel, *The religious condition of Ireland 1770–1850* (Oxford: Oxford University Press, 2006)

Zeller, Alfred, *Irische Agrarbewegungen 1760–1880* (Frankfurt am Main: Peter Lang, 1989)

Zimmermann, Georges Denis, *Songs of Irish rebellion: Irish political street ballads and rebel songs, 1780–1900* (Dublin: Four Courts Press, 1966)

2c General

Archer, John E., *'By a flash and a scare': incendiarism, animal maiming, and porching in East Anglia 1815–1870* (Oxford: Clarendon Press, 1990)

Idem, *Social unrest and popular protest in England 1780–1840* (Cambridge: Cambridge University Press, 2000)

Baker, Alan H. R., and Robin A. Batin, eds., *Studies of field systems in the British Isles* (London: Cambridge University Press, 1973)

Belchem, John, *Popular radicalism in nineteenth-century Britain* (Hampshire and London: MacMillan, 1996)

Idem, *Merseypride: essays in Liverpool exceptionalism* (Liverpool: Liverpool University Press, 2000)

Bentley, Michael, 'Liberal Toryism in the twentieth century', *Transactions of the Royal Historical Society*, 6th series, vol. iv, 1994

Brock, W. R., *Lord Liverpool and liberal Toryism 1820 to 1827*, second edition (London: Frank Cass & Co., 1967)

Bush, M. L., 'Captain Poverty and the pilgrimage of grace', *Historical Research*, vol. lxv, no. 156, 1992

Charlesworth, Andrew, 'The development of the English rural proletariat and social protest: a comment', *Journal of Peasant Studies*, vol. viii, no.1, 1980

Cookson, J. E., *Lord Liverpool's administration: the crucial years 1815–22* (Edinburgh: Archon Books, 1975)

Idem, *The British armed nation 1793–1815* (Oxford: Clarendon Press, 1997)

Darvall, Frank Ongley, *Popular disturbances and public order in regency England: being an account of the Luddite and other disorders in England during the years 1811–1817 and of the attitude and activity of the authorities* (London: William Clowes and Sons, 1969), reprint

Derry, John W., 'Governing temperament under Pitt and Liverpool', in John Cannon, ed., *The Whig ascendancy: colluquies on Hanoverian England* (London: Edward Arnold, 1981)

Idem, *Politics in the age of Fox, Pitt and Liverpool: continuity and transformation* (Basingstoke: Macmillan, 1990)

Dinwiddy, J. R., *Radicalism and reform in Britain, 1780–1850* (London: Hambledon, 1992)

Emsley, Clive, and James Walvin, eds., *Artisans, peasants and proletarians, 1760–1860: essays presented to Gwyn A. Williams* (London: Croom Helm, 1985)

Fisher, D. R., ed., *The history of parliament: the House of Commons 1820–1832, v, members E-K* (Cambridge: Cambridge University Press, published for the History of Parliament Trust, 2009)

Idem, ed., *The history of parliament: the House of Commons 1820–1832, vii, members S-Y* (Cambridge: Cambridge University Press, published for the History of Parliament Trust, 2009)

Gash, Norman, 'Lord Liverpool and the foundation of conservative policy', in Lord Butler, ed., *The conservatives: a history from their origins to 1965* (London: George Allen & Unwin, 1977)

Idem, 'After Waterloo: British society and the legacy of the Napoleonic wars', *Transactions of the Royal Historical Society*, 5th series, vol. xxviii, 1978

Idem, *Lord Liverpool: the life and political career of Robert Banks Jenkinson, Second Earl of Liverpool 1770–1828* (Cambridge, Mass.: Harvard University Press, 1984)

Gilmour, Ian, *Riot, risings and revolution: governance and violence in eighteenth-century England* (London: Hutchinson, 1992)

Gordon, Barry, *Political economy in parliament 1819–1823* (London: Macmillan, 1976)

Idem, *Economic doctrine and Tory liberalism 1824–1830* (London and Basingstoke: Macmillan, 1979)

Griffin, Carl J., 'Swing, Swing Redivivus, or something after Swing? On the death throes of a protest movement, December 1830-December 1833', *International Review of Social History*, vol. 54, no. 3, 2009

Harling, Philip, *The waning of 'old corruption': the politics of economical reform in Britain, 1779–1846* (Oxford: Clarendon Press, 1996)

Harrison, J. F. C., *The second coming: popular millenarianism 1780–1850* (London and Henley: Routledge & Kegan Paul, 1979)

Hilton, Boyd, *Corn, cash, commerce: the economic policies of the Tory governments 1815–1830* (Oxford: Oxford University Press, 1977)

Idem, 'The political arts of Lord Liverpool', *Transactions of the Royal Historical Society*, 5th series, vol. xxxviii, 1988

Idem, *The age of atonement: the influence of evangelicalism on social and economic thought, 1785–1865* (Oxford: Clarendon Press, 1991)

Idem, *A mad, bad, & dangerous people? England 1783–1846* (Oxford: Clarendon Press, 2006)

Hobsbawm, Eric, *Bandits* (London: Abacus, 2001), first published in 1969

Idem, *Primitive rebels: studies in archaic forms of social movement in the 19th and 20th centuries*, third edition (Manchester: Manchester University Press, 1971)

Idem, 'Social bandits: reply', *Comparative Studies in Society and History*, vol. xiv, no. 4, 1972

Idem, 'Peasants and politics', *Journal of Peasant Studies*, vol. i, no. 1, 1973

Idem, and George Rudé, *Captain Swing* (London: Pimlico, 1993), first published in 1969

Jones, Peter, 'Swing, Speenhamland and rural social relations: the "moral economy" of the English crowd in the nineteenth century', *Social History*, vol. 32, no. 3, 2007

Jupp, Peter, *Lord Grenville 1759–1834* (Oxford: Clarendon Press, 1985)

Idem, *The governing of Britain: the executive, parliament and the people* (Oxon and New York: Routledge, 2006)

Kondo, Kazuhiko, 'The Church and politics in "disaffected" Manchester, 1718–31', *Historical Research*, vol. 80, no. 207, 2007

Idem, 'Lost in translation? documents relating to the disturbances at Manchester, 1715', *Manchester Region History Review*, vol. 19, 2008

Landsberger, Henry Adolf, ed., *Rural protest: peasant movements and social change* (London: Macmillan, 1974)

Lee, Stephen M., *George Canning and Liberal Toryism, 1801–1827* (London: Royal Historical Society, 2008)

Lüsebrink, Hans-Jürgen, *Histoires curieuses et véritables de Cartouche et de Mandrin* ([n. p.]: Montalba, 1984)

Machin, G. I. T., *The Catholic question in English politics 1820 to 1830* (Oxford: Clarendon Press, 1964)

Magagna, Victor V., *Communities of grain: rural rebellion in comparative perspective* (Ithaca: Cornell University Press, 1991)

Mills, Dennis Richard, and Brian Michael Short, 'Social change and social conflict in nineteenth-century England: the use of the open-closed village model', *Journal of Peasants Studies*, vol. x, no. 4, 1983

Neal, Frank, *Sectarian violence: the Liverpool experience, 1819–1914: an aspect of Anglo-Irish history* (Manchester: Manchester University Press, 1988)

Neveux, Hugues, préface de Jean-Claude Perrot, *Les révoltes paysannes en Europe (XIVe-XVIIe siècle)* (Paris: Albin Michel, 1997)

O'Malley, Pat, 'Social bandits, modern capitalism and the traditional peasantry: a critique of Hobsbawm', *Journal of Peasants Studies*, vol. vi, no. 4, 1979

Palmer, R. R., *The age of the democratic revolution: a political history of Europe and America, 1760–1800*, 2 vols (London: Princeton University Press, 1959–64)

Philips, David, and Robert D. Storch, eds., *Policing provincial England, 1829–1856: the politics of reform* (London: Leicester University Press, 1999)

Quinault, R., and J. Stevenson, eds., *Popular protest and public order: six studies in British history 1790–1920* (London: George Allen & Unwin, 1974)

Randall, Adrian, '"Captain Swing": a retrospect', *International Review of Social History*, vol. 54, no. 3, 2009

Reed, Mick, 'Social change and social conflict in nineteenth-century England: a comment', *Journal of Peasants Studies*, vol. xxii, no. 1, 1984

Idem, 'The peasantry of nineteenth-century England: a neglected class?', *History Workshop*, vol. xxviii, no. 1, 1984

Idem, 'Nineteenth-century rural England: a case for "peasant studies"', *Journal of Peasants Studies*, vol. xiv, no. 1, 1986

Reed, Mick, and Roger Wells, eds., *Class, conflict and protest in the English countryside, 1700–1880* (London: Cass, 1990)

Royal Historical Society, ed., *Transactions of the Royal Historical Society*, 6th series, vol. x (Cambridge: Cambridge University Press, 2000)

Royle, Edward, *Revolutionary Britannia? Reflections on the threat of revolution in Britain 1789–1848* (Manchester and New York: Manchester University Press, 2000)

Rudé, Gorge, *The crowd in history* (London: Serif, 1995), first published in 1964

Idem, *Protest and punishment: the study of the social and political protesters transported to Australia 1788–1868* (Oxford: Clarendon Press, 1978)

Rule, John, and R. Wells, *Crime, protest and popular politics in southern England 1740–1850* (London: Hambledon Press, 1997)

Sack, James J., *The Grenvillites 1801–29: party politics and factionalism in the age of Pitt and Liverpool* (Urbana and London: University of Illinois Press, 1979)

Idem, *From Jacobite to Conservative: reaction and orthodoxy in Britain, c. 1760–1832* (Cambridge: Cambridge University Press, 1993)

Scott, Geoffrey, '"The times are fast approaching": Bishop Charles Walmesley OSB (1722–1797) as prophet', *Journal of Ecclesiastical History*, vol. xxxvi, no. 4, 1985

Scott, James C., *The moral economy of the peasant: rebellion and subsistence in Southeast Asia* (New Haven: Yale University Press, 1976)

Idem, 'Everyday forms of peasant resistance', *Journal of Peasants Studies*, vol. xiii, no. 2, 1986

Shaw, Brent D., 'Bandits in the Roman empire', *Past and Present*, no. 105, 1984

Skyrme, Sir Thomas, *History of the justices of the peace: vol. 2 England 1689–1989*, 3 vols (Chichester: B. Rose, 1991)

Smyth, Jim, 'Republicans and conservatives: British politics and ideology, c. 1750–1832', *Historical Journal*, vol. xxxvii, no. 3, 1994

Stevenson, John, *Popular disturbances in England, 1700–1832*, second edition (Harlow and New York: Longman, 1992)

Thomis, Malcom I., and Peter Holt, *Threats of revolution in Britain 1789–1848* (London: Macmillan, 1977)

Thompson, E. P., *The making of the English working class*, revised edition (Harmondsworth: Penguin Books, 1968), first published in 1963

Idem, 'The moral economy of the English crowd in the eighteenth century', *Past and Present*, no. 50, 1971

Idem, '"Rough Music": Le Charivari anglais', *Annales. Économies, Sociétés, Civilisations*, vol. 27, no. 2, 1972

Idem, *Customs in common: studies in traditional popular culture* (New York: The New Press, 1991)

Thorne, R. G., ed., *The history of parliament: the House of Commons 1790–1820, ii, constituencies* (London: Secker & Warburg, 1986)

Idem, ed., *The history of parliament: the House of Commons 1790–1820, iv, members G-P* (London: Secker & Warburg, 1986)

Idem, ed., *The history of parliament: the House of Commons 1790–1820, v, members Q-Y* (London: Secker & Warburg, 1986)

Tilly, Charles, 'Collective violence in European perspective', in Hugh Davis Graham and Ted Robert Gurr, eds., *The history of violence in America: historical and comparative perspectives* (New York: Bantam Books, 1969)

Idem, *Popular contention in Great Britain 1758–1834* (Cambridge, Mass.: Harvard University Press, 1995)

Turton, Andrew, 'Patrolling the middle-ground: methodological perspective on "everyday forms of peasant resistance"', *Journal of Peasants Studies*, vol. xiii, no. 2, 1986

Waterman, A. M. C., *Revolution, economics and religion: Christian political economy, 1798–1833* (Cambridge: Cambridge University Press, 1991)

Wells, Roger Anthony Edward, 'The development of the English rural proletariat and social protest, 1700–1850', *Journal of Peasants Studies*, vol. vi, no. 2, 1979

Idem, 'Social conflict and protest in the English countryside in the early nineteenth century: a rejoinder', *Journal of Peasants Studies*, vol. viii, no. 4, 1981

Wilkes, A. R., 'Adjustment in arable farming after the Napoleonic wars', *Agricultural History Review*, vol. xxviii, pt. 2, 1980

Index

For Product Safety Concerns and Information please contact our EU representative GPSR@taylorandfrancis.com
Taylor & Francis Verlag GmbH, Kaufingerstraße 24, 80331 München, Germany

www.ingramcontent.com/pod-product-compliance
Ingram Content Group UK Ltd.
Pitfield, Milton Keynes, MK11 3LW, UK
UKHW011014180926
475701UK00004B/736

9780367594701